# CO-OP
# ADVERTISING

## Bob Houk

*Printed on recyclable paper*

Published in conjunction with the
Association of National Advertisers, Inc.,
by NTC Business Books

ANA
Association of National Advertisers, Inc.

NTC Business Books
a division of *NTC Publishing Group* • Lincolnwood, Illinois USA

**Library of Congress Cataloging-in-Publication Data**

Houk, Robert F.
    Co-op advertising : the authoritative guide to promotional
allowance marketing for advertisers, retailers, and distributors /
[Robert F. Houk].
      p.  cm.
    "Published in conjunction with the Association of National
Advertisers, Inc., by NTC Business Books."
    Includes bibliographlcal references and index.
    ISBN 0-8442-3417-6
    1. Cooperative advertising—United States.  I. Association of
National Advertisers.  II. Title.
HF5827.4.H68  1995
659—dc20                            94-37023
                                            CIP


Published in conjunction with the Association of National Advertisers, Inc.,
155 East 44th Street, New York, New York, 10017.


Published by NTC Business Books, a division of NTC Publishing Group.
4255 West Touhy Avenue
Lincolnwood (Chicago), Illinois 60646-1975, U.S.A.
© 1995, by NTC Publishing Group. All rights reserved.
No part of this book may be reproduced, stored
in a retrieval system, or transmitted in any form or by any means,
electronic, mechanical, photocopying, recording or otherwise, without
the prior permission of NTC Publishing Group.
Manufactured in the United States of America.

5 6 7 8 9 BC 0 9 8 7 6 5 4 3 2 1

# Promotion/Merchandising Committee

Robert C. Pifke, Chairman    *Visa USA*

Debra E. Alloway          *Wendy's International, Inc.*
Charles A. Blackmon       *Xerox Corporation*
Matthew M. Freeman        *Block Drug Company, Inc.*
Maryalice Grubbs          *Sara Lee Knit Products*
Steve Hale                *The Goodyear Tire & Rubber Company*
Barabara Jacobi           *AT&T Universal Card Services*
Donald H. Keaton          *Archway Cookies, Inc.*
David J. Kmetz            *General Foods, USA*
Paul Knouse               *R. J. Reynolds Tobacco*
Herman Livingston         *Warner-Lambert Company*
Carole Lundgren           *3M Consumer Products Group*
Kathleen Maguire          *Schering-Plough HeathCare Products*
Robert Powers             *Combe, Inc.*
Diane Slayton             *The Pillsbury Company*
Maureen Stratton          *American Greetings Corporation*
Gary Yost                 *L&F Products*

# Contents

# Foreword

In the ever-changing business world, cooperative advertising (traditional funds allotted to retailers to feature brands in their advertising) has evolved to encompass almost any area of promotional marketing to the trade and to the consumer through the trade.

Manufacturers, suppliers, retailers, and other participants in co-op still seek the perfect, measurable program, one that consistently benefits all sides in the co-op equation. That goal is elusive, but not impossible, as Bob Houk demonstrates in this book. This guide covers co-op advertising from A to Z, from its infancy to the present and (sure-to-change) future. Whether you are just starting to use co-op or have been for some time, Bob Houk expertly guides you through the ins and outs of the process. He helps you sidestep the pitfalls of promotional allowance marketing and even points out which programs work well—and why.

Many of the member companies of the Association of National Advertisers (ANA) include co-op advertising in their marketing mix, hence ANA's interest in disseminating the latest information on the topic. This publication is a natural successor to *Cooperative Advertising* by Edward C. Crimmins, published under ANA auspices, in 1984 and ANA is pleased to recommend it as a resource whether you are just implementing a program or utilizing an existing plan, whether you're the manager of the program or a field person on the front lines.

Thanks go to the members of ANA's Promotion/Merchandising Committee who undertook the text review, in particular to Bob Powers, Co-op Advertising Manager at Combe, Incorporated, and to Phil Shyposh of the ANA staff.

Matthew M. Freeman  
Manager, Co-operative Advertising  
Block Drug Co., Inc.

# *Preface*

Two books on the subject of cooperative advertising under the aegis of the Association of National Advertisers is enough for any author, so I was delighted when my suggestion that Bob Houk do the next one was accepted.

Reading his manuscript made me feel what a long way we have come since my first book was published in 1970 and even since the second book was published in 1984. A comparison of the glossary in this book with the glossary in the 1984 book is the best evidence of the changes that have taken place. More than half the items in the glossary in this book were not included in the earlier one mainly because these concepts didn't exist as recently as 1984. Another striking example is the discussion of profitability by account. This concept was not taken into account in designing co-op plans in 1984. Most manufacturers simply tried to respond to the demands of their largest customers without breaking the law. No account was taken of the possibility that acceding to these demands might be a way of insuring lower profits. Naturally I do not agree with everything in this book. What two authors could be expected to agree on everything when so complicated a subject as cooperative advertising is at hand? For example, although I share Mr. Houk's impatience about the way the Robinson-Patman Act has been enforced—or not enforced—I do not take quite so dim a view of the Act itself as he does. Some of this difference may be generational in nature. For example, business people of my generation who went through the Great Depression are inclined to be a little less starry-eyed about the efficiency of the market place than later generations who have never experienced the joys of bank closing without the cushion of the FDIC.

But all differences aside, what Mr. Houk has done is to provide a practical guide to any supplier who offers a co-op program or is considering one. It should be the source book on the subject for years to come. And what a pleasure to read a book of this sort—that reads as though it were written by someone who knows how to write rather than by a committee!

Both Mr. Houk and the Association of National Advertisers who made this work possible are to be congratulated.

Edward C. Crimmins
New York, New York

## Acknowledgments

Many individuals have generated ideas and offered insights that are to be found in the following pages. Specifically I'd like to thank Ed Crimmins of Crimmins Co-op Marketing; Rob Hand, a former colleague at both ACB and MEDIANET; John Langdon of MEDIANET; and Dr. Robert Young of Northeastern University.

Neil Averitt, Staff Attorney at the Bureau of Competition of the Federal Trade Commission, has been patient and helpful in answering my questions. I hasten to add that this does not mean the FTC endorses anything about this book, or approves the legality of any proposals or suggestions we've made.

My wife gave me the time to write.

Bob Houk
Austin, Texas

# Introduction

This book is intended to provide both an in-depth study of the subject of promotional allowances and a basic how-to guide. The reasons for the how-to approach are self-evident. You (assuming most readers are marketing professionals employed by manufacturers) are spending thousands or even millions of your employer's dollars and you need some guidelines for structuring the programs that allocate those dollars to maximize their effectiveness in moving your product profitably. Your perspective differs if you are with a distributor, a retailer, or the media, but your interests are the same.

Readers should read the book cover to cover to understand the themes and to see how various issues tie together. The book is arranged in sections and short, mostly single-issue, chapters to assist you in quickly finding subjects of interest. After your initial reading, it will serve as a valuable reference manual for specific problems and opportunities. To that end, many of the definitions in the glossary at the end of the book include chapter references telling where each subject is discussed in the text.

The primary emphasis of this text is profit—specifically, the tactical use of promotional allowances to advance marketing strategies aimed at increasing profits. We will also talk about increasing sales and market share.

## Definitions

The terms listed in this section are used consistently throughout the text. Although they also appear in the glossary at the end of the book, you should become familiar with them now to facilitate your understanding of the rest of our discussion.

**Cooperative Advertising.** Any arrangement by which a product or service is brought to public notice over the names of both a supplier and any intermediary who comes between that supplier and the ultimate purchaser. The intermediary may be a retailer who buys the product for resale or a distributor who sells to retailers, or other intermediaries. This arrangement results in consumer or trade advertising as well as other types of promotion. The cost of the promotion may be shared by the supplier and the intermediary, or the supplier may pay all costs.

**Market development funds (MDF).** Any nonaccrual-based program initiated by the supplier to provide extra funding to specific retailers. These programs are also referred to as key city funds, over-and-above funds, or many other terms.

**Nontraditional media.** Promotional (usually nonmedia) vehicles that were mostly unavailable in co-op programs before the 1980s. These include spiffs, seminars, technical and sales training, spare parts, telemarketing, trinkets and trash, executive briefings, event sponsorships, and hot-air balloons.

**Promotional allowance marketing.** A term used to encompass the full spectrum of marketing programs offered by suppliers to their customers.

**Vendor support funds.** Recipient requests for extra funding from suppliers for specific promotional activities.

In discussing funding, the provider is generally referred to as the *manufacturer* and the recipient as the *dealer, retailer,* or *reseller.* These terms are used for the sake of convenience, because both providers and recipients may fall into a variety of categories.

# Reasons for Co-op

It would be easy to say that marketers offer promotional allowance programs because they work; however, although they usually do provide positive results, this is always the reason for using such programs. In fact, many marketers cannot say whether their programs work, because they have never set quantifiable goals by which to measure them. These companies offer co-op because it is expected, and their programs are structured to match competitors' programs rather than to achieve their own marketing needs. This widespread practice is most common for product categories such as apparel and accessories, hardware, and automotive parts and maintenance, in which virtually identical programs are used across the category and have not changed significantly in 20 years or more, despite the fact that the marketplace for these products has changed dramatically and repeatedly. This is not to say these programs are ineffective; it merely indicates that they are not used principally for effectiveness and they are not, therefore, as effective as they could be.

Besides matching competitors' programs, there are several other good reasons for offering co-op. Dr. Bob Young, in his doctoral thesis, "The Uses and Effectiveness of Vertical Cooperative Advertising," includes the chart of marketer objectives shown in Exhibit 1. Other than competitive pressures, the most frequently cited reasons for offering co-op are the first items listed as short-term objectives for trade and consumer audiences. These items are usually referred to as "sell-in" and "sell-through". A well-structured program should also be able to achieve the other short- and long-term objectives.

Whatever the program goals, it is important that management clearly understand what those goals are and review and revise them regularly. These goals, once set, need to be clearly communicated to personnel involved in the programs's administration and to any outside vendors involved. If goals are not set, the program will drift and never be as cost-effective as possible. If goals are not communicated to those responsible for implementing the program, the results will be the same—or worse if the implementation is aimed at goals contrary to those intended.

**EXHIBIT 1**  Marketer Objectives

|  | Intended Audience | |
|  | Trade | Consumer |
| --- | --- | --- |
| Short Term | Sell-in<br>General influence<br>Competitive parity<br>Generate retail advertising<br>and promotion | Immediate purchase (sell-through)<br>Establishment of price & location |
| Long Term | Build trade relationships<br>Position in merchandise mix | Brand message reminder<br>and reinforcement<br>Image |

Goals naturally imply measurement, a subject we discuss in Chapters 1 and 7. It is necessary to point out that there is a central conflict in promotional allowance marketing, because the goals of the manufacturer (provider) and dealer (recipient) only partially converge. Both want to sell product, but the dealer does not care which merchandise gets sold, and the manufacturer does not care who sells it. This discrepancy has caused a lot of trouble through the years. The solution is profit. Manufacturers care who sells the product when they know which dealers are most profitable (see Chapter 10), and dealers, who already know which products are most profitable, push those made most profitable by the manufacturer.

## The Money Factor

In the mid-1960s, conventional wisdom said that about $4 billion (the number is suspect) was spent each year in co-op advertising. That same $4 billion, adjusted periodically for inflation, still crops up. The fact is, nobody really knows how much money is available, or how much of what is available actually gets spent. Estimates vary wildly—from $10 billion to $55 billion. Why the huge discrepancy? The primary problem is the definitions used. One source may use "co-op advertising" to mean the funding of advertising (and only advertising) by retailers (an old concept that most marketers have moved beyond). On the other hand, another source may refer to "trade promotion" as any payment a manufacturer makes to its customers, although many such payments (such as slotting or order size and annual volume discounts) have no promotional aspects.

Using the definition of cooperative advertising from page X, we can calculate the total amount of money involved by determining, from readily-available sources, the total U.S. sales of each major retail channel. This number is then applied to typical mark-up, co-op accrual, and co-op usage percentages:

Total retail sales for a channel – the channel's normal mark-up =
Total wholesale sales.

Total wholesale sales × Average co-op accrual rate for the channel =
Total co-op accrual.

Total co-op accrual × Typical co-op usage rates for the channel =
Total co-op usage.

You can expand this estimate to include a breakdown by media, by applying a "typical" usage rate reflecting the spending patterns of each channel to the results. The final estimates are shown in Exhibit 2. This approach is not perfect, since it involves averages and estimates, but it is arguably more accurate than other methods. This estimate also attempts to include all current forms of promotional allowance marketing—both media and non-media—while excluding nonpromotional trade payments, such as slotting and rebates. The final estimate is between $30 billion and $33 billion (allowing a margin on either side of the $31.4 billion calculated). The most interesting point of these calculations is that advertising accounts for only 62 percent of expenditures, with newspaper down to 36 percent. Newspapers once accounted for almost all co-op spending, but their current percentage still represents over $11 billion. There also has been no shrinkage of co-op spending in newspapers, such spending continues to grow. The percentage decrease is due solely to the tremendous growth of other spending categories, and reflects the newspaper industry's long-term decline.

It is also interesting to see from the exhibit that advertising totals more than $19 billion (far more than estimated earlier)—although if the questionable mid-1960s estimate of $4 billion was accurate, then co-op *advertising* has only held roughly even in real terms, and may be slightly down, over the last 25 or 30 years.

The grocery and drug channels are clearly the most lucrative co-op sources, accounting for more than half the total. According to a 1994 Nielsen study (*Fifth Annual Survey of Manufacturer Trade Promotion Practices*), manufacturers in packaged goods, on average, allocated 13 percent of their 1993 sales for trade promotion (more than 20 percent of the respondents allocated more than 20 percent of their sales). However, more than half of that 13 percent were non-performance payments. Nielsen reported that the payments broke down as follows:

| | |
|---|---|
| Off-invoice allowances | 49% |
| Bill-back advertising allowances | 13% |
| Market development funds | 15% |
| Accrual programs | 11% |
| Bill-back display allowances | 6% |
| Slotting allowances | 5% |
| Other | 1% |

**EXHIBIT 2**  Estimate of 1994 Co-op Expenditures by Retail Channel and Media/Promotion Type

| Retail Channel | Typical Breakdown of Co-op Spending (%) | | | | | Typical Breakdown of Co-op Spending (Millions of $) | | | | | |
|---|---|---|---|---|---|---|---|---|---|---|---|
| | News-paper | Broadcast | Other | In store | Nontra-ditional | News-paper | Broadcast | Other | In store | Nontra-ditional | Total |
| Grocery | 26 | 6 | 14 | 38 | 16 | 3,675 | 848 | 1,979 | 5,371 | 2,261 | 14,133 |
| Drug | 26 | 8 | 12 | 39 | 15 | 533 | 164 | 246 | 800 | 308 | 2,050 |
| Department stores | 64 | 9 | 16 | 10 | 1 | 2,259 | 318 | 565 | 353 | 35 | 3,529 |
| Other general merchandise | 47 | 15 | 13 | 19 | 6 | 541 | 173 | 150 | 219 | 69 | 1,151 |
| Apparel and accessories | 66 | 13 | 12 | 8 | 1 | 871 | 172 | | 106 | 13 | 1,320 |
| Hardware, building materials, and lawn and garden | 45 | 10 | 18 | 21 | 6 | 1,035 | 230 | 414 | 483 | 138 | 2,301 |
| Automotive | 35 | 16 | 26 | 15 | 8 | 811 | 371 | 602 | 347 | 185 | 2,316 |
| Home furnishings | 42 | 12 | 24 | 19 | 3 | 743 | 212 | 425 | 336 | 53 | 1,770 |
| Appliances, electronics, and computers | 36 | 8 | 13 | 22 | 21 | 527 | 117 | 190 | 322 | 307 | 1,463 |
| Catalog and mail order | 5 | 5 | 90 | 0 | 0 | 25 | 25 | 457 | 0 | 0 | 508 |
| Other | 40 | 10 | 24 | 19 | 7 | 351 | 88 | 211 | 167 | 61 | 878 |
| Total | 36 | 9 | 17 | 27 | 11 | 11,371 | 2,717 | 5,397 | 8,503 | 3,431 | 31,419 |

Source: MEDIANET, Inc.

It should be noted this estimate is only for the United States. Because the Canadian co-op situation is so similar to the United States' and many U.S. marketers include both countries in their programs, we should add about 10 percent to our totals if we want to include Canada. This is approximately the ratio of Canadian gross domestic product to U.S. GDP. Chapter 13 has more information on international co-op, but reliable data on the amount of money being expended outside North America is scarce.

We can use the original estimate of $4 billion from the mid-1960s to check some of the estimates being made today. Four billion dollars from 1965 would be about $21 billion in 1994, allowing for inflation, so the lower-end estimates in the $10 billion to $15 billion range imply that co-op growth has not kept pace with inflation, which is highly unlikely. As another measure, we can compare co-op to the U.S. GDP. Gross domestic product has increased by a factor of about ten since the mid-1960s, which would increase the original $4 billion to $40 billion. It is possible to come up with an estimate that indicates co-op growth has not kept pace with GDP, since much of the increase in GDP during the past 30 years has been in services, where co-op is less prevalent. An estimate that comes in midway between $20 billion and $40 billion seems reasonable.

## What This Book Covers

In the following chapters, we will deal with co-operative advertising from several angles. Chapters 1 and 2 give you background information on research into co-op and its effect on sales, as well as the various types of government legislation and regulation that effect co-op programs. Chapters 3 through 7 provide practical, hands-on advice for setting up and using co-op. A big-picture view is achieved in Chapters 8 through 13, including how real-world economic occurences affect co-op and what the future may hold for these programs.

# Does Co-op Advertising Work?

Every company has someone, usually from the finance or sales department, who would like to discontinue the promotional allowance program. Their reasons are nearly always the same:

1. Half the dealers do not use the program.
2. It is difficult to administer.
3. The dealers would prefer to receive another 2 percent off-invoice instead.

Marketers' response, of course, is that cutting the program would result in less advertising and promotion, decreased brand awareness, and, therefore, decreased sales. The difficulty comes in proving this point of view.

## Effectiveness Research

This chapter will discuss research performed for and by a number of manufacturers showing a direct correlation between the use of promotional allowance programs and sales increases. New research has gone beyond this point to showing correlations between the percentage of promotional spending relative to sales volume and the percentage of sales increases. This relationship has also been shown to be channel specific.

In the late 1970s, Bob Wilcox, who then headed the co-op department for Armstrong World Industries (a flooring company) performed a study on a random sample of his dealer base. Since this took place before the personal computer era, he had to keep the study fairly small and simple. He selected only dealers who had been customers for three successive six-month periods. These remaining dealers (165) were sorted into two groups; those who had done any advertising through the program and those who had not. About two-thirds had done some advertising. He then compared the average sales growth for each group. The sales growth rate of the group that had advertised was more than three times higher than that of the other group (comparing their purchases of Armstrong products from two consecutive years).

These results were interesting, and over a decade later, armed with computers, Medianet decided to replicate and expand on Wilcox's work. These studies were, in most cases, performed with much larger samples, involved several different industries, dealt with both growing and declining markets, and were fine-tuned to relate the percentage of allowance usage to the percentage of sales growth. The findings were consistent with the earlier work. Wilcox found that co-op drives sales, a finding that Medianet confirmed with an added corollary: More co-op drives more sales.

One study dealt with one of the objections to Wilcox's study. Since bigger customers are more likely than small ones to use promotional allowance programs, his dealers who did some advertising were substantially larger, on average, than those in the other group. His figures showed that advertising group averaged 41 percent more in Armstrong purchases in the first year of the study and 61 percent more the second year. Thus, it is possible to argue that all Wilcox's study showed was that big dealers are more likely to advertise and that the big dealers grew faster.

In 1989 the sales figures of a large housewares manufacturer were examined . The manufacturer had several thousand customers, but the study dealt with only their 50 largest dealers, comparing their purchases for two consecutive years. The study determined co-op usage rates (the amount of promotional allowance funding the dealers had been paid in the second program year as a percentage of that year's purchases) and growth rate (total purchases in the second year compared to those in the first year) for all 50, and divided them into two groups: those who used more than the average percentage of co-op funds and those who used less. The average was defined as a factor of 1.00, and the ratio of the numbers for the high usage group

**EXHIBIT 1.1** Sales Growth and Co-op Usage, 50 Largest dealers, Housewares Manufacturer, 1987–1988

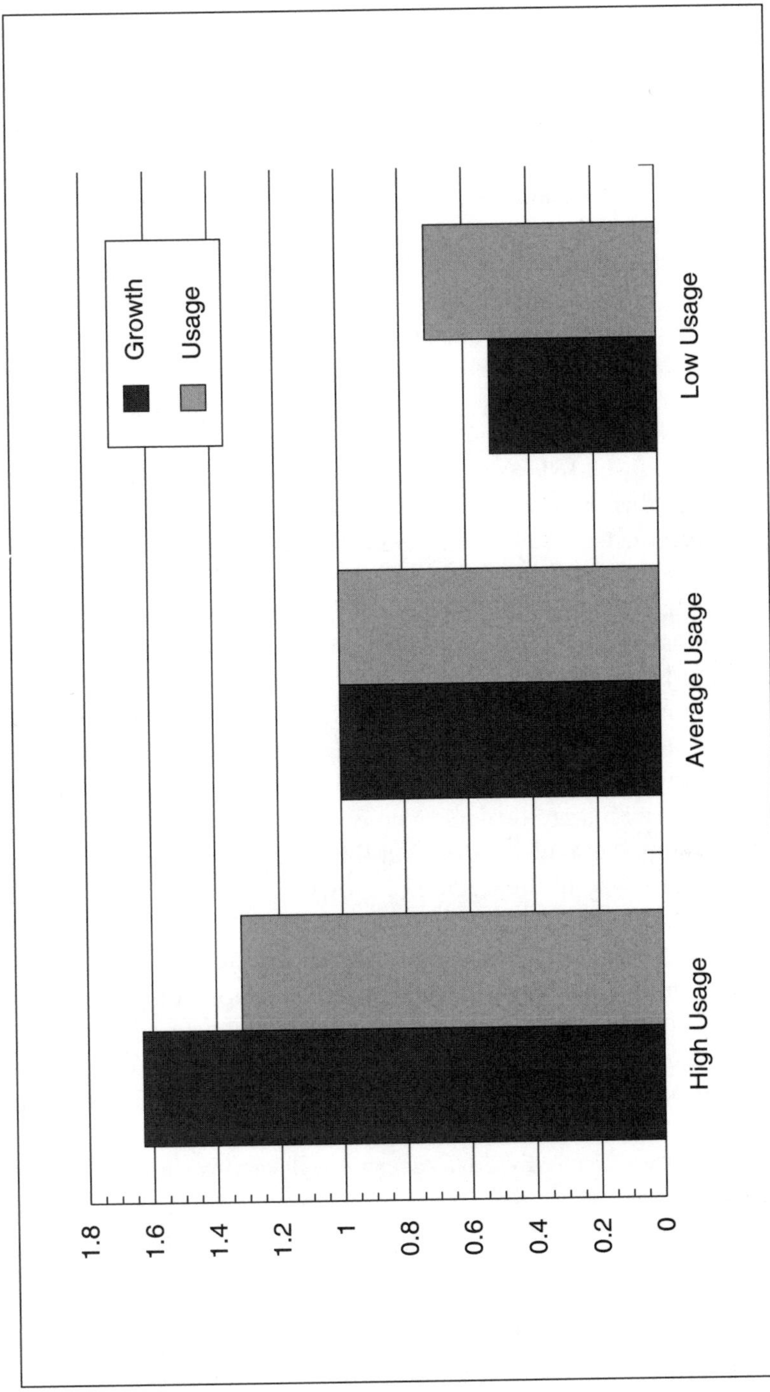

Source: MEDIANET, Inc.

3

and the lower group were compared to the average. As shown in Exhibit 1.1, the high usage group used about 25 percent more co-op than the average, the low group about 25 percent less. The high group's sales increase was more than 60 percent above the average, whereas the low group's was almost 50 percent below.

In 1992, the same study was done for the same manufacturer, with almost the same results. Those customers who used higher percentages of promotional allowances had better results than those who used lower percentages. The results differed, however, in line with the relative performance of the overall economy in the two studies. Whereas, in 1988, relative rates of sales *growth* were measured, 1991 was a poor year for this manufacturer (and many others), and relative rates of sales *decline* were compared. In 1991, the high usage group had slower rates of decline than the low usage group. Although this indicates that promotional allowance programs have a positive effect on sales regardless of the economy (or whether the product is in growth or decline), the later study showed a smaller differential between the groups, perhaps indicating that co-op has an even more positive effect in growth situations (this point is discussed again in Chapter 8).

The methodology of this study counters most of the substantive objections to attempts to the Armstrong study. Whereas the Armstrong study could be criticized for overweighting large dealers, this study dealt *only* with large dealers. Wilcox's study classified dealers only as advertising or nonadvertising, but this study correlated the degree of allowance usage to the degree of growth.

Some other studies have shown a correlation between growth in the *amount* of co-op funding used from one year to the next with a growth in sales. These studies were justifiably dismissed on the grounds that the amount of co-op a dealer used naturally would grow if sales grew, because as the sales grew, the amount of co-op available for use would grow proportionately. This study avoids that trap by dealing with percentages of co-op usage in the second year—a factor that can (and, in individual cases, does) vary without reference to sales increases.

Studies of real-life markets in action, however, cannot be performed under laboratory conditions. Therefore, on the basis of the studies described in this text, we will simply say that there is a direct correlation between the use of promotional allowances and sales growth; other factors are expected to enter into the equation and affect the degree of that relationship. Some would argue that these studies do not show a cause-and-effect relationship between co-op and sales, merely a statistical correlation. Although this is true, until methods are developed to measure cause and effect in advertising and promotion, statistics are all we have to use. Tobacco companies use the same argument with regard to the statistical link between smoking and certain health problems, and the proper reply is the same in both cases: When a statistical relationship is shown to exist consistently and affects your livelihood (or your life), it becomes foolish to ignore it.

One "outside" influence does enter into these studies. It is smart to use promotional allowances, and, therefore, smart dealers use them. Smart dealers also do all the other smart things that increase sales, from selecting good job merchandise to keeping the parking lot swept.

A study similar to the housewares manufacturer's was done for a major computer manufacturer, this time using the entire dealer base. The list of dealers for two succeeding periods (ending in October 1991) was compared and all those dealers who did not purchase product in both periods were eliminated. The remaining dealers' purchases for both periods were compared, their growth rates were calculated, and the percentages of their available promotional allowance funds (often called "soft dollars" in the computer industry) spent in the final period were determined.

The dealers were then separated into groups, according to what percentage of their funds they had used, and the average growth rates of each group were compared. The results were quite dramatic, as shown in Exhibit 1.2. The dealers who used more than 90 percent of their funds had an annualized growth rate of over 80 percent (1991 was a good year for this computer company). Those who used 76 percent to 90 percent of their funds grew about 40 percent, and each lower group had successively smaller growth rates. Note that the huge sales decline for the group that used no funds overstates the effects of not promoting, since this group probably includes a significant number of dealers who became inactive during the period.

For consistency, the same technique was used on the computer dealers as had been used for the housewares manufacturer's big dealers. They were divided into only two groups: those who used more than the average amount of their available funds and those who

**EXHIBIT 1.2** Sales Growth by Co-op Usage, Percentage for a Computer Manufacturer, 1990–1991

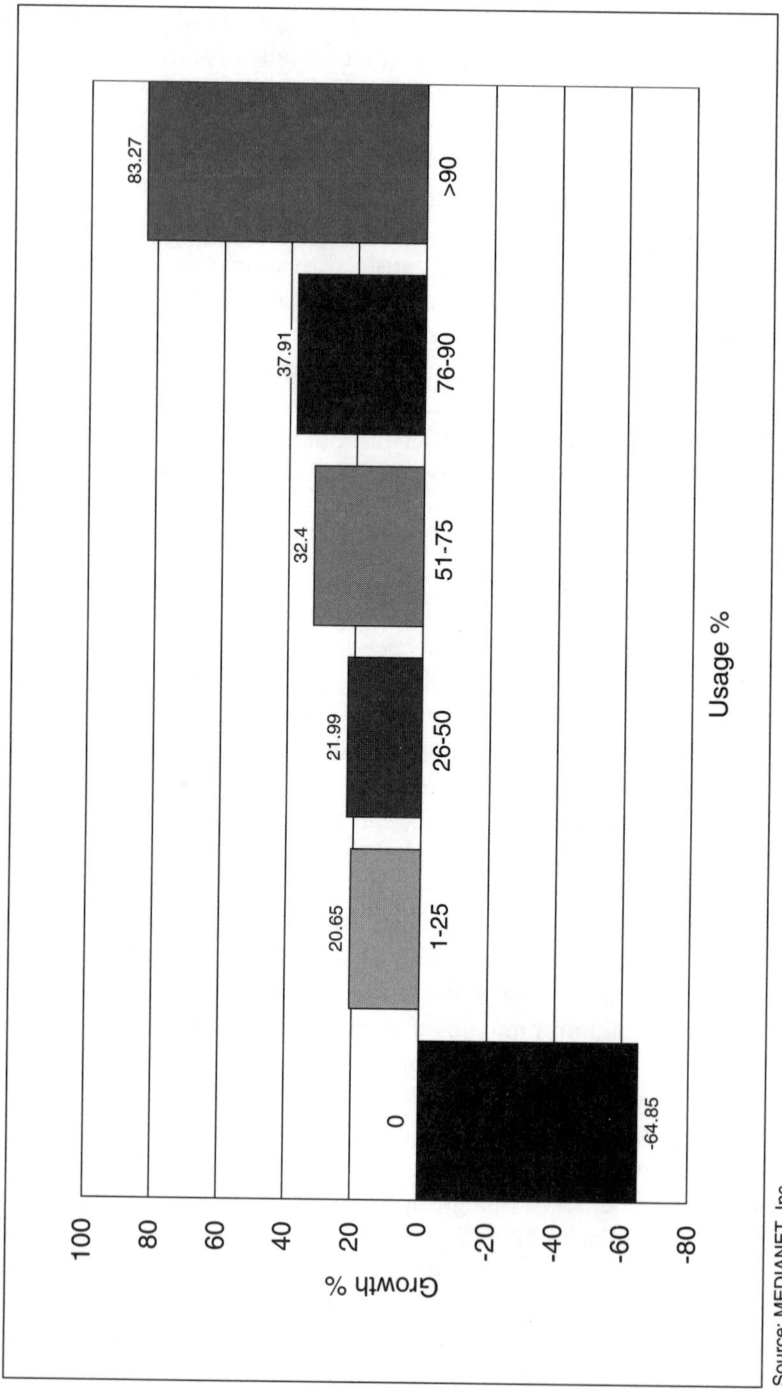

Source: MEDIANET, Inc.

used less. The results shown in Exhibit 1.3 were startlingly similar to those of the housewares manufacturer for the good growth year. The high usage group of computer dealers used about 20 percent more than the average; the low group about 33 percent less. The high group's sales increase was about 45 percent over the average; the low group's 50 percent below.

# Return on Investment

Can we get a sales return-on-investment (ROI) figure from these results? Not a totally valid one, because, as mentioned above, there are other differences between dealers who use most of the promotional funds available to them and those who do not; therefore all growth difference between the two groups cannot be attributed to co-op usage. Nonetheless, we can figure out what the total differences in sales growth are and relate them to usage. To the degree that other factors remain the same from one period to another, a manufacturer can use this ratio to measure increases or decreases in a program's effectiveness.

Researchers calculated how much larger the computer manufacturer's sales growth and promotional allowance expenditures theoretically would have been had all dealers promoted and grown at the same rate as the highest group. The incremental sales were 14.11 times the incremental expenditures. The conclusion is that for this manufacturer each additional dollar of co-op expenditure related to $14.11 in additional sales. Similar comparisons in other cases have shown return rates ranging from below 1:1 to over 20:1. These variances are believed to relate to economic conditions, industry, channel, and competitive conditions, as well as the quality of the promotional allowance program.

Exhibit 1.4 shows the amount of incremental gross profit generated by varying degrees of sales ROI at various gross margin percentages. If, for example, your product has an average gross margin of 60 percent, and you run a promotion generating a 15:1 sales ROI, your gross profits on the promotion will be 8:1 on your investment (if your investment were $2,000, you would generate $16,000 additional gross profits for your company).

No research background would be complete without mention of a case in which co-op did not work. It is instructive to discuss this

**EXHIBIT 1.3** Sales Growth and Co-op Usage for a Computer Manufacturer, 1990–1991

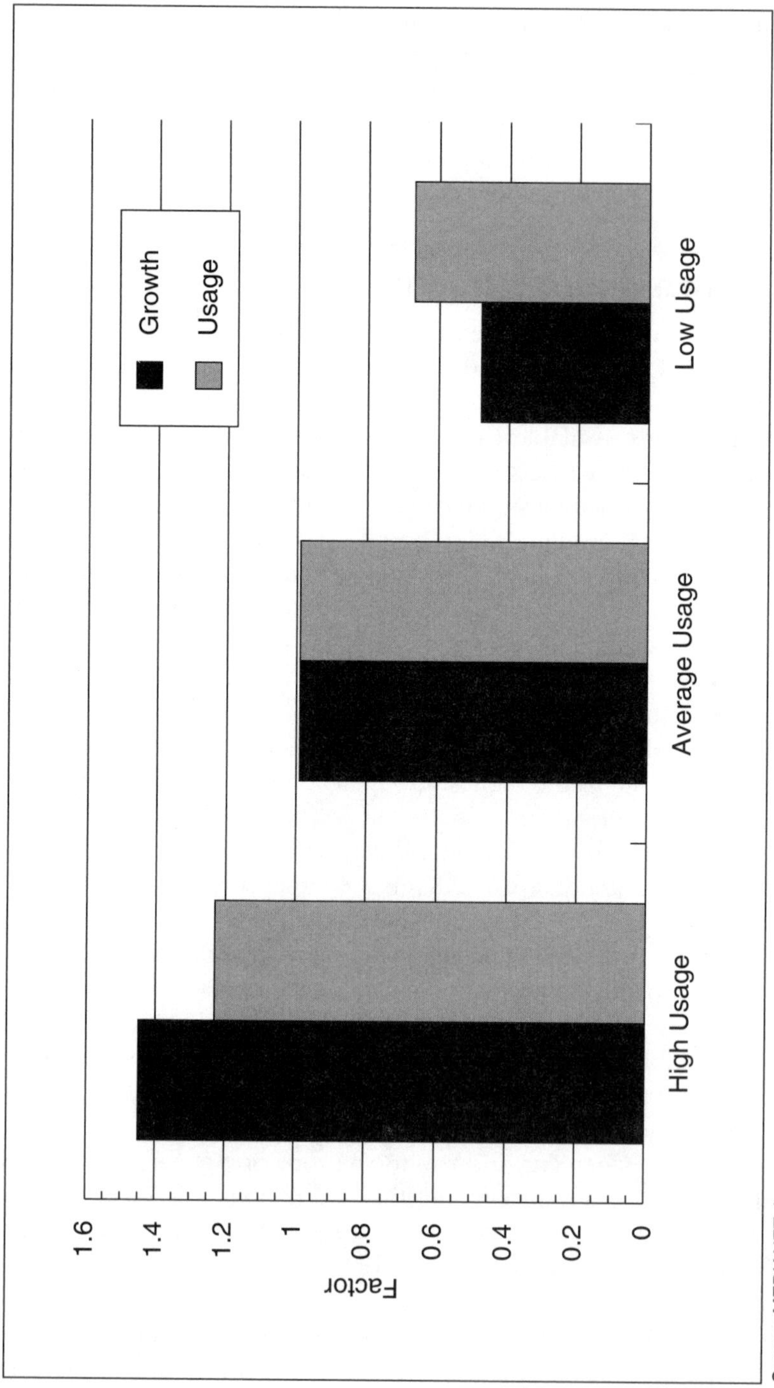

Source: MEDIANET, Inc.

8

**EXHIBIT 1.4** Gross Profit-on-Investment at Varying Return-on-Investment and Gross Margin Levels

| ROI | Average Gross Margins | | | | | | |
|---|---|---|---|---|---|---|---|
| | 80% | 70% | 60% | 50% | 40% | 30% | 20% |
| 20 | 15.00 | 13.00 | 11.00 | 9.00 | 7.00 | 5.00 | 3.00 |
| 19 | 14.20 | 12.30 | 10.40 | 8.50 | 6.60 | 4.70 | 2.80 |
| 18 | 13.40 | 11.60 | 9.80 | 8.00 | 6.20 | 4.40 | 2.60 |
| 17 | 12.60 | 10.90 | 9.20 | 7.50 | 5.80 | 4.10 | 2.40 |
| 16 | 11.80 | 10.20 | 8.60 | 7.00 | 5.40 | 3.80 | 2.20 |
| 15 | 11.00 | 9.50 | 8.00 | 6.50 | 5.00 | 3.50 | 2.00 |
| 14 | 10.20 | 8.80 | 7.40 | 6.00 | 4.60 | 3.20 | 1.80 |
| 13 | 9.40 | 8.10 | 6.80 | 5.50 | 4.20 | 2.90 | 1.60 |
| 12 | 8.60 | 7.40 | 6.20 | 5.00 | 3.80 | 2.60 | 1.40 |
| 11 | 7.80 | 6.70 | 5.60 | 4.50 | 3.40 | 2.30 | 1.20 |
| 10 | 7.00 | 6.00 | 5.00 | 4.00 | 3.00 | 2.00 | 1.00 |
| 9 | 6.20 | 5.30 | 4.40 | 3.50 | 2.60 | 1.70 | 0.80 |
| 8 | 5.40 | 4.60 | 3.80 | 3.00 | 2.20 | 1.40 | 0.60 |
| 7 | 4.60 | 3.90 | 3.20 | 2.50 | 1.80 | 1.10 | 0.40 |
| 6 | 3.80 | 3.20 | 2.60 | 2.00 | 1.40 | 0.80 | 0.20 |
| 5 | 3.00 | 2.50 | 2.00 | 1.50 | 1.00 | 0.50 | 0.00 |
| 4 | 2.20 | 1.80 | 1.40 | 1.00 | 0.60 | 0.20 | minus 0.20 |
| 3 | 1.40 | 1.10 | 0.80 | 0.50 | 0.20 | minus 0.10 | minus 0.40 |
| 2 | 0.60 | 0.40 | 0.20 | 0.00 | minus 0.20 | minus 0.40 | minus 0.60 |
| 1 | minus 0.20 | minus 0.30 | minus 0.40 | minus 0.50 | minus 0.60 | minus 0.70 | minus 0.80 |

Source: MEDIANET, Inc.

case, because it is an instance of the exception not only proving the rule, but yielding more information.

In 1992 a study similar in all respects to the one done for the computer manufacturer was performed on the program performance of a large fashion accessories manufacturer that sells through mostly up-market outlets, including a great number of leading department stores. The comparison covered sales and promotion in the company's 1992 program year (which ended in mid-1992) against the preceding year. As with the second study for the housewares manufacturer, this had been a poor year in the fashion accessories business.

Surprisingly, the results were the opposite of every other case: the dealers who advertised more had *poorer* sales performances.

In searching for an explanation for this anomaly, it was decided to see whether the situation might be caused by the manufacturer's heavy reliance on the department store channel of distribution, a channel that has been deeply troubled in recent years. This seemed the most likely explanation.

The dealer base was split into two groups: department stores and "other" (mostly smaller specialty outlets, both chain and independent). When these two groups were analyzed, it was found that the department stores used 75 percent of their funds but had a negative 13 percent growth rate, whereas the others used about 18 percent of their funds and declined less than 4 percent. Clearly, the department store group was dragging down the overall results.

When the sales growth and co-op usage analysis was performed for each of the two groups, it showed that in each case the heavier users had better growth rates than those who used the program less. In the department store group, however, the difference was so small that the ROI analysis showed that each additional dollar expended by the high usage group resulted in only eighty-six cents of additional sales. In the other group, the return was a much more impressive $6.55.

This is consistent with the conclusion drawn from the two studies on the housewares manufacturer's program: Co-op appears to have a greater effect in high-growth situations. In this case, we find that in an extremely low-growth environment—the already-moribund department store channel in the middle of a recession—those who used their co-op more did grow more, but very marginally.

On the basis of this study, we could draw the conclusion that any promotional funding put into an environment like the department store channel, beyond whatever might be needed to maintain basic promotional levels and meet competition, appears to be a waste of effort. Another possibility is that the poor results shown among high users in the department store group may be a reflection of some inflated claims from this group of stores. The extra money paid out to the high usage group may not have bought a significant amount of additional promotion, just as it did not buy significant additional sales.

In any event, the further analysis of this case in which promotional allowances did not, at first, seem to work, instead showed that it does work when analyzed on a channel-by-channel basis and that the same analysis can be used to determine which channels are most effective.

## Best Situations for Cooperative Advertising

We have shown that promotional allowance marketing works, but it would be foolish to argue that it works equally well (or at all) for every product in every situation. Let us examine the particular market circumstances in which co-op is most (and least) effective.

As a starting point, we will use infomation presented by Dr. Robert Young of Northeastern University in his doctoral dissertation, "The Uses and Effectiveness of Vertical Cooperative Advertising," and in an article in the May 1990 issue of *Proclaimer*. Young shows a chart listing product characteristics as they relate to the importance of co-op advertising in a product's marketing plan (see Exhibit 1.5).

The characteristics listed are generalizations, so exceptions can be found. Within the garment industry, for example, women's designer dresses, although they meet most of the criteria for promotional allowances as a major factor, they generally do not receive as much manufacturer support funding as the basic stock ready-to-wear and accessory lines. As a general guide, this list is an excellent tool for determining whether co-op should play a major role in a given product's marketing plan. For example, consider peanut butter and computers. Peanut butter meets almost all the criteria of the manufacturer-dominated category (except perhaps, brand loyalty), whereas computers meet practically all the criteria for retailer dominance. At a 1990 meeting of marketing personnel of several computer manufacturers, distributors, and retailers, the IBM attendee stated flatly, "Co-op is our most important marketing program." One would be shocked to hear the same statement from a Jif representative.

**EXHIBIT 1.5**  Product Characteristics Relative to Co-op

| Co-op Plays a Lesser Role in the Marketing Mix | Co-op Plays a Larger Role in the Marketing Mix |
| --- | --- |
| Convenience goods | Shopping goods |
| High repurchase rate | Infrequently purchased |
| Brand loyalty high | Brand loyalty low |
| Impulse purchase | Considered purchase |
| Utilitarian purchase | Purchase for ego enhancement |
| Packaged goods | Durable goods |
| Simple product concept | Complex product concept |
| Easily observed product attributes | Hidden qualities |
| Relatively inexpensive | Relatively expensive |
| Self-service retailing | Personal service retailing |
| Broad distribution | Selective distribution |

Source: "The Uses and Effectiveness of Vertical Cooperative Advertising." Robert F. Young.

One of the points Young makes in his *Proclaimer* article is the importance of determining the manner in which target consumers will respond to "dual-signature" ads. The fact that two brand names—the manufacturer's and the retailer's—appear in ads has an effect on the way the consumer will perceive the message and on how they react to each name (see more on this in Chapter 2). Manufacturers must consider whether consumers will give more credence to their name or the dealer's.

Some of these considerations may be changing as the nature of retailing changes. For example, in the days when department stores carried tremendous weight with their customers, and customers were fiercely loyal to one store or another, manufacturers who marketed through the department store channel placed great value on associating their brand name with good store names. Being featured in an ad by Joseph Horne, Sanger-Harris, or Goldwaters was an endorsement that carried considerable weight with people in Pittsburgh, Dallas, and Phoenix, respectively. As department stores lost their local focus through acquisition by national chains like Federated Department Stores and Associated Dry Goods, and then began to lose their preeminent place in the distribution chain to specialty stores and discounters, the purpose of dual-signature ads changed.

Although to a far lesser degree than in the past, some department stores and other retail outlets still carry an endorsement power that a manufacturer may wish to pay for. But no one looks to a Kmart ad for product endorsements, such an ad is merely a listing of product availability and pricing. As the value of the retailer's signature has decreased, however, the sheer size of these retailers has increased. In their promotional allowance dealings with discounters, manufacturers are no longer paying for an endorsement, but for the announcement of availability.

Using promotional allowances as a means of announcing avail-ability is most extreme in the grocery trade, although the announcement is done less in advertising than in stores. An article in the October 15, 1992, issue of *The Wall Street Journal*, quoting information provided by Information Resources Inc. (IRI), asserts that in-store displays can cause short-term increases in grocery sales of as much as 200 percent and more. The article also quotes the Point-of-Purchase Advertising Institute as saying that manufacturers spent $15.2 billion on in-store promotions in 1991, and would spend 18 percent more in 1992. (The figures related to all types of stores, not just grocery).

The effectiveness of displays in moving products means that retailers are raising the rent on display space. The word "rent" is used intentionally—as the publisher of *P-O-P Times* said, "Retailers (are) in the real-estate business, and the price of that real estate is going up." *The Wall Street Journal* reports a rate of $200 per display per week per store, although the rates vary considerably, depending not only on the market and the retailer's market influence, but also on the display's location in the store. A New Jersey retailer says "it's the guy who comes in with the best price and the most promotional dollars who gets the best display."

Displays are obviously most important and most productive for impulse items: IRI's data for the 13 weeks ending September 13, 1992, showed that frozen food displays resulted in a 245 percent sales increase, salty snacks on display were up 172 percent and soft drinks were up 138 percent. Meanwhile, necessities, such as disposable diapers and toothpaste, showed more modest (though still impres-sive) gains in the 60 percent to 65 percent range.

Some manufacturers in impulse categories appear to be almost totally dependent on displays to move their products. Pepsi, for example, sold over 60 percent of its product from displays in the period studied, with Dr Pepper and 7-Up at almost 50 percent. The major snack marketers—Frito-Lay, Eagle, Keebler, and Nabisco— were all in the 30 percent to 40 percent range. These numbers indicate why some manufacturers are so willing to pay the stores' prices.

It is interesting to note that the results in this study were reached with displays and, usually, a reduced price; the products in the study were not advertised. A Campbell Soup representative is quoted as saying that when a retailer uses a display, a price cut, *and* an ad, they can get sales increases of over 600 percent. A 1990 article, also quoting IRI data, in *The Marketer,* showed similar result (see Exhibit 1.6). The *Wall Street Journal* article did not deal with long-term gains from such displays, but we can presume any such gains are minimal. However, a study on price cuts alone, whether promoted through displays or ads or not, shows they result in *no* sustained sales gains.

In 1991, the London Business School (LBS) published the study, "The After-Effects of Large Consumer Promotions," written by A.S.C. Ehrenberg of the LBS and Stern School of New York University, Kathy Hammond of the LBS, and G.J. Goodhart of City University. It covered more than 100 brands of 25 grocery products in the United States, the United Kingdom, Germany, and Japan. The study used scanner data and consumer diaries from several thousand households in each country to determine when "promotional sales peaks" (increases of at least 25 percent over normal weekly sales) occurred. The authors found and tracked 170 such peaks. The study did not attempt to

**EXHIBIT 1.6**  Sales Volume Increases by Type of Promotional Support

| Product | Price Cut | Cut + Ad | Cut + Display | Cut + Both |
|---|---|---|---|---|
| English muffins | 26% | 200% | 260% | 450% |
| Toilet tissue | 62% | 441% | 709% | 1008% |
| Cough drops | 32% | 103% | 110% | 182% |
| Yogurt | 27% | 168% | 421% | 624% |
| Sausage | 40% | 190% | 430% | 975% |

Source: Information Resources, Inc., from "Trade Promotion Junkies" by Monci Jo Williams in *The Marketer,* October 1990, page 31.

correlate the increases to their causes, though presumably most were related to significant price reductions or something equivalent. These peaks were matched with four- to 8-week "clean" periods before and after that contained no such peaks. These clean periods were then measured to determine if the promotion had produced lasting sales increases and/or an increase in repeat buying by the consumers who had bought during the peak.

The study's authors admitted that sales during the clean periods might have been affected by a variety of "noise" factors in the market, such as competitive promotions, weather, out-of-stock items, and so on. Their feeling, however, was that since the study covers 170 instances, the law of large numbers would tend to eliminate any such effects.

The analysis of the 170 clean four-week periods before and after the peaks showed average sales increases of 1 percent across the four countries, ranging from 0 percent in the United States to 3 percent in Japan (see Exhibit 1.7).

**EXHIBIT 1.7** Average Sales Increases by Country

| Country | Increase |
|---|---|
| Germany | 1% |
| Japan | 3% |
| United Kingdom | 1% |
| United States | 0% |
| Overall | 1% |

Source: "The After-Effects of Large Consumer Promotions," London Business School, 1991

To study before-and-after repeat buying patterns, the study analyzed 50 clean eight-week periods. Analysis showed that theoretically-expected norms of repeat buying for the products without any promotion would average 40 percent. The study found actual repeat buying to be 40 percent (see Exhibit 1.8), meaning the promotions had no effect. A further analysis to determine whether such promotions attracted new buyers showed that 82 percent of consumers buying during the promotional peaks had bought the brand during the previous year.

15

**EXHIBIT 1.8** Average Repeat Buying by Country

| Country | Expected | Actual |
| --- | --- | --- |
| Germany | 41% | 47% |
| Japan | 32% | 34% |
| United Kingdom | 42% | 37% |
| United States | 44% | 42% |
| Overall | 40% | 40% |

Source: "The After-Effects of Large Consumer Promotions," London Business School, 1991

The authors concluded that promotions do not result in long-term sales increases, do not build repeat-buying habits in consumers, and do not attract large numbers of new buyers. They recommended that promotional money be put into "brand-building" activities instead, although they offered no evidence that such activities are more successful in long-term product movement. In fact, they admitted that their favored vehicle, media advertising, "generally has little or no immediate effect on . . . sales. Nor does it usually increase . . . sales or market shares in the longer term."

The LBS study calls to mind another study, "The Double Jeopardy of Sales Promotions," published in the September/October 1990 issue of the *Harvard Business Review*. In this article, the author argues that price cuts, even when they result in increased sales, have drastic effects on profits. For example, for a product with a fairly typical price elasticity of minus-1.8, variable costs of 50 percent, and normal net profits of 10 percent, the author calculated that the 18 percent increase in sales that would result from a 10 percent price cut would cause a 28 percent *decrease* in profits. Higher variable costs, lower elasticity, or lower normal margins would result in even greater losses.

If we put together the results of the two studies, we come to the conclusion that price promotions result in no long-term benefits and have a negative effect on price in the short term.

Throughout this section, we have talked about what work and what does not in trade marketing. In Chapter 13 we will discuss trade loading—the practice of forcing product into distribution channels by offering it at reduced prices—and how at least some manufacturers are beginning to react against it and move to everyday low pricing, or at least toward less excessive swings in pricing. Which leaves us with the question: How do all these things tie together into a cohesive approach to trade marketing and promotional allowances?

More and more people are deciding that trade loading, is wasteful, expensive, and, ultimately, counterproductive. The only reason more companies do not give it up is because too many people's jobs depend on maintaining it and because nobody knows for sure that anything else will work better.

So, if trade loading does not work, perhaps in-store promotions will do the job. The data cited in this chapter tell us in-store displays move tremendous amounts of merchandise in supermarkets, particularly in certain product categories and when combined with other promotion. But does in-store promotion produce lasting results? Not according to the London Business School.

So, what does work? If channel stuffing does nothing but clog up the distribution channel and interfere with production schedules; if, even when a manufacturer gets the trade to pass some of the deal money on to the consumer and gets them to run an ad and put up a display, all that manufacturer is doing is giving itself a temporary lift that goes away as soon as the price goes back to normal; and if all any of this does is cut into manufacturers' profits, what should be done?

The authors of the London Business School study, in agreement with representatives of Procter & Gamble (who were among the sponsors of the study) say that manufacturers should put more promotional funds into brand-building, specifically into media advertising, although they admit that this does not have any short-term and little long-term effect. Their plea for media advertising is somewhat forlorn and based mostly on faith. "[A]dvertising," they say in their summary, "unlike many or most promotions, is at least *aimed* at reinforcing the brand in the longer term, and most of us believe that it often does this successfully. . . ."

Brand-building is important (more than important to the packaged goods industry covered in the LBS study). Nonetheless, increased spending on national advertising is not the answer either. Review the previous sections, and Exhibit 1.6. Promotional allowance marketing works, the statistical analyses and case studies cited earlier prove that. It moves product in the short-term, which is what it is designed to do.

Although it has never been proven to have major long-term effects, that has also never been its purpose. Promotional allowance marketing is intended to have short-term results and is ineffective only when its short-term results are insufficient to justify its cost.

# Co-op Legalities and Legislation

The Federal Trade Commission (FTC) publishes the rulebook for promotional allowance marketing, properly titled *Guides for Advertising Allowances and Other Merchandising Payments and Services*. For obvious reasons, no one ever uses the full title, references are to the Guides, the FTC Guides, or the Fred Meyer Guides.

## Legislative Background

Some form of co-op has been around since the turn of the century. And from the time co-op programs began, there has been legislation aimed at regulating them. The following list identifies the most important acts and actions pertaining to promotional allowance programs. These descriptions will give you a basis for our future discussions of legal issues and concerns.

**Clayton Act (1914).** The primary intent of this act was to deal with preferential pricing. For the first time, the government said that a seller could not favor one purchaser over another. Those who drafted the law, however, left a large loophole; manufacturers could charge everyone the same price, but offer their key customers a "promotional allowance" or some other form of rebate.

**The FTC Act (1914).** This act established the Federal Trade Commission to enforce the Clayton Act and to oversee trade in general. The idea was that a commission would have more specific knowledge of trade issues and could act more quickly and effectively than the courts.

**The Robinson-Patman Act (1936).** Passed as an amendment to the Clayton Act, Robinson-Patman was the result of small grocery retailers' complaints to the federal government that they could not compete with the large chain supermarkets that had begun to spring up around the time of the Great Depression. We look at this act in more detail later in this chapter, but we will say here that its primary intent was to outlaw discriminatory allowances that amounted to discriminatory pricing in favor of larger retailers. Although it has been enforced strenuously at different times, it did not save the small grocers who originally prompted its establishment.

**The FTC Guides (1960).** The FTC issued its first set of co-op guide-lines telling manufacturers what they could and could not do when offering support programs to their dealers. These guides are discussed in more detail in the next section.

**FTC v. Fred Meyer, Inc. (1968).** Fred Meyer, a chain headquartered in Portland, Oregon, argued that they were entitled to larger allowances than their smaller competitors because they bought direct from manufacturers, whereas the small retailers bought through wholesalers. The Supreme Court upheld the FTC's contention that all customers, direct and indirect, had to be treated equally.

## SPECIFICS OF ROBINSON-PATMAN

The Robinson-Patman Act is actually Section 2 of the Clayton Act. Section 2, in turn, consists of six subsections, 2(a) through 2(f). Of these, only 2(d) and 2(e) greatly interest us, though we will need to take a quick look at 2(a), 2(b), and 2(f). For the terminally curious, 2(c) forbids brokerage payments by one party to another party except for services rendered in connection with the sale, and thus could never have any connection to co-op.

Section 2(b) allows for a meeting competition (popularly known as "meetcomp") defense against charges of violating Robinson-Patman, and also says that after a *prima facie* finding, the defendant must prove innocence.

Section 2(f) says that buyers cannot induce an unfair price. Interestingly, 2(f) is not the legal basis for extending the Guides to buyers, since it only forbids buyers to induce unfair *prices*, not unfair allowances. According to the law books, it is Section 5 of the FTC Act that says buyers cannot induce unfair allowances. It says: "Unfair methods of competition in commerce, and unfair or deceptive acts or practices in commerce, are hereby declared unlawful." Vague enough for you?

The differences between 2(a) and 2(d-e) are often confusing to marketers. The essential point is that 2(a) deals with the sale of the product (the sell-in), whereas 2(d-e) deal with the resale (sell-through).

The rules governing the subsections are slightly different, but the differences are very important. First, 2(a) allows for a cost-justification defense, whereas 2(d-e) specifically forbid such a defense. Thus, you can offer WalMart a lower price than other dealers get, based on the tremendous volume you do with them, but you cannot use that volume as a justification for also giving them a disproportionate promotional allowance. Perhaps as important, violations of 2(d-e) are *per se* violations, whereas a violation of 2(a) must be shown to have caused "competitive injury" or it is not a violation. This makes 2(a) a "no harm, no foul" rule—if you did something Robinson-Patman says you should not, but it did not hurt your competitors or your customer's competitors, then the FTC cannot act against you. Violations of 2(d-e) being *per se* violations means that the FTC does not need to show any competitive injury, just that you violated the rules.

# The FTC Guides

## GUIDE 1: PURPOSE OF THE GUIDES

The Commission says the purpose is to help you comply with Sections 2(d-e), that the Guides are based primarily on legislative history and court decisions, and that the Commission attempts to give guidance where there is no case law.

It also points out (very important) they are *only* guides, and do not have the force of law. In theory, this should concern you, because it means you could do everything the Guides tell you to, and still get in trouble if the Commission or the courts changed their minds. Realistically, that is pretty unlikely, although an example of changing enforcement is covered later in this chapter.

## GUIDE 2: APPLICABILITY OF THE LAW

Here the Commission tells us who and what Sections 2(d-e) regulates. The most important points are that the Guides apply to the resale of products (not services), that are sold in interstate commerce, in situations in which the reseller is in competition with other resellers of the same seller's goods of "like grade and quality." These points are expanded on in the next few Guides.

This Guide also points out the difference between 2(d) and 2(e): Section 2(d) deals with payments to the reseller for promotion, whereas 2(e) deals with the provision of those services. In either case, Guide 2 tells us, the rules apply whether the payments or services are provided directly or through an intermediary. Guide 2 also makes reference to Section 5 of the FTC Act applying to buyers or third parties, such as media.

## GUIDE 3: DEFINITION OF SELLER

A seller is anyone who sells products for resale, whether or not the products sold will have further processing before resale. This means that co-op programs for products that are ingredients of finished products (such as cotton) are subject to Robinson-Patman rules.

## GUIDE 4: DEFINITION OF CUSTOMER

A customer is anyone who buys for resale from the seller or from an intermediate reseller (for example, a wholesaler). This Guide offers a few exceptions, such as a purchaser of distressed merchandise, someone who purchases only from other retailers, or someone who makes only sporadic or incidental purchases.

## GUIDE 5: DEFINITION OF COMPETING CUSTOMERS

Customers compete if they sell products "of like grade and quality" at the same level of distribution in the same trading area. As everyone knows, it does not matter customers buy direct. This was the basis of the Fred Meyer case. Fred Meyer argued that because it was a direct customer, it was entitled to better treatment than indirect customers.

Department stores have long argued that they were entitled to special allowances as a more prestigious channel, but the revised 1990 Guides added an example specifically forbidding discrimination by class of trade. The fact that all channels must be treated equally, however, does not mean they must all be treated the same (see Chapter 12).

You need not, however, treat distributors the same as retailers— they are not at the same level of distribution. Similarly, if you make a high-end line and a low-end line that you distribute through two separate channels, you do not need to offer equal programs to both channels because the goods are not "of like grade and quality".

### GUIDE 6: INTERSTATE COMMERCE

Unless you are doing business entirely within one state, Robinson-Patman applies to you.

### GUIDE 7: SERVICES OR FACILITIES

The rules cover any services or facilities related to resale of a product. Examples cited include advertising, demonstrators, cabinets, displays, contest prizes, and special packaging.

### GUIDE 8: NEED FOR A PLAN

The Commission advises that anyone who is making payments or furnishing services coming under Robinson-Patman *should* do so according to a plan and "would be well advised" to put it in writing. The plan should be made available to all competing customers on a timely basis. The plan should be proportionally equal and offer alternatives that all eligible customers can use.

### GUIDE 9: PROPORTIONALLY EQUAL TERMS

Here is the tough part. What is proportional? What is equal? The Guide says there is no one way of determining proportionality. Some examples are offered, including basing payments on the cost of a service (the ad or promotion) or paying on a per-unit basis on goods purchased during a given period, or on a combination of both. Most co-op programs have traditionally been based on a combination: X percent of cost up to Y percent of purchases. The Commission then adds that "other methods . . . are acceptable." The Guides specifically state that allowances should *not* be graduated.

This is the Guide around which the infamous "Value War" erupted. In 1988, the Commission staff published a proposed set of new Guides in the Federal Register. Argued in the proposal was the idea that perhaps the Commission should bless a "value standard" as a proportionally equal method of allocation. The chairman of the

Commission at the time, Daniel Oliver, went further in proposing a value standard as the *only* proper method of allocating promotional allowances. The value standard would base payments to retailers on the value of the advertising or promotion to the manufacturer.

All hell broke loose. The Commission received 210 comments on the value standard, which split out 201 to 9 against it (with several of the nine offering only partial support). The principal objection was the subjectivity of such a standard—how do you determine what the value (as opposed to the cost) of a particular newspaper ad is? Who does the determining? This, of course, led to the other major objection, unfairness, since it was obvious to all concerned (except perhaps Chairman Oliver), that the biggest retailers would have a field day with such a proposal, using it to gain even more disproportionate promotional allowance terms than they got already. Many in the industry mounted a full-scale campaign against the value standard and some other provisions of the proposed Guides. Letters were written to Congress, asking that pressure be put on the Commission and proposing Congressional hearings.

When the new Guides were finally adopted in 1990 (without Congressional hearings), the value standard had disappeared and the new Guide on proportional equality was almost identical to the old one.

It must be noted that the motives of the value standard opponents were not totally pure. Two major groups of opponents were co-op administrative services and newspapers. The co-op administrators were concerned that a value standard would mean that manufacturers would dispense with the auditing of claims, a move that would devastate their industry, especially for those who offer little service beyond auditing. The newspapers saw the already strong tide moving promotional allowance funding away from media and into other promotional activities turning into a possible flood.

It should also be noted the Commission did not say a value standard could not be used, only that it was not included in the examples offered in the Guides and that certainly Chairman Oliver's proposal was not adopted.

The Commission, in the commentary released along with the new Guides, said "[T]he law may . . . permit use of the value standard . . . ." It warned, however, that unless such a program were carefully monitored, it could easily be discriminatory. The commentary said this concern was the reason the new Guides included no reference to the value standard.

Having said all this, it should be noted that many of the trends in co-op today are leading toward *de facto* value standards. A value standard is implicit in return-on-investment-based programs (see Chapter 10). Many companies are moving toward what they call plan-based programs, in which they approve or reject proposals submitted by dealers based on the merits of the plan (Chapter 11)—this is a value standard. In recent years, members of the grocery channel have been talking about account-specific marketing, which is similar to a plan-based program (again a form of value standard). The pay-for-performance programs beginning in the packaged goods industry, in which dealers are paid on the basis of sales-out (Chapter 12), are somewhat value-based. So maybe we owe Chairman Oliver a belated apology.

Another lesser controversy concerning this Guide had to do with the question of "mathematical precision." Must the proportional equality be mathematically precise? The old Guides said nothing about it. The proposed Guides said mathematical precision was not required, although a reasonable basis should be demonstrated. The new Guides are again silent, but the Commission's commentary said "mathematical precision has never been required by the law or the Guides."

### GUIDE 10: AVAILABILITY TO ALL COMPETING CUSTOMERS

The services and facilities should be usable "in a practical sense" by all competing direct and indirect customers. If not, then usable, proportionally equal alternatives must be offered. Timely notice of the basic program and of any alternatives must be given to all customers. This allows you to offer different types of programs to different types of dealers, as long as the different programs are proportionally equal (see Chapter 12).

### GUIDE 11: WHOLESALER OR THIRD PARTY PERFORMANCE OF SELLER'S OBLIGATIONS

Use of intermediaries to handle all or part of a program is permitted but does not relieve a company offering promotional allowances of its legal obligations. This means that you are not relieved of your obligations by hiring a third-party administrator, nor by giving co-op money to distributors and telling them they have to pass the money through to their dealers. You are obligated to check that the money goes where it should.

## GUIDE 12: CHECKING CUSTOMER'S USE OF PAYMENTS

This is the Guide dear to the hearts of all administrative services. It was deleted in the proposed revisions, but restored practically unchanged in the new Guides. It says sellers should take reasonable steps to ensure that their customers are actually performing the services being paid for, that they are not being overpaid, and that the allowance is being used solely for the purpose intended. If the seller knows or *should know* that the program is being abused by a customer, the payments should be discontinued.

## GUIDE 13: CUSTOMER'S AND THIRD-PARTY LIABILITY

As mentioned earlier, Sections 2(d-e) refer to sellers, not to their customers. However, this Guide states that customers who know or should know that they are receiving services or allowances not available to their competitors, can be proceeded against under Section 5 of the FTC Act. Examples provided include billing at vendor rates (standard practice among department stores) or failing to pass on volume discounts from the media (standard practice among almost all channels).

Guide 13 also forbids deductions if they result in discriminatory treatment. We deal with deductions at length in Chapter 12.

This Guide also extends Section 5 to the media and to media brokers, citing such practices as double billing and phony rate cards.

## GUIDE 14: MEETING COMPETITION

This is one of the most contentious areas of the Guides. Guide 14 says, in short, that you can make offers violating the terms of your promotional allowance program, if it is necessary to do so in order to meet the deal a competitor is offering. *Meetcomp*, as this is often called, is valid with either existing or new customers, so if a competitor is trying to get your best customer away by offering special allowances, you can meet the offer. Similarly, if you are trying to acquire a new account, but to do so you have to match what your competitor is offering, you can do it. It is also usable on an area-wide basis.

There are catches (of course), including:

- You can only meet an offer, not beat it.
- You can only meet a lawful offer.
- You must act in good faith.

The first is pretty clear. You and your competitor both offer 2 percent co-op programs, and a prospective new account says to you, "Why should I change unless I can get a better deal? Give me 3 percent and I'll switch." You cannot do it. Your program is 2 percent, but your competitor is offering one of your dealers 3 percent to switch. You can offer the dealer 3 percent to stay with you, but not 4 percent.

The second restriction is a little more difficult. If your competitor has a 2 percent program and offers one of your dealers 3 percent, can you match the offer? Even knowledgeable attorneys do not want to commit to an answer. It would appear the competitor's offer is illegal, but maybe they are meeting a third offer you do not know about, or maybe it is a special promotion not yet made public, or there could be some other explanation. If you are acting in good faith, it would be unlikely that you would be cited in by the FTC for matching a competitor's offer, even if it goes beyond the competitor's published program.

But what is "good faith?" This is where the FTC and the courts (to say nothing of theologians and philosophers) trip all over themselves. Good faith is difficult enough to define in the abstract, but virtually impossible to determine in practice. Deciding whether someone was acting in good faith amounts to trying to decide what he or she was thinking at a given moment.

If a buyer tells you he or she got a better offer from a competitor, does good faith require you to verify it? Yes and no. Yes, according to the Supreme Court in *Corn Products v. FTC* (1945) and according to the FTC in their action against Boise Cascade in 1986. But not if past experience indicates you can rely on the buyer's word, according to the Supreme Court in *A&P v. FTC* in 1979.

You probably *should not* try to verify the offer with the competitor. Not only are you unlikely to get a straight answer, but calling a competitor to discuss pricing and allowances could be considered collusion.

So, where does all this leave you? It probably leaves you confused and, hopefully, careful. It is good practice to concentrate less on the law and more on making good marketing decisions. Match an offer if you think it is real and if it makes sense to do so—that is good marketing and generally should be legal. But do not do something stupid just because the dealer says your competitor is doing it—that is bad marketing and may get you into legal trouble. If a buyer tells you about getting an offer that sounds too good to be true, it probably is, unless your competitor really *is* stupid.

Remember, you are in business for profit, not for market share. Take into account *all* the various allowances you offer the dealer (and make sure the dealer is also taking all the various allowances into consideration before saying you do not measure up), and calculate whether the additional point or two needed to match the competitor will shave your margins too thin. If so, it may be better to walk away from the deal.

You should also document completely any decisions to meet competition. Write down exactly what the buyer told you, what you did to try to verify it, why you believed it was a real offer, and what you offered in response.

And talk to your lawyers. To help speed their research, suggest they look at the cases mentioned in this section, plus *US v. U.S. Gypsum* (1978), *FTC v. Staley* (1945), *Hillside Dairy v. Fairmont Foods* (1981), *Exquisite Form v. FTC* (1965), and *Standard Oil v. FTC* (1951).

## GUIDE 15: COST JUSTIFICATION

There is no justification. As mentioned earlier, this means you cannot justify higher allowances or special deals for your biggest customers on the basis of their volume or your reduced unit costs of selling to them. These are legitimate points in regard to Section 2(a) questions, and the law's view is that all such allowances should be made in the selling process.

## ADDITIONAL CONSIDERATIONS

**Slotting.** The Commission spent a considerable amount of time in the commentary accompanying the 1990 revision of the Guides discussing slotting, and decided it is legal as long as it is proportion-ally equal. The major point, though, is that slotting is more closely related to the initial sale rather than the resale of goods (because a slotting allowance is generally required by the dealer as a condition of carrying the product), and it should therefore be dealt with under Section 2(a). Slotting is reduced to a footnote to Example 5 of Guide 9, which says, "The discriminatory purchase of display or shelf space

. . . may violate the (Robinson- Patman) Act . . . (and) Section 5 of the FTC Act." Slotting is covered in detail later in this chapter.

The commentary suggests that an argument could be made that some of the "infrastructure-building" programs so prevalent in the computer industry (programs paying for technical support, sales and technical training, floor planning, and many other such reseller expenses), by making it possible for the dealer to carry a product line, are related to the original sale, not to the resale. This would allow greater discretion in allocating such programs, since they would be subject to a cost justification, and alleged discrimination in their application would not be subject to *per se* interpretation. A staff attorney for the FTC, given as an example programs that pay for training for sales and service personnel, said (with due governmental caution) that it sounded like "a reasonable interpretation."

***Diverting.*** With regard to this practice, some grocery groups asked the Commission to deal with diverting by ruling that wherever promotional goods are diverted, the promotion had to be offered to local retailers. The FTC wisely declined to get involved, saying it would be virtually impossible to track the diversion of goods. Had the FTC followed the grocers' recommendations, it could have killed the entire concept of regional marketing.

***The ABA Lawsuit.*** On May 27, 1994, The American Booksellers Association filed a lawsuit in U.S. District Court against five book publishers alleging violations of the Robinson-Patman Act, involving both price discrimination and co-op advertising violations. The allegations are similar to issues in a Federal Trade Commission investigation of several other book publishers opened in 1988 and still open, though reported to be near settlement.

The two most important allegations would appear to be:

- Publishers participate in vendor support programs ("programs that are designed and developed by the Chains themselves.") which is evidence of discrimination. If this argument is upheld, it could throw virtually every co-op program in the United States into question.

- The different documentation requirements imposed on independents and chains constitute a violation of Robinson-Patman. This could, if upheld, be another industrywide problem, since many manufacturers allow larger retailers to get away without submitting invoices or otherwise fully documenting their claims.

Some manufacturers hire outside services to collect tearsheets of newspaper and insert ads run by their bigger customers (knowing that the customers will not provide the tearsheets themselves), but require their smaller customers to submit tearsheets to receive payment.

The suit summarizes the co-op section by saying that the alleged practices "provide to the Chains a profit source denied to the [independents]."

The ABA asked that the court declare the practices illegal, prohibit the publishers from continuing the practices, and award the ABA costs and fees, and "such other and further relief as this Court deems just and proper."

The publishers responded on August 1, arguing that the court should dismiss the suit or at least stay any action, pending the outcome of the FTC's action against the other group of publishers.

The defendants asked dismissal on several grounds, which can be summarized as follows:

- *The ABA does not have standing.* They argued that only injured parties may sue under Robinson-Patman and that an association, which itself neither buys nor sells products from the defendants, has no basis on which to file a complaint. They also pointed out that the association is bringing an action contrary to the interests of some of its members (the chain stores), which, according to cases cited in the response, undercuts the association's position in court as being a representative of its members.

- *The complaint is generalized.* They argued that the complaint alleges generally that chains get better pricing and promotional deals than independents, but that Robinson-Patman requires specific instances of discrimination. Their position is that a Robinson-Patman complaint over pricing must, for example, cite two contemporaneous sales at differing prices to stores in competition with each other, and which caused competitive injury.

Failing dismissal, the defendants asked that the court delay any action until the resolution of the FTC complaint. The defendants' response cites a recent item in *FTC: WATCH* (April 25, 1994) reporting "that the publishers have reached an agreement with the FTC staff concerning a consent order and that the staff has referred to the Commission proposed consent orders for its formal approval."

The defendants' position is that the FTC action may obviate the need for the lawsuit, or at least clarify the issues and provide grounds for a settlement. In support of this position, they cite a letter the ABA sent to its members on June 27, 1994: "ABA is seeking relief ... that in large part mirrors the relief that several major publishers have reportedly already agreed to with the FTC; if the resolution of the FTC proceeding provides effective relief for ABA members, the association will attempt to coordinate that relief with what it seeks in private litigation."

Observers say that, apart from the issues involved, the lawsuit itself is significant, because it is another reminder that, even if the FTC should remain relatively inactive on Robinson-Patman issues, there is a danger to manufacturers from the "right to private action" aspect of the Act. This was the second major Robinson-Patman lawsuit filed by retailers against their suppliers in one year, alleging discriminatory action in favor of other retailers. In July 1993, Wherehouse Entertainment filed suit in U.S. District Court in Los Angeles against several record distributors, alleging Robinson-Patman violations relative to the distributors' refusal to give co-op allowances to stores dealing in used compact disks. The distributors agreed to change their policies.

# The Debate Over the Robinson-Patman Act

The main concern marketers have with Robinson-Patman is its clearly anticompetitive intent. It is difficult for anyone who believes in free markets to defend the Act. Those who do defend it do so on practical grounds. To present an argument against Robinson-Patman, it is not sufficient (and totally unnecessary) to point out that it is contrary to sound economic theory, and it is an awful piece of legislation. What matters is that, in addition to all its other faults, Robinson-Patman is also contrary to good sense and harmful to the growth and health of the co-op advertising industry.

First, we have to ask if the Robinson-Patman Act has achieved its purpose. When the act was passed in 1936, its primary purpose, as mentioned earlier, was to defend the neighborhood independent retailer (particularly the grocer) against the then-emerging supermarket chains. Did it work? If you take a walk through your neighborhood, you will likely note that most of the mom-and-pop stores are gone.

Would we have been better off if the act had succeeded? As consumers, of course not. The small neighborhood store was inherently inefficient as a vehicle of distribution, and the large chains beat them because they offered the consumer better prices and better selection.

A hint of what kind of prices consumers could expect if Robinson-Patman had worked can be found at convenience stores, which occupy the same slot in the distribution network as mom-and-pops once did. By buying as chains, though, even the convenience stores are more efficient than the independent neighborhood store of old. How would you like to buy *all* your groceries at 10 percent or so above 7-11's prices? That is what Wright Patman wanted you to do.

That is the situation for consumers. How would we have been affected as marketers? The co-op industry would be no better served than consumers if Robinson-Patman had worked. One of the first things everybody in this business learns is that small dealers do not use their co-op funds because they do not advertise. A nation of small independent retailers would be a nation without much co-op—or much retail advertising of any kind.

Since the act did not accomplish its purpose, why not get rid of it? The two main arguments advanced by supporters of Robinson-Patman against its repeal (or weakening) are that (1) it would lead to excessive funding going to major retailers at the expense of smaller businesses, and (2) too much of the funding would be used (and abused) in unmeasurable promotional vehicles like in-store displays and signage. (This latter concern is expressed with greatest vigor, of course, by representatives of measurable media like newspapers and radio.)

Regarding the first argument, most of the funding already goes to the major retailers and since, for the most part, the small dealers do not use what they have available, what difference would it make if less were available to them?

The second argument is a more valid concern, but is this not the sort of thing a free market is good at sorting out? Those retailers who use co-op funding in an unproductive manner and those suppliers who allow their co-op funds to be abused will suffer in the marketplace. As believers in real advertising and promotion (as opposed to the diversion of co-op to the bottom line through rebates and rebate-like payments for nonexistent promotions) should we not be willing to see our beliefs put to the test? Let's not hide behind a law, but let competition determine if co-op, properly used, is an effective marketing tool.

What would things be like without Robinson-Patman? We had a virtual test of that proposition during the Reagan-Bush years. The act was thoroughly ignored by the FTC for 12 years. The result was an explosion of co-op: hundreds (maybe thousands) of new programs; vast expansion of existing programs; innovation; creativity; tremendous growth of fund usage; more and more suppliers seeing the benefits of dealer support and consequently diverting funds from national advertising into co-op, MDF, and vendor support programs; more and more retailers seeing the opportunities and presenting innovative proposals for additional funding to their vendors.

Conversely, what would be the result if Robinson-Patman were once again rigidly enforced, as it was in the 1960s? We might well go back to 1960s-style co-op. Manufacturers, fearful of costly legal battles with the FTC and possible ruinous fines, would be inclined to scale back their programs, simplify them, and offer nothing that was not in writing. Their lawyers would forbid the innovation and expansion we have seen in recent years. Co-op programs would again be "We'll pay for X percent of your ad cost up to Y percent of your purchases for the following list of media. Don't bother asking about anything else." That is not in anybody's interests.

We all know that Robinson-Patman is *not* going to be repealed, at least anytime soon. But our conclusion is that we are well served by the continued inaction of the Federal Trade Commission.

## Slotting Allowances

Slotting has little to do with promotion. Slotting—the practice of paying retailers for shelf space—and failure fees—payments to retailers for discontinued lines—are part of the pricing process.

This view received Uncle Sam's stamp of approval in the FTC's commentary accompanying the 1990 revision of the Guides: "Payments for shelf space concern the original sale from seller to customer, and do not differ in substance from a price cut, the paradigm application of Sec. 2(a)."

Translated from governmental language, this apparently means that slotting allowances are illegal only if they are disproportionate, but in any case they would be violations of Section 2(a) as discriminatory pricing rather than of Section 2(d) as discriminatory promotional allowances. This also means, of course, that a cost-justification defense can be used, and competitive injury must be demonstrated.

When we say that slotting payments are not promotional allowances, we are not referring to payments for displays or for preferential positioning, only to payments for shelf space itself.

## JUSTIFYING SLOTTING

Many in the promotional allowance business have something of a prejudice against slotting and failure fees, seeing them as diversions of money from promotional allowances. This has some validity, since slotting expenses are often included in the promotional allowance budget. As already noted, slotting is part of the cost of selling in and should be viewed as a reduction in price, not as part of the cost of promoting the resale of the merchandise, and therefore should be budgeted as a selling cost, not as a promotional expense. However, this is not to say that slotting is without promotional value; after all, selling-in is one of the purposes of promotional allowances.

A defense of slotting allowances was posited by Kevin J. Arquit, then Director of the FTC's Bureau of Competition, in his speech before the National Grocer's Association in 1991. After presenting the antislotting view, he added:

> Others, however, have offered procompetitive explanations for slotting allowances. They argue that such payments compensate retailers for the costs and risks inherent in allocating shelf space to an increasing number of new grocery products, many of which reportedly fail soon after introduction. If this is true, then slotting allowances may efficiently allocate a scarce resource—retail shelf space—and may actually tend to increase new product innovation rather than restrict procompetitive entry. Slotting allowances may be a way to get products on the shelves quicker and cheaper than other means, such as waiting for national advertising to create sufficient demand for new products that stores are then willing to stock them. In addition, some analysts of slotting allowances contend that they promote efficiency by transmitting valuable information from manufacturers to retailers about the likelihood that a new product will succeed. To the extent that it communicates the manufacturer's willingness to absorb some of the retailer's risk in stocking the product, the slotting allowance is said to inform the retailer of the degree of the manufacturer's confidence in the product's ultimate success.

However one views slotting, it is certainly a fact of life. Nonetheless, we will take the approach that payments directed only at getting or maintaining shelf space or paying for removal of unsuccessful merchandise, although important marketing functions involving tremendous amounts of money, are outside the focus of this book and will be discussed only tangentially. Payments for preferential position, however, are within the scope of our discussion.

## Spiffs

The FTC has a specific set of guidelines dealing with spiffs, Rule 14.7. These guides would appear to render many common practices in several industries illegal. The guides say, for example, that sales contests are illegal. Example (b) says that spiffs are an unfair trade practice "[W]hen the terms and conditions of the agreement or understanding are such that any benefit to the sales person or customer is dependent on lottery. . . .."). However, it should be noted that at least one prominent attorney in the field said that he could not think of a single instance of Rule 14.7 being invoked.

## Restrictions on off-price advertising

One of the more interesting examples of the shifting tides of regulation can be found in analyzing the FTC's various stances over the years on the use of promotional allowance marketing funds to support or discourage off-price advertising.

Prior to the mid-1970s, many manufacturers' promotional allowance programs, including almost all programs in the apparel industry, specifically banned all off-price co-op advertising. In the related fashion accessories trade, especially women's hosiery and intimate apparel, programs typically allowed off-price ads only during certain time periods, during which every department store in the country would be running ads offering the same brands at much the same discounts.

In the mid-1970s, the San Francisco office of the FTC undertook an investigation of Levi Strauss, whose program was fairly typical in this regard. The investigation resulted, as such things so often do, in a consent decree, the gist of which was that the company would no longer refuse payment for ads offering Levi's at discount prices.

In the course of the Levi's investigation, the FTC took a look in the files of the Advertising Checking Bureau, which administered the

Levi's program and a great many other apparel and accessory programs. The Commission found, of course, that most of the programs were similar to Levi's. It then put ACB under a consent decree, in which ACB agreed not to enforce off-price restrictions in any of its clients' programs.

These events took place during 1976-1977. The following years of the Carter Administration saw continued enforcement of this and other provisions of the Robinson-Patman Act, although the FTC under Carter was far more active on consumer issues than on trade practices.

Beginning in the Carter years, however, and much more so with the onset of Reaganism, regulation, both at the FTC and in the courts, has gone out of fashion. Several court decisions in the early 1980s cut away at earlier decisions, and eventually the FTC reversed itself and once again approved restrictions on off-price advertising. At this point, ACB, still under a consent decree for doing something that was now okay, asked for and received (in May 1987) a release from the decree.

The issue is still a live one, though. The FTC Guides continued until recently to include an example citing restrictions on off-price promotion as being improper. And when the new Guides were issued in 1990, few issues other than the value standard elicited as much debate as the elimination of that example. In the FTC's accompanying commentary to the Guides, it devotes several pages to its reasons for the deletion, and to the public comments on it.

Most comments (13 of 18) opposed the FTC and said the example should be retained. The source of most of these comments was predictable—off-price retailers, including Kmart, Service Merchandise, the National Association of Chain Drug Stores, and others. Their position, not surprisingly, was that deletion of the example would encourage manufacturers to go back to their old restrictions, and that such actions would put retailers who rely on price-cutting at a competitive disadvantage.

The FTC's position was that they were not approving restrictions on off-price advertising, but that such restrictions did not constitute a *per se* violation of Robinson-Patman. This means the possibility exists that the FTC might proceed against manufacturers in cases where an off-price restriction can be proven to create a competitive disadvantage for a retailer (the "rule of reason" interpretation). Such proof, of course, is notoriously difficult to obtain.

Since the FTC in recent years has shown little inclination to interpret Robinson-Patman strictly under any circumstances, the question of *per se* versus "rule of reason" interpretation may have been academic. If, however, the FTC becomes more activist as Clinton appointees become the majority on the Commission, and if they have an interest in trade practices, we could see the pendulum swing again. To summarize those pendulum swings:

1. *Prior to 1976.* Restrictions on off-price are okay

2. *Late 1970s, early 1980s.* Restrictions are illegal

3. *Late 1980s, early 1990s.* Restrictions are mostly okay again

4. *Future.* It is anyone's guess

The problem, of course, is that a lot is riding on a guess. You might, in good faith, put restrictions on off-price promotion into your program today, only to find yourself signing a consent decree in 1996 because a new set of Commissioners decided to change the way the rules are interpreted again.

You should generally stay away from restrictions on off-price because they are more dangerous than they are worth. And they are probably not worth much. To explain why, let us again look at Dr. Bob Young's thesis, "The Uses and Effectiveness of Vertical Cooperative Advertising." Young refers to Osgood's Congruency Theory, which holds that when we see two items in an ad that seem not to belong together, we will adjust for the discrepancy by adjusting our opinions of the items, with the amount of the adjustments depending on how strongly we held the original opinions. In psychology this is called cognitive dissonance.

To put it into co-op terms, if you were to see a Kmart ad for Calvin Klein apparel, you would have to upgrade your image of Kmart and downgrade your image of Calvin Klein. If you are like most people, your opinion of Kmart is founded on day-to-day experience, whereas your knowledge of "who's in" and "who's out" this week in the world of fashion is probably less solid. Therefore, according to Osgood, your opinion of Kmart would come up only slightly, whereas Calvin Klein would drop like a rock.

The point is, however, that the damage to Calvin Klein's fashion image would not come from being advertised off-price, it would come from being associated with an off-price merchandiser. If you do not want your product to have such an association in consumers' minds, do not sell to discounters. If you want the volume the discounters produce, then let them do business their way.

One popular alternative is to create a separate line for the discounters. This allows you to get the discounters' volume, while protecting your brand name. To say nothing of your price points, and your relationships with your full-price channels. By having separate lines, you can also have separate co-op programs.

## Osgood and Competitive Products

Mentioning the Osgood Congruency Theory brings up an interesting, somewhat related, application of it—the effect it has, not on relative images of stores and products, but on competitive products. If, for example, your product is the market leader in terms of quality image, are you not tarnishing your image and helping your competitors every time you appear in a multiproduct ad with them? You are if Osgood is right, and many programs used to forbid competitive products in the same ad, though this sort of rule is seldom imposed (or, when imposed, seldom enforced) these days.

If Osgood is right, there may be a ratchet effect created by mixing products with strongly differing public images; a ratchet effect causing, over time, a leveling in the images. A supporting case could be made based on the experience of IBM when they first entered the personal computer field in the early 1980s. At that time, the conventional wisdom in the infant personal computer trade was that IBM's entry had "validated" the industry. History has shown that this might be one of those rare cases of conventional wisdom being correct.

However, in validating the industry, IBM also appears to have validated their competitors. If Osgood is correct, every time a Computerland store ran an ad featuring IBM and another PC, the clone's image jumped in the eyes of the reader. (IBM's image being much more firmly established, the clone would pull IBM's image down only slightly, although the cumulative effect of tens of thousands of such ads would be significant in damaging IBM's reputation.) Is it not possible that much of the reason for the speed with which such no-name clones as Compaq became respected brand names was because they consistently appeared in ads next to the one computer name that everybody knew and respected—IBM?

Assuming this is true, however, what could IBM have done differently? They could have sold their products themselves, thus keeping themselves separate from competitors. They tried this, although not selling exclusively through their own outlets. It was unsuccessful, and they soon closed or sold their IBM Business Centers. They could have demanded exclusivity from their resellers. At the time IBM had the clout to do this, but the FTC and the Justice Department would likely have come after them.

What IBM might have tried was using promotional allowances. At the time, IBM did not offer a co-op program to its dealers, figuring (correctly) that there was no reason to pay for what the dealers would do anyway. The dealers *wanted* to run ads for IBM (the dealers didn't need Osgood to tell them that advertising themselves as IBM dealers was good for them), but they saw no reason not to include products from other manufacturers in the ads. Especially since the others were willing to pay for the privilege. If, however, IBM had offered to pay for ads, but only if there were no competitive products in them, or if IBM had offered their dealers a supplier-controlled program, they might have delayed at least much of the deterioration of their position *vis-a-vis* their PC competitors that ensued throughout the 1980s.

An interesting corollary to this would be that a new product trying to create a better brand image might consider paying dealers *extra* to be featured next to the category leader. It is a bit Machievellian, but it should have the effect of creating an impression of parity between the products in the public's mind.

# Enforcement Considerations Other Than Robinson-Patman and the FTC

As mentioned in regard to the American Booksellers Association lawsuit, the Robinson-Patman Act includes a "right to private action" provision allowing parties believing they have been injured by proscribed activities to sue, independent of the Federal Trade Commission. As discussed, resellers, while not covered under Robinson-Patman, are constrained from inducing unfair treatment under the Federal Trade Commission Act. Beyond these statutes, however, and beyond the FTC, there are other sources of potential legal danger that manufacturers and resellers need to be aware of.

Two additional areas of danger are illustrated in widely publicized actions in December 1994 by other government agencies. The first was an investigation of Intelligent Electronics, a large computer reseller, by the Securities and Exchange Commission. The second was an investigation of appliance manufacturers by the Justice Department.

In the Intelligent Electronics (IE) case, *The Wall Street Journal* reported that IE had been overcharging its suppliers by millions of dollars for co-op. Documents in a civil suit, brought by a former employee alleging he was fired for complaining about the overcharges, appeared to support the major points in the *Journal* article.

IE denied any wrongdoing. Interestingly, they didn't deny overcharging their vendors. They argued, however, that the vendors were aware they were being overcharged, and that such overcharges are standard practice.

Regardless of the merits of this case, the point to consider here is that the SEC was the agency undertaking the investigation. The SEC's interest in the case was that IE had not made public the source of a large portion of their profits, and that investors might therefore be misled.

In the second matter, the Justice Department was reported to be investigating whether appliance manufacturers were using the minimum advertised price provisions in their co-op programs in ways that amounted to price-fixing.

The issue of requiring a minimum price in co-op ads was discussed earlier in this chapter. The point about this latest investigation is that it is being conducted by the Justice Department.

Given that a state attorney general in at least one case has successfully taken on Wal-Mart for predatory pricing practices and that trade allowances can easily be interpreted as affecting pricing, we should not rule out the possibility that state AGs, if properly motivated, could get involved in co-op.

CHAPTER 3

# Developing a
# Co-op Program

All programs consist of certain basic elements. In this chapter we will list and define these elements and then provide further detail on the most important ones.

First, however, a few points need to be made. It has become fashionable in recent years for some manufacturers to compete with each other to produce the largest and most elaborate program kits. These are very nice, and if you feel having a 20-pound program serves a genuine marketing purpose, such as giving you increased visibility or credibility with the trade, you should produce one. Under normal circumstances, however, there is no real need for a program's terms and conditions to run more than four to eight pages. You should also take into account that no dealer is going to read an extensive program—it is difficult enough to get them to read a four-page program.

Complicated programs reduce program usage. Sherry Qualls, head of Armstrong World Industries' co-op program, commented at a Newspaper Adevertising Co-op Network meeting a few years ago that Armstrong, bothered by a 45 percent usage rate, looked at their program and asked themselves, "Would we use it?" When they answered no, they decided it was time to simplify.

Another point to remember is that you should not try to develop your program until you have a clear idea of what your program goals are. The following steps are standard in creating programs:

**Step 1:** Define your marketing goals.

**Step 2:** Using these goals as a guideline, define the goals of your promotional allowance program.

**Step 3:** Develop the program, choosing each element based on how well it helps you fulfill your goals.

# Defining goals

No one can tell you what your goals should be. Asking yourself the following questions may help you determine them:

- Are your goals short term—immediate sell-in and/or sell-through—or longer term—building your brand and your relationship with the trade?

- Do your goals involve counteracting the effects of seasonality or, alternatively, exploiting those effects?

- Do you want to concentrate on your bigger dealers or build up your small accounts?

- Do you want to generate retail advertising and/or promotion?

- Are you seeking competitive parity or competitive advantage?

- Do you want to coordinate your retail message with your national advertising?

If, like most marketers, you answered "All of the above" to the preceding questions, you need to be realistic in assigning relative weight to each. In any case, these are some of the questions you need to consider before you begin the design of your program. In the following sections, you will see how program features can be adapted to achieve specific purposes.

# Organizing Program Elements

Each of the following subsections describes an element that you will need to cover in your program and provides guidelines for deciding what information to include.

### ELIGIBILITY

Define who is eligible to participate in your program. Is it limited to distributors or dealers, or is it open to both? Do they have to enroll?

If so, you will need to explain how. If you have authorized and unauthorized dealers, are they both eligible, or is eligibility limited to the authorized dealers? This could be a violation of the Robinson-Patman Act, but if the authorized dealers have to do certain things to gain or retain authorization, you may be able to justify giving them something (a co-op program) in return. Detail any geographic limitations.

## TIMING

When does the program begin and end? What are the dates during which purchases earn allowances, and when can the allowances be spent? In Chapter 10, we will discuss the comparative merits of fixed-period programs and rolling programs. Even if you have a rolling program, you should have an ending date to cover liability questions, you may extend it over and over, but you need to have some protection.

A further precaution is to say you have the right to end the program on 30 days' notice. Some programs are written with a provision that they can be withdrawn without notice, but this is of questionable legitimacy, since advertising and promotion cannot be stopped in midstream, and a manufacturer is clearly liable for any promotions already underway, or so close to execution that they cannot be stopped at the time the program is withdrawn.

## ACCRUAL PERCENTAGE

How much do your dealers earn, and how do they earn it? For example, will they earn a 3 percent allowance on all purchases of first-quality merchandise, but earn no allowance on close-outs and seconds? A typical restriction is that spare parts do not earn an allowance. The apparel industry often restricts special-purchase goods and out-of-season merchandise. This is also where you would list any special periods (for example, the toy industry often gives higher allowances on orders placed early in the year to encourage advance ordering). If you offer different allowances on different lines, it should be detailed here.

## REIMBURSEMENT PERCENTAGE

How much are you going to pay? For example, will you reimburse 100 percent of dealers' net cost of qualifying ads or promotions, up to the limit of their available allowances? Some variations appear in programs that offer different percentage reimbursement on different media or different product lines.

## ELIGIBLE COSTS

What will you pay for? Typically you should state that you will reimburse the customer for his or her net cost of advertising after all discounts and rebates. This is to protect you against arrangements by which the media bills dealers at higher rates for co-op purposes, and then provides a month-end rebate. If you are willing to pay some portion of production costs, you should state *very specifically* what sort of expenses you will cover, and/or a cap (such as, production costs cannot exceed 3 percent of the media cost). Let the dealers know whether you will pay for color in print ads.

## ELIGIBLE MEDIA

Which media can your customers use? List any media (or other types of promotion) you are willing to automatically approve, then cover the rest by saying something like, "If none of these media choices fit your promotional needs, we will consider any other options you may propose."

This phrase accomplishes three important goals:

- It covers your Robinson-Patman responsibility to make sure your media choices do not effectively eliminate small dealers from your program.

- It covers other media choices you might like, but that you want a chance to approve in advance (preapprovals are discussed again later in the chapter).

- It allows you to engage in innovative new programs (which in practice come mostly from the larger customers) and lets those customers know you are open to new ideas.

Most programs limit their blanket approval to traditional media (usually newspaper, radio, and television—sometimes direct mail, magazines, or outdoor) to maintain more control over the nontraditional, which can be very productive, but also easier to abuse.

## ART AND COPY REQUIREMENTS

For each of the media that received blanket approval in the previous section, list what has to be in the ad for it to be paid. Typically, this means your name and/or logo (if you require a logo, be reasonable about the size) in print ads and television, and your name (a certain number of times, often three) on radio. Usually an illustration is required for print and television. Tell the dealers whether competitive products can be in the same ad and under what restrictions. List minimum size (for print) and length (broadcast) requirements.

Something that many people forget is that research has shown that listeners/viewers have a difficult time taking in several different concepts from broadcast ads. Nonetheless, dealers persist in running radio (as an example) ads that mention a dozen different products. Given that the ad will probably run in a cluster with five or six others, the likelihood that your product, as one of several products in one of several ads, will get any recall is poor at best. Limit multiproduct ads in broadcast.

## DOCUMENTATION REQUIREMENTS.

For each of the media that received blanket approval, list the types of documentation the customer will have to submit. Be realistic and only list documentation you really need and expect to get (for example, if your customers are big department stores, it will accomplish nothing to tell them to submit newspaper invoices, because they will not).

Unrealistic documentation requirements lead to deductions. If you return a claim for additional documentation that the store has a policy not to provide, it is more likely you will get a deduction rather than the documentation.

## SUBMISSION DEADLINE

Many programs require claims to be submitted within 60 or 90 days of performance. This is an unnecessary holdover from the days when most co-op was for newspaper advertising and the Advertising Checking Bureau, then the only auditing service, kept 90 days worth of papers on hand. If your customers are in no hurry to get paid, why should you be in a hurry to pay them? It does make sense to have a deadline at the end of the program (or at the end of the calendar year in a rolling program), in order to keep outdated claims from resurfacing, and to allow your finance people to close the books.

## CLAIMING INFORMATION

Tell dealers where to send their claims. Remind them to use a claim form if you require one. Tell them how they will be paid—

check, credit memo, credit advice, electronic fund transfer, and so on. Also give them a reasonable amount of time in which to expect payment (or a response). It should take no more than two weeks to process claims (an efficient operation can usually do it in less time), so, allowing for mail each way, they should be promised a response within about three weeks, although a month is reasonable. Keep your own terms in mind. Is it reasonable to take six or eight weeks with claims, when you expect the dealers to pay you in 30 days?

## DEDUCTIONS

Remind dealers they are not allowed to take deductions. See Chapter 12 for more on this subject.

## PENDING

Let dealers know what will happen if they claim more than the amount of funds they have available. Various options are detailed later in this chapter.

## INQUIRIES

Tell dealers who to call if they have any questions.

## WARRANTIES

For legal reasons, many programs include a disclaimer that ads cannot include any unauthorized warranties and cannot make unsubstantiated performance claims. Similarly, many say the ads cannot violate any laws, which appears to be self-evident.

## SPECIAL PROGRAMS

If you have special programs such as programs in which the customer orders an ad or promotional service or materials from a third party (like the Yellow Pages), with the cost deducted from allowances (see Chapter 9) - let dealers know they have these options.

This is all the information that needs to be in the program, and it should easily fit on four to eight pages. Some perfectly good programs get by with all their rules on both sides of a single sheet. If you feel the need to have something big and elaborate, you can add some bulk by putting the whole thing into a fancy binder with special pockets for claim forms and ad slicks. You can also have sections telling the dealers how to put together different types of ads and how to make media selections. Your ad agency will appreciate this, because they get outrageous upcharges on the production costs involved in putting those binders together. There are also services that specialize in producing such binders.

## Program Periods and Structure

One of the most important decisions in determining the structure of your co-op program is what your calendar will be. There are two basic ways of structuring the calendar, with a number of variations.

Programs can be either fixed or rolling. A *fixed program* is one that has a beginning and an end (for example, a program that runs for a calendar year); a *rolling program* never ends (theoretically), with new funding constantly being added and funds left unused dropping off.

The two systems each have their benefits and drawbacks, and each can be used to assist in achieving certain goals.

### FIXED PROGRAMS

Fixed programs are easier to administer and easier for the reseller to understand. Anybody can understand the idea that all of his or her 1995 purchases will earn 3 percent accruals, and the 3 percent must be spent in 1995. However, it is almost always necessary to create an overlap period. Because dealers do not know in December what they have earned for December and do not have time to spend it sensibly, you have to give them another two or three months into 1996 to spend the 1995 funds. The overlap period also ameliorates the other problem with fixed programs: At the beginning of the year, the dealers have no funds, so you have dead periods when there is no promotion for your product.

These examples assume an annual program, but it is also common to have two six-month programs each year. This is particularly popular in highly seasonal industries or in industries where there are frequent introductions of new products.

The biggest problem with fixed programs is that they tend to encourage "splurge" spending. This is particularly true if you have a lot of small dealers who earn small accruals. They will be tempted to run one ad or promotion at the end of the spend period to use up all the funds they have earned. This is a problem exacerbated by overlaps, since most programs with overlaps allow dealers who run ads in the overlap period to collect funds from both periods. For example, a calendar year 1995 program with a three-month overlap into 1996 would allow a dealer running an ad in March 1996 to collect any funds left over from 1995, *plus* any funds earned for January through March 1996. This type of program feature can create spending patterns in the program that do not correspond to sales patterns.

## ROLLING PROGRAMS

In general, rolling programs are more likely to meet your strategic marketing needs, in most instances. Exceptions may arise where instituting such a program might put you at a competitive disadvantage; if everyone else in your industry has calendar year programs and your dealers are therefore unfamiliar with rolling programs, they would very likely be confused (and probably rather annoyed) if you switched to a rolling program. Program usage would, at least initially, probably be quite low.

We mentioned that a disadvantage to fixed programs is that they tend to encourage splurge spending at the end of the program. One reason this happens is that small dealers might not accrue enough funding to run promotions on a regular basis. An advantage or disadvantage (depending on your viewpoint) of rolling funds is that many small dealers might *never* accrue enough money to use your program. This is a disadvantage if you want to encourage program use by all your dealers; it is an advantage if you would like to concentrate your spending on your biggest dealers. Usage by small dealers can be encouraged under a rolling fund by lengthening the roll (for example, using a nine-month rolling fund, instead of the more usual six-month model). If, conversely, you want less usage by small dealers, you could shorten the roll.

All of these examples have assumed the unit of measure to be a month, although a number of programs base accruals and/or spending on quarters (some rolling programs have earnings by month, but have the funds roll off by quarters). The idea of using shorter periods—weeks, for example—has been broached but never implemented, because of the logistical problems. This is still a possibility for the future, however. As just-in-time distribution becomes more popular and as electronic data interchange (EDI) networks are more commonly used, there is no reason why accruals could not be updated simultaneously with shipment of or payment for goods, with the retailer having immediate access to the update by EDI instead of waiting until the next monthly statement is mailed out. When this is possible, why not have the accruals expire six months to the day from when they were earned? (For more information on these and related issues, see Chapter 12).

## UP-FRONT ALLOWANCES

Another possibility, and the simplest of all, is the up-front allowance, usually based on the previous year's purchases. In this scenario, the manufacturer figures the dealers' purchases for the corresponding six-month period of the previous year and gives each dealer 3 percent (for example) as an up-front accrual. That is the dealer's fund for the coming six months, regardless of what actual purchases are (usually, it actually works as a base accrual, and if dealers go over the base, they can earn more). This has obvious advantages. As noted, it is simple, everybody understands it, and it is easy to administer. It is also great for planning purposes; dealers know in October exactly how much money they have for the January-June period.

The negative aspect is that this kind of program is less effective for products that are volatile either in terms of growth or decline, which is why it is most popular in such static markets as apparel. It also tends to overfund declining channels of distribution, such as department stores, and underfund growing channels, at least in the up-front allocation stage. Since this is the opposite of what most marketers want to do, it is a problem to watch for. If, however, you have a steady product and steady channels, you might want to consider this type of program. Some programs find a partial solution by providing only a portion, perhaps two-thirds, of the accrual up front. This guards against excessive overfunding, but exacerbates underfunding.

A variation on this method is to use *projected* sales to give up-front allowances. This might be the only possibility in a new product launch, but obviously it has dangers attached to it. Use this approach only if you have to, only if you have a very disciplined sales force (since you have to rely on them to make responsible projections), and only if you have nerves of steel.

In regard to administrative costs, as always, you can expect that the simpler the program is, the less it will cost you to administer it (whether administered in-house or by a third party). Therefore, all else being equal, a program with up-front allowances should be the cheapest to administer, a fixed program next, and a rolling fund the most expensive.

The complexity of administration itself is only part of the reason for higher costs - the more difficult it is for your dealers to understand the program, the more you will have to spend on telephone support to answer their questions. Rolling funds are particular problems in this regard because dealers always want you to "reinstate" money that rolls off because the money was there when they ran the ad, but it went away before they could get the claim in. You will get these calls regardless of the length of your grace period.

# Pending

Since people use different terms for this concept, we will define *pending* as the practice of making additional payments on a claim if the dealer does not have sufficient accruals to pay it in full at the time it is submitted; when these claims are held awaiting additional accruals, they are considered to be pending. Other commonly used terms are *holding* or *suspense*.

There are several ways of handling pending claims:

- The simplest way to handle insufficient fund claims is to pay the dealer the available funds with notification that nothing more will be forthcoming. In other words, no pending at all.

- The simplest way to offer pending is to pay the dealer the available funds with instructions to resubmit the claim to be considered for additional funds accruing later. There may or may not be a time limit on the resubmission. This puts the administrative burden on the dealer and raises the strong possibility that the claim will never be resubmitted.

- Some programs allow for a payment of available funds, plus one additional payment—either when sufficient funds accrue to complete payment or, if sufficient funds never accrue, a payment of whatever has accrued at the end of the program period.

- Other programs pay what is available, plus additional payments each month until the claim is fully paid, until the program ends, or for a specified time period.

- Another possibility is to hold the claim until sufficient funds accrue, making no payment until then.

- Some programs offer dealers the option of waiting for sufficient funds to accrue for full payment or taking what is currently available.

There are other variations, but these are the most prevalent. Which is best depends on your marketing needs and your competitive situation. Often it may be best to match exactly what is offered by your major competitor(s) because you know your dealers are used to it.

The biggest factor in your decision ought to be how you view promotional allowance marketing. If you think of it as attaching certain funds to certain products and feel those funds should be used to advertise those products, then you should not offer pending at all. The funds accrued after the ad or promotion should be reserved for future advertising to move the product purchased after the ad.

If you feel promotional allowances should be used to generate reorders, it is reasonable to allow accruals earned on those reorders to pay for the ad. Therefore, you should allow a short pending period, the length being determined by the normal reorder cycle in your industry. The quicker the merchandise turns in your business, the shorter the pending period you would allow.

If you see co-op as a sell-in tool, do not offer pending. If you are using co-op for sell-through, offer pending, but always for a limited time period. After all, why should you continue to pay in August for a radio ad that ran in March, especially since doing so means the dealer has no funds for promoting in August? In such a case, you are actually discouraging your dealer from doing additional promotion, and you are paying for promotion that has long ceased to have any effect. There comes a point where it is time to bury the claim and start fresh.

One exception is when the promotion is ongoing. It is not uncommon for marketers who deal with catalog houses such as Service Merchandise to allow for long-term payment of claims for their catalogs, since the catalogs typically have long lifespans. This is also true of Yellow Pages.

If you want to encourage your dealers to run bigger ads and promotions for greater visibility, allow pending so dealers will feel safe in running ads bigger than those allowed by current allowances. Conversely, if you want a constant stream of retail advertising, do not offer pending; this encourages your dealers to spend their money in smaller increments.

Pending drives administrative costs up considerably because you are handling claims multiple times, writing multiple checks or credit memos, and probably answering multiple phone calls from dealers asking what you are going to do about the unpaid portion of a claim. If you must have pending but are concerned about holding down the administrative costs of your program, use one of the simpler variants.

## Accrual and Payment Rates

Accrual and payment rates are closely linked with budgeting (Chapter 6), but we will deal with them separately: Setting accrual rates is part of the program design process, whereas budgeting is an administrative function. You may wish to look at Chapter 6 in conjunction with this section.

Determining what accrual rate to offer your dealers is a function of a number of issues. Most important among them are:

- How much dealer promotional support do you need to meet your marketing goals?

- What do you need to offer in order to be competitive?

- What other programs are you offering?

- How much do you need to hold aside for vendor support programs and other special purposes?

- Of what you make available, how much do you expect to be used?

- What do you expect your administrative costs to be?

- What is your budget?

- What are your profit margins?

Unfortunately, there is no matrix or formula to tell you what rates to use for what situation. Determining accrual rates is more an art than a science, and the arts it involves most often are those of negotiation and compromise, because setting the rate involves balancing the needs and wants of at least the sales, finance, advertising, and marketing departments.

It is nearly impossible to say that one of the questions listed is the key question, because all of them must be examined together. If pressed, however, you could make a good case for the first question, because if you do not give yourself enough support to make your marketing goals, the budget becomes a work of fiction. Of course, the last question is important, too, since if you make your marketing goals, but do not make a profit you will go out of business. All the questions are important, so make sure you come up with an accrual rate that fits the needs implicit in all of them.

According to data provided by Multi-Ad Services (Exhibit 3.1) from their ReCas database of co-op programs, there is no one percentage that dominates:

**EXHIBIT 3.1**   Accrual Percentages in Co-op Programs

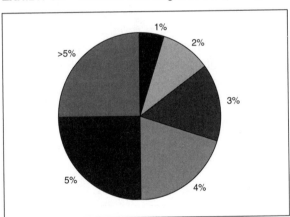

Source: Multi-Ad Services

*Computer Retail Week* (August 8, 1994) reported that computer software distributors averaged receiving 8.3 percent promotional allowances from their suppliers (broken down as 4.4 percent co-op and 3.9 percent MDF).

## UNITS AND PERCENT OF PURCHASES

Most programs in most industries set accruals as a percentage of net purchases. This is an interesting approach, because most manufacturers also spend a good deal of time trying to figure out ways (preferably, but not necessarily, legal ways) to aim their programs at their biggest customers. One simple way to tilt your program *away* from your biggest customers is to base accruals on percentage of purchase. If you want a program in their favor, you should base your accrual rate on units purchased.

Percentage-based accrual programs discriminate against larger customers because the percentage is based on the net amount the customer paid you, and the bigger customers are paying you less per unit because of their volume discounts and therefore are accruing less per unit purchased. If you accrue the same amount per unit for all customers, you are allowing your biggest customers to accrue at a higher percentage.

For example, International Useless Products (IUP) sells to two customers, Joe's Corner Market and Monolithic Multinationals Inc. (MMI). Both receive a 2 percent co-op allowance. Joe buys one unit at a time and pays $50 per unit, earning a $1 co-op allowance. Monolithic usually buys 1,000 units at a time at $40 per unit. A $40,000 purchase earns an allowance of $800, which is only $0.80 per unit. If the International Useless program were based on units, and the company offered a $1-per-unit allowance, Joe would still get his $1, which is 2 percent of his purchases; but MMI would get $1,000, 2.5 percent of its purchases. It is also 25 percent more than MMI got from the percentage-based program. Thus, IUP could discriminate legally in favor of its larger customer (see Exhibit 3.2).

**EXHIBIT 3.2**  Comparison of Percentage and Unit Accruals

| | Units Purchased | Price per Unit | Total Purchase | Amount Accrued | Accrued per Unit | Accruals as Percentage of Purchases |
|---|---|---|---|---|---|---|
| **Percentage Accruals** | | | | | | |
| Joe's | 1 | $50 | $50 | $1 | $1.00 | 2.00% |
| MMI | 1,000 | $40 | $40,000 | $800 | $0.80 | 2.00% |
| **Unit Accruals** | | | | | | |
| Joe's | 1 | $50 | $50 | $1 | $1.00 | 2.00% |
| MMI | 1,000 | $40 | $40,000 | $1,000 | $1.00 | 2.25% |

If you change from percentage-based accruals to unit accruals, you might need to adjust the amounts. In the previous example, IUP would see its liability increase dramatically, because its smaller customers like Joe would be receiving the same accruals, but the biggest customers, as mentioned, would get 25 percent more accruals.

Usage and usage as a percentage of accruals, would also increase. Since small dealers generally do not use their accruals (see Chapter 4 on increasing participation and usage) and this type of program moves a bigger share of the money away from them to big dealers who do use the funding, more of your money will be used. What unit accruals do, in effect, is recycle currently unused funds from smaller dealers to bigger dealers who will use the money.

Unit accruals have long been the standard in some commodity industries and are common in packaged goods. The motor oil business uses unit accruals (per gallon, usually), as do a few computer marketers. Use of this method of accrual is uncommon in soft goods. It is easiest to administer with limited product lines and product lines with relatively stable pricing.

## INDIRECT CUSTOMERS

One of the most commonly asked questions is "How should I deal with indirect customers?" Long a nightmare in several industries, including hardware/do-it-yourself, this problem also affects industries such as computers, many of whose dealers are members of franchise groups, which buy most of their products through a central location, sometimes called an aggregator. In computers, as well, more and more sales are now moving through distributors.

The ideal solution is to get your distributors to tell you how much each of their customers is buying. Unfortunately, a lot of distributors will not or cannot give you this data. This is not surprising—not many people are willing to tell a real or potential competitor (you) who their best customers are. Some vendors have had success through incenting the distributors in one way or another, allowing rollbacks of dealers' unused funds, for example. Although this is probably worth doing if possible, it does create a problem—the incentive (a rollback of accruals) to give you data is a disincentive to pass the accruals through in the first place.

Assuming that you cannot get sales-out data from the distributor, however, what are your other options?

***Require Dealers to Send in Invoices.*** This is the most-used alternative. The obvious drawback is that it puts an administrative burden on dealers that most will choose not to accept, resulting in low usage rates for your program. Also, if one were a lawyer for the Federal Trade Commission, one might argue that the effect of this type of program is discriminatory, since the administrative burden is proportionally larger for small dealers, and that in practice small dealers do not or cannot use such programs. (Even if a rule is the same for everybody, it can be ruled discriminatory under Robinson-Patman if the *effect* is discriminatory, and the FTC Guides say programs must be "functionally available" to all dealers.) This might be reaching a bit, and a bigger objection to this type of program is that it also puts a large administrative burden on *you*, driving up costs relative to usage (the usage will be so low, however, that your total administrative costs will be low).

***Give Dealers Ad Scrip.*** This is the old alternative. Ad scrip (certificates dealers can send in with their claims with each certificate worth a certain amount of co-op funding) has not been used much in recent years, but it may be time for a comeback.

The perceived disadvantage has always been the fear that some distributors might steal the ad scrip (since this has been known to happen), but the manufacturer can offer an accrual-based program to the distributors, limiting ad scrip usage to dealers. If the distributors cannot use it, why would they steal it? One reason is to give it to favored dealers. But this probably would not happen all that much, and if it did, who cares? The distributor's favored dealers are probably your best dealers too. Where this could be a major problem is if the distributors in your industry own their own dealerships as well as selling to independents. If that is the case, forget this alternative, because they would definitely steal all the ad scrip they could get away with for their own outlets.

The biggest concern about ad scrip is that it is not much less of a paperwork burden than sending in invoices, but, interestingly, it is perceived as less trouble—perhaps because scrip has the tangible feel of money. In any case, ad scrip programs, back when they were common, generally got better usage than invoice-based programs.

The administrative burden on you is almost, but not quite, as bad as with invoice-based programs. However, the higher usage will mean that you will probably pay more to administer this program.

*Offer an open-end program.* This is the cleanest alternative. But open-end programs (sometimes called "unlimited" programs) have always had two large negatives: their potential for abuse and the difficulty of budgeting them.

In a standard open-end program, a manufacturer pays 50 percent of whatever advertising the retailer runs without reference to accruals. The theory is that since the retailers have to pay half the cost, they will not run a volume of advertising that is unjustified by stock on hand. The theory works as long as the dealers are honest.

For example, several years ago, the Advertising Checking Bureau handled a number of open-end programs, mostly in the hardware/do-it-yourself and lawn and garden areas. A time brokerage group in the Pacific Northwest got a great idea: They bought blocks of time on low-rated radio stations, during which they broadcast programming like minor-league baseball games. (Such programming costs little because minor-league teams virtually give away broadcast rights in the hope radio exposure might increase attendance.) They sold the time on the games to local hardware stores, with the stores running spots for products with open-end co-op programs. The stores paid for the spots with bartered goods at wildly inflated prices or with gift certificates the time brokers threw away; in other words, the spots were effectively free. The brokers submitted co-op claims for the advertising at rates many times the normal cost of advertising on the stations. When the stores received the co-op payment for 50 percent, they signed it over to the time brokers (maybe getting a small rebate). It was a great deal: The retailers were getting free advertising; the station was selling its time; and the time broker's 50 percent was sufficient to generate a healthy profit. Of course, the manufacturers were getting ripped off, but so what?

Despite this example, open-end may often be the most attractive way of handling promotional programs for indirect customers, if we can find an alternative version of it that keeps most of its benefits and eliminates (or ameliorates) its defects.

One possibility is to marry open-end to a commitment or preapproval system. The program could be presented to the dealers as open-end with two limitations: Any expenditure of more than $500 would have to be preapproved, and any dealer receiving cumulative payments of more than $5,000 in a year would have to have all subsequent expenditures preapproved. (The numbers, obviously, are merely examples).

The preapproval process eliminates all but the most petty abuse and aids in budgeting. Although the preapproval process dilutes some of the benefits of open-end (ease of administration and ease of use), it contributes the benefits of control and forecasting.

The program, in skeletal form, would be something like the following:

**Terms:** Dealers can advertise as much as they want up to the caps; the manufacturer pays 50 percent of the net space cost.

**Per Item Cap:** All claims for individual promotions costing more than $500 (manufacturer share) must be approved in advance.

**Cumulative Cap:** When a dealer has been reimbursed more than $5,000 during a 12-month period, all subsequent claims must be preapproved. (Note: Preapproval criteria includes both promotion value and dealer sales volume.)

**Media:** Newspaper, broadcast, and Yellow Pages. All others require prior approval. All must be fully documented. No barter or trade. (Note: you should spot-check broadcast rates.)

**Usage:** This will be relatively low at first. Unused funds can go into an MDF fund, and/or into contests and incentives to build usage.

**Notification:** Request your distributors to provide mailing lists or do mailings to their dealers, and/or publicize the program in their catalog or price list. Further publicize it in trade magazines and trade shows.

One of the reasons open-end programs are so attractive is that they are administratively cheap and easy. A great portion of the expense related to any promotional allowance program is the cost of maintaining records and reporting on the accruals. Eliminate the accruals, as you do in an open-end program, and you have eliminated much of the cost. On the negative side, you do not have the clear measures of liability you have in accrual-based programs, although the caps will give you some protection.

# Payment Rates

How much you reimburse for promotion is something that will probably be determined more by competitive pressures than by anything else. No single element of promotional allowance programs shows more standardization across given industries than the reimbursement percentage. In those industries in which the standard is less than 100 percent, this allows one of the participants the opportunity to gain a competitive advantage, although it would likely be a short-lived and relatively expensive advantage. In most cases, you should set your reimbursement percentage equivalent to the industry standard, but allow for promotions (such as for special selling seasons or product emphasis) in your budget at higher reimbursement levels.

If the standard in your industry is 50 percent or 75 percent, consider yourself lucky and do not rush to grab an advantage by going to 100 percent, because you may never be able to go back. Dealers who have to put up some of their own money are more likely to use your money wisely. Most of the really wasteful things that are done with co-op money have been done in 100 percent programs, especially at the end of the program when the dealers figure that it is "use it or lose it" time.

Multi-Ad's database tells us (Exhibit 3.3) that more than half of all co-op programs offer 50 percent or less reimbursement:

**EXHIBIT 3.3** Reimbursement Percentages in Co-op Programs

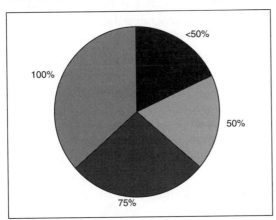

Source: Multi-Ad Services

# Checks or Credits

Another important decision in setting up your promotional allowance program is how to pay. Give it some thought, because it involves a lot of work to change. Luckily, this is not one of those decisions that involves dozens of possibilities with variations on each possibility. There are only two major ways to pay—check or credit. (A very few companies pay with merchandise, but we will ignore them for the moment).

Generally, you should pay with credit memos if you can. The biggest benefits have to do with cash flow, but there are others. The cash benefits are obvious. If you pay by check, you lose the money practically as soon as the dealer receives it. With a credit memo, you do lose nothing until the dealer's next payment cycle. Assuming most of your dealers pay you monthly, you should average 15 extra days of float on your money. Float has been of less importance during the recent years of low interest rates, but if interest rates increase, float will be important again. Additionally, of course, you are effectively paying in merchandise. A check for $500 costs you $500, a credit memo for the same amount costs you merchandise that cost less than $500 to make. There is also the possibility that credit will not be used.

A hidden benefit of credit memos is that they tie the dealer to you. The dealer has to continue to buy from you in order to use the credit memo. This increases the likelihood the dealer will stay with you for the long term. This ties in with our discussion of pending. If you believe the purpose of promotional allowances is to promote sell-through, it makes sense to have your dealers pay for reorders with a credit memo generated by the ad that generated the reorders.

It may be necessary to use checks if your dealer base is primarily indirect. Checks may also be forced on you by competitive necessity if they are standard in your industry, or if you currently are using checks and a change would cause too much unhappiness among your dealers.

If you must use checks and you use an outside service, the most efficient way of handling the checking account is to set up a separate account at your bank. Set it up as a "zero-balance" account, with the bank transferring money from corporate funds to cover each check as it comes in. This ties up a minimum of corporate funds. Your finance people will like it, although they would like credit memos a lot more.

One (infrequently used) variation on credit memos is paying with merchandise. Dealers hate it, and it only works if you are a one-product company. If you can get away with it, go ahead, but not many can. Another variation is a "credit advice" instead of a credit memo. This is a form telling the dealer that a credit for a certain amount has been applied to his or her account. It is simpler than a credit memo, but it sometimes confuses dealers, who think it *is* a credit memo and end up using the credit advice to reduce an invoice that was already reduced.

Wire transfers are the only real alternative to checks and are still difficult to do on a large scale, although they have been used for some programs (particularly international programs ones) on a limited basis. Undoubtedly, various forms of electronic fund transfer will become more popular as more marketers and their large dealers set up EDI and just-in-time programs for ordering. It has terrible cash flow implications, but it is inevitable.

## Preapprovals

Many promotional allowance programs require some sort of preapproval process. Many others offer a preapproval service to their participants and recommend, but do not require its use. How should you handle preapprovals in your program?

Before you decide, you need to consider what you want to accomplish with preapprovals. Do you want to control potential abuse of your program? Do you want to guide your dealers toward the best uses of their allowances? Do you want to cut down on the number of claims you have to reject (and on the number of consequently unhappy dealers)? Or do you want to cut down on the use of your program, particularly by smaller dealers? Preapproval programs can be used to accomplish any or all of these purposes.

Almost all programs have some preapproval requirements, at least for use of unusual media. Earlier in this chapter, we recommended that, after you list the media you will accept without question, you insert a clause to the effect that "If none of these media choices fit your promotional needs, we will consider any other options you may propose." This fulfills your Robinson-Patman requirement to make sure your media choices do not effectively eliminate small dealers from your program, covers the other media choices you might like but that you want a chance to approve in advance, and allows you to engage in innovative new programs.

Some manufacturers want greater control over their programs, however, and require all, or practically all, ads and promotions to have preapproval. If you really feel this is necessary, go ahead, but bear in mind it will have two effects:

- It will drive usage of your program down, because many dealers will not want to deal with the hassle. You will have required them to think further in advance than many of them are used to, and you will have doubled their paperwork. If you want to drive small dealers out of your program, this is a good way to do it.

- It will drive your administrative costs up, at least relative to the usage of the program, because you too will have to handle twice the paper. Of course, this might be offset by the decline in program usage.

Preapproval can serve to protect dealers, as well as cause them hassles, however. Many manufacturers say they offer preapproval programs because it is unpleasant to have to turn down claims from dealers, so they try to protect the dealers by checking the claims in advance. It also gives the manufacturer the opportunity to steer the dealers away from ill-advised promotions and inappropriate media choices.

When the various needs are taken into account, we come up with the following suggestions about how and when to require preapprovals:

1. **If you want or need strong, direct control over all uses of your program,** require preapprovals on everything. But be prepared for the consequent low usage and relatively high cost.

2. **If you want to limit usage of your program, especially by small dealers,** require preapprovals on everything (also, see Chapter 4 on how to increase participation rates and do the opposite).

3. **If you want to protect the dealers from rejected claims and unwise media and promotion ideas,** limit your program to the standard media choices that most dealers can

handle without any problem (such as newspapers, radio, Yellow Pages, or in-store signage and display). Also, put a cap on expenditures, requiring *any* promotion over, say, $2,000 to be preapproved. This limits the pain of rejected claims and also leads into developing a return-on-investment-based co-op program (see Chapter 10 for more on ROI-based programs that require preapprovals on larger claims).

4. **If you want to guard against abuse,** follow the suggestions in number 3, but make sure the types of promotion most subject to abuse (including in-store signage and display, if applicable) require preapproval. When you give the preapproval, be very detailed and specific as to the type of verification you will need. Again, have a cap, to limit your own pain instead of the dealer's.

An important thing to clarify, in your own mind and in the dealer's, is what you are approving. Many programs have created unnecessary ill-will by preapproving media choices and then rejecting the claim when it comes in, because the ad did not meet copy or art requirements. The dealer's reaction, naturally enough, is "But you approved it!" It is best, if you do preapprovals, to approve both the media and the execution.

It also makes sense, if possible, to say on the prior approval how much you will pay for the ad, since this can avoid further protests if you refuse to pay an approved ad in full. The form should also state, if the ad is to be paid from an accrual fund, that the approved amount will be paid only if the dealer has sufficient accruals available when the claim is submitted. (An alternative is to approve the ad only if the dealer has sufficient accruals and then put a freeze on the account.)

Another control is to put a time limit on the approval. Some dealers have been known to continue to run an ad a manufacturer approved long before, even though the ad's themes are contrary to the manufacturer's current positioning.

# Conclusion

To summarize the points we have made throughout this chapter, Exhibit 3.4 lists the program elements described, and how they can be adapted to achieve various results.

**EXHIBIT 3.4** How to Use Program Elements to Achieve Goals

| Program Element | Major Variations | What You Can Accomplish | Potential Problems |
|---|---|---|---|
| Eligibility | Geographic | Concentrates funding in key markets to exploit strengths and/or shore up weaknesses. | Complications involving multimarket dealers, and possible legal problems if they are exempted from geographic limits. |
| | Distributors only or dealers only | Concentrates funding on the distribution tier where you can have the most effect. | Possible competitive disadvantage in the tier you are not covering. |
| | Authorized dealers only | Concentrates funding on the dealers who are most committed to you. | Legal questions. |
| | Enrollment required | Cuts down on database size; concentrates funding; eliminate small dealers (who are less likely to do the paperwork). | More administration; eliminates small dealers; FTC could see it as discriminatory. |
| Timing | Fixed 12-month | Simple. | May encourage splurge spending at the end of the year. |
| | Fixed other (eg, 6-month) | Almost as simple. Allows for seasonal variations. Less funding in each period could eliminate some small dealers. | Still allows splurges at the ends of the periods. Less usage because some small dealers are eliminated. |
| | Very short period (eg, monthly) | Forces dealers to promote on a regular basis; keeps your name before the public. Only big dealers have enough for practical use. | Seen as inflexible by your customers. Less participation and usage, because small dealers are forced out. |
| | Carryover periods | Avoids dealers starting periods without funding, which can cause dead periods in promotion. | Encourages even more splurges—dealers combine carryover funds with current-period funds. |
| | Rolling | Avoids splurges; makes sure dealers always have funding; should lead to funding being used at the most effective | Administratively more difficult than fixed periods; more difficult for some dealers to |

**EXHIBIT 3.4**  (Continued)

| Program Element | Major Variations | What You Can Accomplish | Potential Problems |
|---|---|---|---|
| | | periods of the year for each dealer. | understand, especially in channels where it is not common. Liability accounting issues. |
| | Longer or shorter rolls | A shorter roll (eg, 3-months) discourages usage by small dealers, since they will never accrue enough to use practically. A longer roll encourages more usage by small dealers. | A shorter roll (eg, 3-months) discourages usage by small dealers, since they will never accrue enough to use practically. A longer roll encourages more usage by small dealers. |
| Accrual percentage | Higher | More usage, especially by smaller dealers. | Increased liability, decreased profits. More usage. |
| | Lower | Less usage, especially by smaller dealers, who may be effectively eliminated. | Less usage, especially by smaller dealers, who may be effectively eliminated. |
| | Vary by product | Encourages purchase of key products. | Some product managers may feel they are subsidizing others. |
| | Vary by channel or tier | Flexibility in dealing with the needs of different channels. Concentrates on more profitable channels. Incents dealers to higher levels. | Major potential for FTC problems, although there may be ways around them, (eg, by offering other benefits to balance co-op inequities.) |
| | Unit accruals | Allows tilting to larger dealers. | Difficult to use with volatile pricing. |
| Accruals for indirects | Ad scrip (co-op in a box) | Easy. Encourages usage. | Adds paper. Some types can be abused by distributors. |
| | Open-end (unlimited) | Effective way to deal with indirects. Administratively easy. | Potential for abuse. Accounting will object to the liability questions. |

**EXHIBIT 3.4**   (Continued)

| Program Element | Major Variations | What You Can Accomplish | Potential Problems |
|---|---|---|---|
| | Dealer submits proof of purchases | May concentrate usage on bigger dealers. | Small dealers will not bother with paper-work—low usage. Administration intensive for you and dealer. Dealers hate it. |
| | Distributors certify purchases | Easy administration (for you). | Adds administrative burden for distributors; some distributors may abuse it; more paper for dealers, too. |
| Reimbursement percentage | 100% | Standard in many industries, may give you a competitive advantage in others; increases usage. | May be more than is needed in some industries. Dealers may not be as careful if none of their money is at stake. |
| | <100% | Spreads your money farther, gives the dealer a stake in promotion decisions. | May not be competitive. Lower usage. |
| | >100% | Increases usage; can be very effective for special periods. | Uses up funding faster. |
| | Vary by media | Can be used to encourage use of the media you want or to discourage popular but inefficient media. | Adds complexity. Potential FTC problem if some media are not practically available to smaller dealers. |
| | Vary by product | Gets dealers to concentrate promotion on key products. | Some product managers may feel they are subsidizing others. |
| | Vary by channel or tier | Flexibility in dealing with the needs of different channels. Concentrates on more profitable channels. Incents dealers to higher levels. | Major potential for FTC problems, though there may be ways around them (eg, by offering other benefits to balance co-op inequities.) |

**EXHIBIT 3.4** (Continued)

| Program Element | Major Variations | What You Can Accomplish | Potential Problems |
|---|---|---|---|
| Eligible costs | Production costs | Can encourage better advertising. May be required by some channels (eg, department stores). | Can be abused. Uses up funding faster. Less advertising and promotion. |
| Eligible media | Standard | Newspapers and broadcast are expected. Easiest to document, least abuse. | May not be the best choices; alone may not be enough for all channels. |
| | Other media | Some may be required for certain channels or product types. Widens reach. | Some types are difficult to document. |
| | Nonmedia | Allows flexibility in meeting the needs of differing channels. Allows co-op to support full marketing plan, instead of advertising only. | Often abused. Sometimes merely pays for things the dealer would have to do anyway. Sometimes used to lower the street price of your products. |
| Art and copy requirements | Illustration | Gains more reader notice. May force dealer to give you more space. | Meaningless for some products. Requires you to provide up-to-date product art. Dealers often use outdated art. |
| | Color | Gain more reader notice. Of value especially to color-sensitive products (eg, fashion). | Uses up funding faster. Paying for more color means you get less space. |
| | No competing products | Exclusivity. Discourages price-comparison in ads. | May not be possible in some channels. You may want comparisons. |
| | Price restrictions | Supports full-price dealers. Discourages pricecutting. | Murky legal history. Discourages some high-volume dealers. |
| Documenta-tion | Full documenta-tion | Standard in most industries. Avoids abuse. | Some channels (the biggest) balk. Administratively burdensome all around. |

**EXHIBIT 3.4**  (Continued)

| Program Element | Major Variations | What You Can Accomplish | Potential Problems |
|---|---|---|---|
| | Back-end | Better cash flow for dealers. Best with commitment programs and preapprovals. | Bad cash flow for you. Sometimes hard to get money back when necessary. |
| | Random | Cuts administrative costs for you and dealers. | Could anger dealers required to submit. May encourage dealers to chance abuse. Dealers see inconsistency. |
| Submission deadline | 60 to 90 days | Evens out your administrative burden, avoiding a last-minute flood of claims. | Hurts your cash flow, angers dealers who are rejected and see it as an unnecessary requirement. |
| | No deadline | Seen as flexible by dealers; better for your cash flow. | If you have a year-end deadline, you may get flooded. If not, your liability never ends. |
| Payment format | Checks | Dealers like checks. May be the only practical way to pay indirects. | Poorer cash flow than credits. |
| | Credit memo | Better cashflow; encourages repurchases. | Dealers prefer checks. Difficult or impossible for indirects to use credits. May encourage deductions. |
| | Both | Combines the benefits. | Adds to administrative burden. Directs may demand checks, and see it as unfair. |
| Pending | None | Administratively easy; limits liability; makes dealers advertise again. | Dealers do not like it; may cut size of promotion to funds on hand. |
| | Unlimited | Dealers like it. Encourages dealers to run bigger promotions than what can be paid for with funds on hand. | Discourages repeat promotion, forces you to pay with today's funds for promotion |

**EXHIBIT 3.4**   (Continued)

| Program Element | Major Variations | What You Can Accomplish | Potential Problems |
|---|---|---|---|
| | | | from months past. Administration intensive. |
| | Pay for a limited period | Combines the benefits | Combines the drawbacks, too. Dealers will not like it as much as unlimited. |
| Other features | Direct deduct | Good for dealer cash flow; directs dealers to preferred media and art/copy approaches. | Administration intensive and expensive. |
| | Supplier control | Allows co-op to more closely support national advertising; avoids wasteful media and bad advertising. | Even more administration intensive and expensive (some cost may be offset by media commissions). Possibly not responsive to local marketing needs. |
| | Signback programs | Encourages support of your program by the media or distributors; encourages pooling by small dealers; may allow you greater control of the message. | Some media and/or distributors may abuse it. Can increase your administrative costs. |
| | Commitment system | Gives the opportunity to work closely with dealers to plan promotions and expenditures. Your sales reps will like the flexibility it gives them in working with their dealers. | Administration intensive. Your salespeople will hate the paperwork burden; they will be tempted to favor big dealers to such an extent that you may have legal liabilities. |
| | Preapprovals | Lets you help dealers with advertising and promotions; avoids some hard feelings by avoiding rejected claims. | More administrative burden and cost. Some dealers may not like the requirements. |
| | Two-for-one or free ads | Good for concentration on certain products or during certain periods. | Makes projection of liability difficult. Uses up the budget faster. |

**EXHIBIT 3.4**   (Continued)

| Program Element | Major Variations | What You Can Accomplish | Potential Problems |
|---|---|---|---|
| | Higher payments for repeat ads | Encourages frequency and repetition; effective for encouraging heavy advertising during specified periods (eg, introductions). | Administrative burden; difficulty in recognizing ads as repeats if they are not sent in at the same time. |
| | Rollbacks | Gains greater loyalty from distributors; increases overall usage rates. Can be used as incentive (eg, to provide sales-out information). | Adds some administrative burden. May give the distributor a reason to discourage pass-through. |
| | Redistribution | Allows greater funding for bigger dealers without going to MDF programs. | If coupled with barriers to use by smaller dealers, could be seen by FTC as evidence of an intention to discriminate. |

CHAPTER 4

# Co-op Goal Achievement

It is very common to talk about using co-op as a marketing tool, but it seems to be talked about a lot more than it is done.

The most common reason for this is that the strategist (such as the vice president of marketing) does not communicate the strategy to the tactician (the co-op director or channel marketing manager). So there is a tendency to go on with the same programs year after year.

But let us assume your company is different. People talk to each other and work together to set the objectives for the promotional allowance programs in concert with the marketing strategy. So how do you achieve those objectives?

## Program Goals

The following are some of the most common goals set for co-op programs and some tactics that have been used to reach those goals, starting with advertising goals.

1. **More ads during certain time periods.** You know that certain short time periods during the year are and always will be your major selling seasons. Naturally you want a lot of ads during those periods. The Justin Boot Company, for example, knows they sell a lot of boots when the rodeo is in town. They offer a 50 percent co-op program (standard in their industry), but added a special offer: If a dealer runs an ad during the two

weeks before the rodeo, Justin pays the usual 50 percent; the second time the same ad runs in the same two weeks, they pay 75 percent; the third time, it is 100 percent. The result is that a lot of Justin ads run during the hottest selling period for boots. Others with similar goals have allowed the second ad to be paid without being subtracted from the dealer's allowance, which not only increases frequency, but also tends to achieve the next goal, bigger ads.

2. **Bigger ads.** You need to create an image of prestige and industry dominance by getting bigger ads (recognizing that it may mean fewer ads). Offer dealers one ad per quarter for which only half the cost of the ad will be deducted from their accrual. The dealer will spend the entire allowance for the quarter on that one ad. On a spot-use basis, this can be used to get bigger ads during a new product introductory period, or when you are attempting to reposition a product.

3. **More color.** Many manufacturers have allowed color charges to be paid without subtracting them from the co-op accrual. This is particularly valuable for color-sensitive products, such as apparel or fashion accessories.

4. **Constant, Steady Advertising.** Switch to a rolling fund (see Chapter 3) to try to give the dealers a steady supply of funds. Toyota wanted a steady stream of parts and service mailers and ads in the sports pages every Saturday in the 1970s. They cared less about size than frequency. So they gave their dealers a *monthly* accrual—January funds could be spent only on January ads. Although extreme, this measure resulted in the desired behavior; dealers were forced to advertise regularly. Toyota added a bonus by rewarding dealers with points toward dealer-of-the-year awards for each month in which they ran an ad. The more ads, the closer the dealer was to winning a trip or some other prize.

5. **Focus on Certain Products.** Some companies in the household appliances field, with their large product lines, encourage their dealers to advertise certain products by subtracting only half the cost of ads on those products from the dealer's accruals.

Obviously, not all your marketing goals relate to advertising. Perhaps you would like your dealers to have better sales training, send their sales reps out to sell your product instead of waiting for walk-in traffic, or give you better shelf space.

How do you get your dealers to do these things? You pay them.

A few years back, promotional allowance programs paid for advertising only. Now, developing concurrently in two very different industries—groceries and computers—and spreading rapidly, some programs pay for the following:

6. **Dedicated sales personnel.** You want the dealers to have an outside sales force pitching your product. Offer to pay all or a portion of the salary. But make sure the rep you are paying for is selling *your* product.

7. **Floor planning.** You want the dealers to carry your full line and have a decent inventory. They complain about the interest cost to finance the inventory. Let them use co-op funds to pay the interest, but only if they agree to expand their inventory.

8. **Spare parts.** Your product is not perfect, it will occasionally break down. That is not a problem as long as repairs are done quickly. But your reputation for reliability will suffer if consumers have to wait for simple fixes. You want your dealers to stockpile spare parts, but they do not like the expense. Let them pay for a reasonable number of spares from their co-op funds, and allow them to accrue co-op funds on the purchase of spare parts.

9. **Sales and service training.** Your dealers hire a lot of minimum-wage salespeople. If you want them to sell your product, you need to train them yourself. Contract with a sales-training firm to set up seminars around the country and bring in the salespeople. Deduct the cost of the seminars from the dealers' co-op funds. You will probably also have to pay for airfare, hotels, and meals. Service is also important, so fly their technicians into your headquarters and train them yourself.

10. **Displays and demos.** Some consumers will walk in and ask for your product, but most will buy what they see. The way to make sure they see your product is to pay the dealer to put it

out front. People are even more likely to buy things they can touch and feel, but dealers do not like people touching and feeling because they cannot sell shopworn merchandise. So let them use their co-op funds to buy demos at a cut rate. But limit them to (for example) one per product family every six months, otherwise they will use this allowance to cover ordinary product purchases.

11. **Shelf space.** The more and better shelf space you have, the more product you are going to sell. Pepsi and Coke have known that for years. How do you get more? Pay for it, obviously. But remember that dealers do not sell shelf space, they just rent it, so be prepared to keep paying, and to have to meet your competitors' offers. The price will keep going up.

Here is a suggestion to move this sort of payment out of the slotting allowance category and into the realm of promotional payments that motivate the dealer. Try tying a portion of your market development funds (MDF) to shelf space; give more of your over-and-above funds to the dealers who are giving you an over-and-above share of their shelves. Or have a bonus allowance tied to the number of SKUs displayed.

These are just a few of the possibilities, but you get the idea. With most of these examples, the same two problems crop up:

- Manufacturers must structure these programs so they are paying for additional services as opposed to paying for something that already exists. If you offer to pay for something the dealer is already doing for free, unless you get something in return, you are just making a charitable contribution to the dealer.

- Some of these programs are invitations to abuse. Whereas traditional co-op advertising programs are abused often enough, the more recent variants are much more difficult to document and to audit. Many of these programs can involve charges for things that perhaps never existed, and are certainly not documentable. How "dedicated" is that dedicated salesperson? Did the dealer just put that display you paid $500 to have for a month up long enough to take a picture of it?

There are generally solutions for these questions, mostly involving having a sales force that consists of more than order-takers. Sales reps must be people who are knowledgeable about their dealers' businesses, work with the dealers to set up programs that are right for the dealer and the manufacturer, and monitor the success of the program.

For that reason, these programs should almost always be on a prior approval and/or commitment basis only. They should also involve goal-setting mechanisms for the additional sales targeted for the activity. Many manufacturers have separate allowances for advertising and for "infrastructure-building programs," or limit the portion of each dealer's promotional allowance budget that can be used for nonadvertising purposes. Finally, the sales reps should be given a budget for these activities and held accountable for showing results in line with the expenditures.

All this implies, as mentioned earlier, a sales force that is close to its dealer base. Therefore, manufacturers who have extremely large dealer bases and/or extremely small sales forces should probably steer clear of extensive infrastructure-building programs. Such manufacturers *might* offer some such options, controlling abuse through such mechanisms as mystery shoppers. Or they might offer such programs only to their largest dealers, the ones who are serviced closely by sales reps, and offer some offsetting program to other dealers to maintain proportional equality.

## Usage and Participation

Usually, you will want to increase or decrease usage and participation rates in your program as a means to another end (if you are seeking to increase usage, you usually want more promotion; a decrease is sought most often for budgetary reasons). In this section, however, we will ignore the reasons and treat increased or decreased usage and participation as goals in themselves.

Before deciding whether to try to increase participation and usage, however, you need to determine whether your current rates are, in fact, low. People are constantly quoting "average" participation and usage rates for co-op programs (60 percent usage is the most commonly heard number), but any such average is meaningless, because the variances are so great.

The variances are caused by a number of factors, which we will examine to help you determine where your program should be. The most important factors, not surprisingly, are the type of product, the type of program, and the channels of distribution. By the way, the program effectiveness report mentioned in Chapter 7 will come in handy in making the assessments in this chapter.

First, you should look yet again at Dr. Young's chart in the introduction, showing some of the product attributes that lend themselves to co-op and those that do not. This will be a good guide to how much dealers are likely to promote your product.

Then look at your program. Dealers will use a program paying 100 percent of their costs more than they will use one paying 50 percent. They also will use a program that is simple and written in a short, easy-to-understand format more than they will use one of those that run 100 pages and come in a binder. They will use one with lots of different ways to spend the money more than one limited to only a few choices. They will use one in which the spend options are appropriate for their needs more than one where they are not. Since the usage and participation rates depend in part on whether dealers feel they have enough money to be worth using, a program with higher accrual rates will get more usage than one with low rates.

Are all these things painfully obvious? Yes, but they are, nonetheless, things you should consider in assessing your program's usage rate.

Some other factors to consider are the channels of distribution: Department stores and drug and grocery chains use a lot more of their available funds than most other channels. If your distribution chain consists of a relatively few large dealers you will get more usage than if you have a dealer base of small outlets. As the old line goes, "Small dealers don't advertise, that's why they are small." But also, related to our note on accrual rates, dealers do not use your program if they do not earn enough to make it worth bothering with. You will get more usage from dealers who buy direct than from those who buy through distributors (in part because the ones who buy direct are usually bigger, but also because the direct relationship encourages participation). To study these points in chart form, see Exhibit 4.1.

Use these factors and those on Dr. Young's chart to figure out whether your program's usage rate is in line with what it should be. For example, if the left column of each chart is generally closer to

**EXHIBIT 4.1**  Factors Affecting Participation in and/or Usage of a Co-op Program

| Low Usage | High Usage |
| --- | --- |
| Low payout (such as 50 percent) | High payout (such as 100 percent) |
| Many small dealers, few large | Mostly large dealers |
| Poor administration (for example, poor phone service, slow pay) | Good administration |
| Low accrual rate | High accrual rate |
| Indirect distribution | Direct dealers |
| Complex, difficult to understand program | Simple program |
| Few (or wrong) spend options | Many (and appropriate) spend options |
| Low-usage channels (such as independent specialty stores) | High-usage channels (such as grocery or department stores) |

describing your situation, and you are getting something anywhere close to the 60 percent mythical average, then you are probably doing about as well as can be expected. You will get significantly more only by changing your program (or your product or your channels of distribution).

It is important to clarify whether you want to increase usage (the amount of available funds that are spent) or participation (the number of dealers who use some portion of their funds) or both. The suggestions offered in this section will sometimes do both, sometimes just one or the other.

If you think you could be doing better, it is time to set your goals and checkpoints and to assess your resources, for example, can you use some of the unused funds to offer incentives? Having figured out where you are, where you want to be, when you expect to get there, and what tools are available, here are some of the steps you might want to take:

- **Compare your program.** The most obvious step is to find out what your competitors are doing. If your program is not as good as your competitors', you should expect to get lower usage than they do. If you aren't the category leader, you may have to have a slightly better program than the leader's just to keep even.

We are talking here about both the published programs *and* the programs as they exist on the street. The published programs are easy enough to compare. To determine how they compare in practice will require some research.

One suggestion: *do not* ask your sales reps how your program stacks up against the competition, or more realistically, do not put too much stock in what they report. To sales reps, the competition is always stronger, richer, and wiser. They will tell you the competition is offering 12 percent accruals and pays every claim immediately upon receipt, even if it exceeds accruals and even if it is an ad for someone else's product. They will tell you this because it is what the dealers tell them. The dealers, of course, are trying to scare an extra couple of points out of the reps.

Do a telemarketing or mail survey among the dealers (ideally without identifying yourself), and ask them to compare the important points of your program and those of your top competitors. Ask about accrual rates, payout rates, administration, availability of MDF, help with problems, willingness to consider nonstandard media or special events, and anything else that might be relevant.

Bear in mind that dealer (and sales rep) surveys, unless carefully conducted, have a tendency to skew upwards. Realistically, nobody's self-interest is served by *under* estimating what the competition is offering. So the replies to a survey will range from totally honest to mildly inflated to wholly imaginary.

- **Analyze your program.** Look at your program and see whether its rules and the way it is used are in keeping with your company's marketing strategy. If your marketing strategy and the co-op program aren't in sync, you are sending conflicting messages to your dealers and they will often respond by ignoring the program. This sort of analysis is important not only to increase usage, but to get better, more effective usage.

  Analyze it also in terms of your dealers' marketing strategies. Examine your participation and find out which of your dealers are and are not using the program. The patterns may give you hints as to what your problems are. If particular channels have unnaturally lower participation and/or usage rates than others, it may be a signal that your program does not contain elements that are appropriate for them. Do some research among those channels, and find out what you need to do to get them into the program.

If your usage rate is higher for some products or product lines than others, it may be an indication that you need to vary your program by product.

- **Offer incentives.** It should be fairly obvious that the easiest way to get people to do something they aren't currently doing is to make it worth their while.

To get to dealers who haven't used a program, you can offer a First Claim program. Send a mailing to all the dealers who have not used the program in the past year or so. Send them a special claim form (for example, the usual form on colored paper). If they submit a claim using that form within three months, they will be paid (for example) 125 percent of the cost of the ad or promotion. The special form also tells your claims processing department or service to give the claim special handling. Tell them to move it to the top of the stack of claims to be processed and to use very loose standards in auditing it. Do not refuse payment if it comes anywhere near the normal standards for payment. Instead, pay the claim and attach a form letter telling the dealer, "Future claims cannot be paid unless you meet the following criteria . . . ." Better yet, if practical, call the dealers and tell them about the problems with the claim and how to fix them in the future, and that the claim will be paid this time anyway. The entire process should leave the dealers with a positive feeling about your program and get the desired goal—repeat usage.

Bonuses, such as the 125 percent payment mentioned, can also be offered more generally to increase participation and usage. They are also frequently used to drive specific types of usage, for example, bonuses during certain time periods, for use of certain media, or for advertising or promoting certain products.

Other dealer incentives might be to make usage of the co-op program a requirement for other programs you offer to your dealers. If you have some kind of dealer-of-the-year program, offering trips or other recognition to your best dealers, you can make co-op one of the ways dealers gain points toward the title.

You can also offer prizes; each valid claim is an entry into the contest. You can drive certain behavior with such contests, in addition to increasing participation. Increase frequency and regularity of program usage by having monthly drawings. Get larger claims by offering prizes for different claim categories; for example, claims of less than $500 are entered into a drawing for a blender, whereas claims over $10,000 can win a trip to Tahiti. (This should be legal as long as there is some degree of proportionality between the prizes and the size of the claims.)

Consider offering incentives to your sales reps. Just as with the dealers, your reps can get points toward a rep-of-the-year prize by getting their dealers to participate in the program. If you have enough support among the right people, you might even be able to have co-op made a part of the reps' bonus plan. Praise and shame also work; track usage by rep and sales region and publish the results among management.

- **Publicize your program among the media.** Make sure the program is listed (with current information) in the Co-op Source Directory, Multi-Ad's database, the Radio Advertising Bureau's co-op directory, and other listings. Mail copies of the program to major media, media groups (Thompson, Booth, Southam, and so on) and media associations. Let the same groups know about upcoming deal periods, special events, promotions, and new product introductions. These types of actions are particularly useful if you sell through indirect channels or if you have a small or weak sales force, because you are getting the media to serve some of the dealer-contact functions that would normally be done by your sales force. Try addressing media groups, distributing dealer names sorted geographically and/or rep names, if your company policies will allow you to do so. (Obviously, media reps are more likely to help you if you make it easy for them to do so by telling them whom to contact.)

- **Educate the dealers and reps.** The reason many dealers do not use your program is because they do not understand it, or co-op, or advertising. And often your reps cannot help them because they do not know much more. You are going to have to educate them to get your usage and participation figures up.

If your company publishes dealer and/or rep newsletters, have a "Co-op Hints" column added to them, publishing basic information and success stories. Conduct workshops on advertising and promotion. (You might let your dealers use their co-op funds to pay for their travel to the workshop.)

- **Simplify the program.** Rewrite your program in simple language and a short format. To repeat a comment made earlier: There is no need for almost any program to run more than four to eight pages, and most could be considerably shorter. Re-examine your rules and determine whether they are necessary. Eliminate as many as possible, or make them suggestions. Do not have rules that are not driven by marketing necessity.

  Offer alternative programs that allow your dealers to have you or your agency place prepared advertising for them. This allows you to control the advertising and the dealers (especially the small ones) to get ad production done for them. This type of program generally allows for the ad cost to be deducted out of the dealers' accruals, thus also improving the dealers' cash flow. (See Chapter 9 for more detail on this type of program.)

- **Provide the right ad materials.** Make sure the ad slicks, scripts, and in-store materials you provide make sense for all your dealers. Make sure the ad slicks are retail; too many manufacturers provide ad slicks that are just copies of their national ads with space at the bottom for a dealer name.

- **Lengthen the accrual period.** If you have a lot of small dealers who never accrue enough to use, you can lengthen the accrual period so they have a better chance to accumulate funds.

- **Change to unit accruals.** This will increase funding for larger dealers and thus increase usage rates. It will do nothing for participation rates. In fact, if you lower the amount available for smaller dealers, which you may have to do to fit your budget, it will probably lower their participation rate. See Chapter 3 for more detail.

- **Redistribute.** Give unused funds to the dealers who are using their funds and/or making their sales goals. This will increase usage, but not participation.

- **Sell it all to management.** Make sure you maintain support for your efforts by reporting results to management. Report on the increase in promotional activity relative to payout (report on how much promotion you got that you *did not* pay for because dealers had exhausted their funds), increases in usage and participation, ROI/POI on usage, percentages of dealer retention among participants and non-participants, and so forth.

- **Cut participation and/or usage.** Cut usage or participation by doing the opposite of some of the things mentioned previously. For example, shorten accrual periods, making it more difficult for smaller dealers to accumulate enough funding to be used effectively and, thus cutting their participation. Since they are small dealers, this will not cut usage rates as much as participation rates. The same can be accomplished, in fixed-period programs, by eliminating the carry-over period at the end of one period and the beginning of the next. If you combine this with redistribution of unused funds to dealers who do use the program, you can effectively take money from small dealers and give it to larger dealers (thus cutting participation while maintaining usage). Adding a preapproval procedure, as mentioned in Chapter 3, will generally drive down both participation and usage, especially among the smaller dealers.

## Summary

Exhibit 4.2 charts some of the points made in this chapter, listing many of the most common goals set for co-op programs and some of the ways those goals can be achieved, together with some of the side effects you might see and problems you might encounter.

**EXHIBIT 4.2**  Ways to Achieve Specific Goals Through a Co-op Program

| Goals | Means | How it Works/Problems/Comments |
|---|---|---|
| Get more usage | Increase payment percentage | The most obvious way to get more usage is to pay more for it. The drawbacks are equally obvious. |
| | Increase accrual percentage | Self-explanatory. |
| | Simplify the program | Eliminating unnecessary rules and writing the program in clear, brief language can increase usage with no or little cost (possibly even savings). A possible drawback is that an excessively simple program may not meet everybody's needs. |
| | Review the program | For example, make sure the media choices are appropriate to the channels. |
| | Improve administration | Dealers will participate more often if claims are processed quickly and accurately, phone calls returned, etc. Provide ad materials appropriate to all channels. |
| | Get more funding to big dealers | Anything that shifts funding from small to large dealers (eg, unit accruals) will increase usage, because big dealers are more likely to use their money. Possible FTC problems. |
| | Institute supplier control programs | These types of programs (including direct deduct and sign-backs) are most effective in providing means for smaller dealers to participate. You could lose some local input and flexibility. Heavy on administration, therefore expensive (media commissions could offset some of the cost). |
| Get more dealers to participate | Institute supplier control programs | These types of programs (including direct deduct and sign-backs) are most effective in providing means for smaller dealers to participate. You could lose some local input and flexibility. Heavy on administration, therefore expensive (media commissions could offset some of the cost). |
| | Simplify the program | Eliminating unnecessary rules and writing the program in clear, brief language can increase usage with no or little cost (possibly even savings). A possible negative is that an excessively simple program may not meet everybody's needs. |
| | Review the program | For example, make sure the media choices are appropriate to the channels. |
| | Improve administration | Dealers will participate more often if claims are processed quickly and accurately, phone calls returned, etc. Provide ad materials appropriate to all channels. |

**EXHIBIT 4.2** (Continued)

| Goals | Means | How it Works/Problems/Comments |
|---|---|---|
| | Increase accrual percentage | Moves smaller dealers' accruals up to the point they are usable. Remember that increasing participation means increasing small dealers' participation. Big dealers need little encouragement. This is the expensive way to do it, because you have to give big dealers a lot more money to give smaller ones a little bit more. |
| | Lengthen the accrual period | Gives small dealers more time to reach the point of having enough money. Cheaper than increasing accrual rates. Works better if you have a rolling fund, since you will see splurge spending at the end of fixed-period programs. |
| Get less usage | Do the opposite of steps recommended for more usage | The best ways to cut usage are to cut accrual and payment rates. You can also slow down claim processing, make the program more complicated, do not publicize it, ask reps not to talk about it, etc. The drawbacks are obvious: unhappy customers. |
| Get fewer dealers to participate | Do the opposite of steps recommended for more participation | The best ways to cut usage are to cut accrual and payment rates. You can also slow down claim processing, make the program more complicated, do not publicize it, ask reps not to talk about it, etc. The drawbacks are obvious: unhappy customers. |
| | Require enrollments, preapprovals, or commitments | Discourages small dealers, who do not have the staff to deal with the paperwork. The money they do not spend can be shifted to the big dealers. Be careful: If you are too obvious about driving out the small dealers, you may attract attention from the FTC. |
| Eliminate small dealers from program | Require enrollments | Most will not enroll. Be careful: If you are too obvious about driving out the small dealers, you may attract attention from the FTC. |
| Increase big dealers' share of funding | Use unit accruals | Gives dealers a bigger share than percentage accruals will. How much the difference is depends on how big your volume discounts are. Perfectly legal. |
| Get more authorized or exclusive dealers | Offer bonus accruals | There may be legal problems. You could get around them if you can show that the offer is functionally available to all dealers without their having to fundamentally change the way they do business. |
| Encourage certain channels | Arrange your program by channels | Potential legal problems, but you can deal with them by letting the dealers choose from various programs, and offer different but basically equal overall packages. |

**EXHIBIT 4.2** (Continued)

| Goals | Means | How it Works/Problems/Comments |
|---|---|---|
| Concentrate on key markets | Limit the program geographically | The problem comes in dealing with multimarket dealers or with channels (eg, direct mail, telemarketing) that are inherently national. |
| Get more distributor support | Encourage signbacks | The distributor gets signbacks on co-op funding from the dealers. Has the same benefits and drawbacks of other types of supplier control, in lesser measure—more local input, less control for you. |
| | Offer rollbacks of unused dealer funds to distributor | The distributors will love it and may offer a *quid pro quo.* But it may discourage them from passing funds through. |
| Get distributors to give sales-out information | Offer rollbacks of unused dealer funds | Effective, but there's a danger—some distributors may see this as an incentive to *not* pass funds through. Administration intensive. |
| | Offer bonus accruals | Give them a bonus for providing sales-out and tie the amount of the bonus to the percentage of dealer funds used by the dealers. Complicated, administration intensive. |
| Get accruals to indirects | Open-end (unlimited) | Administratively easy, but has been badly abused. Hard to forecast liability. |
| | Ad scrip | Easy to understand, encourages usage. Adds paper, sometimes abused by distributors. |
| | Indirects submit through distributors | Distributors may resent administrative burden. Some distributors may abuse it (especially if they own their own dealers). Easy for you to administer. |
| | Indirects submit invoices | Lots of paper, administration intensive. Small dealers will tend to drop out because of the administrative burden. |
| Get involved in the dealers' planning | Offer a commitment program | Allows your rep in at the planning stage for a given season. Helps with forecasting. Sometimes encourages excessive spending on big accounts (legal problems). Can increase administrative costs. |
| Get better ads and promotions by dealers | Require preapprovals | Adds administrative burden and expense. You must be prepared to respond quickly. Lets you help dealers and avoids rejected claims. |

**EXHIBIT 4.2** (Continued)

| Goals | Means | How it Works/Problems/Comments |
|---|---|---|
| Get better ads by dealers | Offer supplier control programs | The ads will be better (from your viewpoint), but the dealers may not like them; you lose some flexibility and local input. Administration costs are high, but media commissions could be an offset. |
| Tie co-op to national | Offer supplier control programs | Your local ads will reflect national themes, but the dealers may not like them. You lose some flexibility and local input. Administration costs are high—but media commissions could be an offset. |
| Direct dealers to the best media choices | Require preapprovals | Adds administrative burden and expense. You must be prepared to respond quickly. Lets you help dealers and avoids rejected claims. |
| | Offer supplier control programs | The media selection will be better (from your viewpoint), but the dealers may not like it; you lose some flexibility and local input. Administration costs are high, but media commissions could be an offset. |
| Get more ad frequency | Offer two-for-one or free ad programs | Higher payment rates can be offered for repeat ads, either during the same period or in another season. Or the repeat ad is not deducted from allowances, or is deducted at a reduced rate. Administration can be complicated. Dealers may be confused. |
| Get bigger ads | Offer a higher payment rate for one ad per period | Offering higher percentage reimbursement on one ad during a period will encourage dealers to use all their money on that ad, therefore the ads will be bigger. It will mean fewer ads. |
| Get more ads during peak periods | Offer higher payment rates for repeat ads | Higher payment rates can be offered for repeat ads during the target period. Or the repeat ad is not deducted from allowances, or deducted at a reduced rate. Administration can be complicated. Dealers may be confused. |
| Discourage price-cutting | Do not pay for off-price ads | Courts and FTC have been back and forth on the legality of this approach. Could be a serious problem if much of your volume is through discounters. |
| | Do not allow any price in ads | Works with a few products, but usually consumers like to see a price. |
| | Do not allow competitive products in the ad | Discourages comparison pricing. Some channels will reject this kind of limitation, although they can still cut prices. |

**EXHIBIT 4.2** (Continued)

| Goals | Means | How it Works/Problems/Comments |
|-------|-------|-------------------------------|
| Get dealers to expand inventory | Offer inventory financing from co-op | Paperwork intensive. Structure the program to pay for *increased* inventory. Watch the turns, because this could cause holes in reorders. Also watch returns. |
| Get more shelf space | Offer bonus accruals | Tie bonus programs to increased shelf space. Somebody has to monitor it, so you either have another job for the rep or you have to hire a service to spot-check displays. |
| Get more demo units out | Offer bonus accruals | Tie bonuses to the number of demos in use. Allow a reasonable number of demo units to be purchased with co-op funds. Police carefully: this is easy to abuse; make sure you track the serial numbers. |
| Get more displays | Offer bonus accruals | Besides bonuses for displays, provide display units free or cheap. Make sure you are providing displays appropriate to the targeted channels. Monitoring is a problem. |
| Get dedicated sales personnel | Pay for them from co-op funds | Abuse is rampant, do this only under the tightest of supervision. |
| Train the dealer or distributor personnel | Fund training through co-op | Can be useful, but be leery of training that is not specific to your product. Specify training suppliers if you do not do it yourself. Audit expenses closely. |
| Get dealers to carry more spare parts | Pay for them from co-op funds | Structure the program to make sure you are paying only for increased supplies. Also, allow spares to accrue co-op funds. |
| Encourage reorders | Pay by credit memo | Credit memos force dealers to continue doing business with you. Some may never be used—no reorder, but no cost. Tough to do with indirects. Dealers may object. |
| | Offer pending payments | Making incremental payments on past claims encourages dealers to overpromote, then they have to reorder to collect the funds. The problem is that you can keep paying forever, and meanwhile the dealer has no funds to promote you again. |
| Get short-term sales spike | Offer high accruals | If you do not offer a way to spike the dealers' sales at the same time, you will have a clogged channel. |
| Emphasize certain products | Offer higher accrual rates | Encourages increased purchase of targeted products. |

**EXHIBIT 4.2** (Continued)

| Goals | Means | How it Works/Problems/Comments |
|---|---|---|
| | Offer higher payment rates | Encourages increased advertising on targeted products. If these two approaches are not done together, you will get complaints from one product manager or the other. |
| Improve dealer cash flow | Improve administration | Move claims through quickly. |
| | Pay in advance | Use a commitment system, pay all or some upfront, audit on the back-end. Problems are the potential for abuse, difficulty in getting back-end documentation (what is the dealer's incentive?), difficulty with repayment for nonfulfillment of commitments. |
| | Pay by check | Self-explanatory. |
| Improve your cash flow | Pay by credit memo | Dealers will not like it. May be impossible with indirects. |
| Avoid rejecting claims | Require preapprovals | Lets you help dealers avoid mistakes. Your turnaround must be fast. Some deviation from what is approved must be expected. Expensive. |
| | Pay all claims | Keeps dealers happy. Not effective at getting the most possible promotion for your money, however. Robinson-Patman compliance problems. |
| Cut administration costs | Simplify the program | Examples: fixed period instead of rolling; no pending; no pre-approvals or commitments; limited media choices; direct dealers only (indirects submit through their distributor.) Good ideas, but can be over-done. Watch out for making the program so simple it is not meeting everybody's needs. |

# Co-op Program Administration

Should you administer the program yourself or should you let an outside service do it? This is a tough question and one with a lot of pitfalls either way. How do you decide whether the program should be in-house or to subcontracted out? And if you decide to go outside, how do you choose a good administrator? And, either way, how much is it *really* going to cost?

## In-House Administration

Generally it is cheaper, in terms of direct out-of-pocket costs, to handle the administration of your program yourself. It may not be as cheap as you think, but it will usually be cheaper. We will discuss how to do comparative budgets in a later section.

The other major benefit to handling the program yourself is that nobody knows your customers better than you do, and nobody else can present your policies and personalize your service philosophy as well as you can.

There are drawbacks to in-house administration, however. Some of them pertain to costs. You are taking on a lot of fixed costs when you bring the program in-house: overhead you may not have considered (space, equipment, and so on) and the obvious salary and benefit costs. These costs may be difficult to jettison in times of tight budgets. In addition, you are bringing in one or more administrative workers who need supervision and will force you to deal with turnover and other personnel concerns. (Although you will also likely have the same problems with an outside service, your concern there will be to deal with the results of the problem; the personnel questions are someone else's responsibility.

Another problem is difficult to quantify, but it has to do with amateurism. Your specialty is not administration of co-op programs. Third-party administrators are specialists, and the good ones will, to be blunt, make fewer mistakes than you will.

A question you need to address is how complicated your program is and therefore how difficult it will be for you to handle it yourself. A few major overpayments to your big dealers or a few dealers angered because their claims have been mishandled, and you may have lost the savings you were expecting.

## Third-Party Administration

To some extent, this situation is simply the reverse of everything we have said so far. Third-party administration will generally cost you more out of pocket and diminish your direct control of the program, sometimes resulting in poorer communication between you and your dealers. It is often more difficult to manage an outside vendor than your own employees.

On the other hand, you are hiring specialists and will get the benefits of their expertise—there should be fewer expensive mistakes. Another benefit to hiring a third party is that it makes it easier to say no to your dealers and/or salespeople when they are making unreasonable requests; you can let your outside service be the bad guy. Another (sometimes hidden) benefit to an outside service is consulting, free and paid. Your service should have much wider knowledge of trade promotion programs than you do, and they should be able to give you ideas, or good feedback on your ideas, based on all that experience. It can be valuable for a tire manufacturer to know how an approach they are thinking about worked out when it was tried a few years ago in the fashion accessories business. Most third parties will give this sort of advice, on an off-the-cuff basis, for free. Even if you want them to do a larger consulting project that you will have to pay them for, you will at least save money over the cost of bringing in consultants who would have to first familiarize themselves with your program before even beginning their research.

Related to the consulting question is the value of an independent outside opinion. Internal staff are often too close to issues to give honest opinions. An outside service, though not always without their own agenda, is more likely to be free of internal pressures.

We talk about reporting in Chapter 7, but a good outside service, being specialists, has a better package of standard reports and can usually customize them to your needs better than you can yourself (at least, unless you are willing to spend a lot of money on your own report development).

A factor that could go either way is availability of programming and other computer resources. Depending on your own information systems staff and equipment, it might or might not be better to go outside to get better and/or quicker service. But remember that everybody has programming backlogs, including outside administrators.

Some of the problems you will have in-house can also show up with a third party. We mentioned that you are more likely to make mistakes and cause dealer problems than a good outside service will, because of your lack of specialized expertise. The operative phrase is "than a *good* outside service." If you choose the wrong service, it will be worse than doing it yourself. You will get a steady stream of calls from angry dealers whose claims were mishandled or late, or whose statements are wrong; you will be making decisions based on inaccurate reports; your company auditors will uncover a dozen mistaken payments; your finance department will call you, screaming that the monthly liability report does not balance; and on and on.

## Budgeting In-House Costs/Savings vs. an Outside Administrator

When determining how much your in-house program administration costs are or would be compared to using an outside service, it is important to recognize all the costs. The figures in the exhibits in this section taken from real-world situations. The figures have been changed a bit to disguise the sources, but have been kept in the same proportions to present legitimate results without revealing proprietary information. They represent the high and low ranges of costs for a very large and complex program and for a small, simple program. In both cases the companies were with a third-party and wanted to assess the cost of moving in-house.

The costs included under set-up are office furniture and supplies, office equipment (copiers, PCs, phone systems, and so on), hiring and training costs, software development, research and planning costs (which you will incur either in the form of consultants' fees or your own time), forms (checks/credit memos, form letters, claim forms, and so forth). Plus 10 percent to cover the things nobody ever thinks of.

For the large program, to which the service had dedicated 15 clerical employees, three supervisors, and a manager, we assumed the company would use the same numbers in-house, plus three technical support people, and one-fourth of the salary of an executive who would oversee the operation. The company looked into various off-the-shelf software packages, but decided none met their very specific and complex needs, so they started from scratch to develop their own software. The amount estimated as the cost for this exercise was close (although a bit on the low side).

The set-up cost estimate is shown in Exhibit 5.1.

**EXHIBIT 5.1**   Set-Up Costs for Internal Administration, Large Program

| Description | Estimate ($) | Basis for Estimate |
|---|---|---|
| FURNITURE | 33,000 | 22 PEOPLE @ $1,500 EACH |
| SUPPLIES | 3,300 | 22 PEOPLE @ $150 EACH |
| PCS/OFFICE EQUIPMENT | 25,000 | GUESS |
| HIRING | 5,000 | 2 PEOPLE INTERVIEWING, ONE MONTH, @ $2,500 EACH |
| TRAINING | 58,800 | SIX WEEKS' SALARY FOR ALL EMPLOYEES |
| | 9,000 | SIX WEEKS' SALARY FOR TWO TRAINERS @ $3,000/MONTH |
| BENEFITS | 21,800 | 30% OF SALARIES |
| PLANNING/DEVELOPMENT | 50,000 | CONSULTANTS AND/OR INTERNAL COSTS |
| SOFTWARE DEVELOPMENT | 200,000 | PROGRAMMERS AND INTERFACE COSTS |
| PHONE SYSTEM | 5,000 | GUESS |
| FORMS | 12,000 | GUESS |
| CONTINGENCY | 42,000 | THE UNKOWN—ADD 10% |
| TOTAL | 464,900 | |

To estimate the ongoing costs, the salaries and benefits for personnel, space rent, the cost of disk space on the company's computers, plus materials, supplies, and depreciation were included. The set-up costs were amortized over a five-year period, since that would be the soonest anybody would be brave enough to reconsider the $465,000 decision to bring administration in-house. Annual costs worked out as shown in Exhibit 5.2.

The next step was to compare these costs with what the company was paying the administrative service. Two factors had to be added in before a straight comparison could be done. The company had three internal people working with the administrators who could be eliminated or, more likely, absorbed into the internal operation. That was a substantial savings. On the other hand, the company needed to take into account that their internal operation would not be as effective in auditing as an outside firm, for two reasons: First, because the outsiders are specialists and have long collective experience at pro-

**EXHIBIT 5.2**  Annual Cost of Internal Administration, Large Program

| Description | Estimate ($) | Basis for Estimate |
|---|---|---|
| CLERICAL STAFF | 240,000 | 15 @ $16,000/YEAR |
| SUPERVISORS | 90,000 | 3 @ $30,000/YEAR |
| MANAGER | 50,000 | 1 @ $50,000/YEAR |
| EXECUTIVE OVERVIEW | 18,800 | 0.25 @ $75,000/YEAR |
| TECHNICAL SUPPORT | 114,000 | 3 @ $38,000/YEAR |
| BENEFITS | 153,800 | 30% ON ABOVE SALARIES |
| SPACE RENT | 66,800 | $250 PER PERSON PER MONTH |
| AMORTIZE SET-UP | 93,000 | $464,900 AMORTIZED OVER FIVE YEARS |
| COMPUTERS | 96,000 | GUESS, $8,000/MONTH FOR USE OF COMPANY COMPUTERS |
| MATERIALS | 144,000 | $12,000/MONTH (FORMS, PRINTING, PHONES, POSTAGE, ETC.) |
| OFFICE SUPPLIES | 13,400 | $50 PER PERSON PER MONTH |
| DEPRECIATION | 15,000 | GUESS, $1,250/MONTH |
| TOTAL ANNUAL COST | 1,094,800 | |

cessing co-op claims (over time this difference would diminish as the internal operation gained experience); and, more importantly, outsiders are less susceptible to pressure from dealers and salespeople to "just make an exception this one (or one more) time and pay the claim." An internal operation will almost always end up paying claims that an outside service would not.

How much is difficult (perhaps impossible) to quantify. To some extent it depends on how firm a stance your marketing situation will permit you to take, and how the internal political situation stands between sales and the department within your company that will oversee the program administration.

A good administrative service will probably come up with savings through their auditing amounting to about 20 percent to 25 percent of the amount claimed. Some will say they are getting much higher numbers. It may be true, depending on the industry involved and the channels of distribution submitting the claims, but 20 percent to 25 percent is typical. (Sometimes the higher percentages some services say they get are based on counting claims short-paid due to insufficient funds as savings, or by counting claims returned to the dealer for additional documentation as savings, even if the claim was later paid when the documentation was provided).

If we assume 5 percent to 10 percent of the claims that would have been disallowed by an outside administrator will be paid by an internal operation (a conservative estimate, based on experience), the additional cost of an internal operation will be between 1 percent and 2.5 percent of your current annual payout. This example takes the low side, 1.25 percent of the client's annual $64 million payout. This is not to argue, by the way, that such an additional expense may not be justified in terms of customer satisfaction. Any co-op operation, internal or external, pays otherwise invalid claims in order to keep people happy. If paying 2 percent more on those claims makes everybody 10 percent happier, it may be a good idea to do so. Taking these factors into consideration, we come up with the numbers shown in Exhibit 5.3.

The numbers for this program may not all apply to you, but they will give you an idea of where to start in making your own decisions. Your personnel and space costs could be radically different depending on local conditions. If your company has empty office space, the incremental space cost would actually be zero on the company's

**EXHIBIT 5.3**   Savings Analysis vs. External Administration, Large Program

| Description | Estimate ($) | Basis for Estimate |
|---|---|---|
| COST OF INTERNAL OPERATION | 1,094,800 | SEE EXHIBIT 5.2 FOR DETAIL |
| INTERNAL PERSONNEL SAVINGS | 90,000 | SALARIES FOR THREE POSITIONS ELIMINATED |
| | 27,000 | BENEFITS ON ABOVE @ 30% |
| LOSS THROUGH INTERNAL AUDITING | 800,000 | 1.25% OF $64,000,000 |
| NET INTERNAL COST | 1,777,800 | |
| FEES PAID TO OUTSIDE SERVICE | 1,800,000 | |
| NET ANNUAL SAVING | 22,200 | |

overall budget, although depending on your company's accounting practices, it might affect your departmental budget if the cost moves from being a corporate overhead item as empty space to being part of your departmental expense.

In this company's case, a savings of $22,200 meant nothing in terms of their overall budget (about 0.03 percent of the total promotional allowance budget), and was not enough to justify financially the program disruption such a major move would entail. For other reasons, mostly having to do with gaining greater control over such a large and vital part of their marketing budget, the decision was made to bring the program in-house. But, importantly, the decision was made for the right reasons, not because they believed it would save them a significant amount of money.

The same evaluation was performed for a small company that felt their program was too small to justify the expense of an outside administrator. The set-up cost estimate (see Exhibit 5.4) is based on hiring only one person, a co-op coordinator, and using off-the-shelf software with minimal customization—a realistic option for their program.

In estimating ongoing annual costs, it was assumed the co-op coordinator would absorb one-third of his or her supervisor's time, who would in turn absorb one-third of a manager's time. No executive cost was allocated, and 10 percent of a technical support person was added in. Other costs were reduced similarly from those of the larger program (see Exhibit 5.5).

**EXHIBIT 5.4** Set-up Cost for Internal Administration, Small Program

| Description | Estimate ($) | Basis for Estimate |
|---|---|---|
| FURNITURE | 1,500 | 1 PERSON @ $1,500 |
| SUPPLIES | 150 | 1 PERSON @ $150 |
| PCS/OFFICE EQUIPMENT | 4,000 | GUESS |
| HIRING | 375 | THREE DAYS' INTERVIEWING @ $2,500/ MONTH |
| TRAINING | 2,500 | SIX WEEKS' SALARY FOR CO-OP COORDINATOR |
| | 1,500 | TWO WEEKS' SALARY FOR TRAINER @ $3,000/ MONTH |
| BENEFITS | 1,300 | 30% OF SALARIES |
| PLANNING/DEVELOPMENT | 5,000 | CONSULTANTS AND/OR INTERNAL COSTS |
| SOFTWARE | 20,000 | PURCHASE AND LIGHT CUSTOMIZATION |
| PHONE SYSTEM | 500 | GUESS |
| FORMS | 1,200 | GUESS |
| CONTINGENCY | 4,200 | THE UNKNOWN—ADD 10% |
| TOTAL | 42,225 | |

**EXHIBIT 5.5** Annual Cost of Internal Administration, Small Program

| Description | Estimate ($) | Basis for Estimate |
|---|---|---|
| CO-OP COORDINATOR | 22,000 | |
| SUPERVISORS | 10,000 | 0.333 @ $30,000/YEAR |
| MANAGER | 5,600 | 0.111 @ $50,000/YEAR |
| TECHNICAL SUPPORT | 3,800 | 0.1 @ $38,000/YEAR |
| BENEFITS | 12,400 | 30% ON ABOVE SALARIES |
| SPACE RENT | 4,600 | $250 PER PERSON PER MONTH |
| AMORTIZE SET-UP | 8,400 | $42,225 AMORTIZED OVER FIVE YEARS |
| COMPUTERS | 0 | USE PC PURCHASED IN SET-UP |
| MATERIALS | 6,000 | $500/MONTH (FORMS, PRINTING, PHONES, POSTAGE, ETC.) |
| OFFICE SUPPLIES | 900 | $50 PER PERSON PER MONTH |
| DEPRECIATION | 1,500 | GUESS $125/MONTH |
| TOTAL ANNUAL COST | 75,200 | |

**EXHIBIT 5.6**  Savings Analysis vs. External Administration,
Small Program

| Description | Estimate ($) | Basis for Estimate |
|---|---|---|
| COST OF INTERNAL OPERATION | 75,200 | SEE EXHIBIT 5.5 FOR DETAIL |
| INTERNAL PERSONNEL SAVINGS | 10,000 | SALARY FOR 0.333 POSITION ELIMINATED |
| | 3,000 | BENEFITS ON ABOVE @ 30% |
| LOSS THROUGH INTERNAL AUDITING | 18,750 | 1.25% OF $1,500,000 |
| NET INTERNAL COST | 80,950 | |
| FEES PAID TO OUTSIDE SERVICE | 65,300 | |
| NET ANNUAL LOSS | MINUS 15,650 | |

Using the same criteria (this company had one internal person interfacing with the administrative service who devoted about one-third of her time to the task) in comparing internal and external costs as with the larger company, we come up with the totals shown in Exhibit 5.6.

This company decided to stay with their outside service.

# How to Choose an Administrative Service

Some of the major factors to consider when selecting an administrative service include reputation for quality, cost, stability, technology, industry/marketing knowledge, innovation, and dealer and sales force phone support.

### QUALITY

A reputation for quality can be assessed most obviously by checking references. But remember that anybody can give you a list of clients who are happy with them. The Co-op Source Directory lists programs and administrators (though it is often out-of-date). Use it to find the clients your prospective service did not tell you about. When you call the references they gave you, ask the contacts to tell you who some of the service's other clients are. Look around when you visit. When you take a tour of their facilities you will probably have chances to mark down the names of several clients. If they are not on the list of references, there might be a reason.

A subset of the quality question, but one worthy of separate attention, is reporting accuracy. The reports provided by your administrators are many times the most vital part of their service to you. They can also be among the most expensive to provide properly. One way some companies cut their costs is simply to send the reports to you exactly as they come off the computer, without any quality checking. We all know computers *do* make mistakes, people *do* sometimes input strange data, and programmers *do* write programs that make no sense. Insist that *correct* reports be part of the specs; require your administrators to submit copies of the reconciliation sheets with the reports to prove they have been quality-checked and to allow you to check their checking; and insist there be a financial penalty in the contract for significant report inaccuracies or lateness. Otherwise, your internal auditors will lay all the problems on *your* doorstep.

The question of guarantees is one that should have a broader application than just reports. Co-op services, like all other vendors, will make a lot of promises when seeking your business. It makes sense to ask them if they are willing to reduce their service fee in some way if they fail to meet those promises. It also makes sense, though fewer clients are willing to do this, to offer bonuses for exceeding the service guarantees.

## COST

Cost is naturally of great importance and is dealt with in detail elsewhere in this chapter. Make sure you know *exactly* what is included and what is not. Most firms, for example, will charge extra for materials. Fair enough, but find out what they are including in the materials and how they will document the costs.

Some of the billing options are:

- **Time and materials.** This is the most common method of billing. The advantage is that everybody understands it. The drawbacks are that it is difficult to budget and rewards inefficiency.

- **Fixed monthly fee.** This is the simplest billing method. The drawback is that programs that are likely to change and grow are poor candidates for flat fees. How can you logically lock in a set fee on a program that may be very different before the fee expires? The best bets for this kind of fee arrangement are programs in mature industries with static marketing programs, where volume can be estimated solidly on last year's figures, and the program never changes much (examples abound in hardware/building materials and the automotive aftermarket).

- **Per claim.** This method is growing in popularity, since it deals with the volume problem inherent in fixed monthly fee programs. It does not deal with the problem caused by major changes in the program, but if you are not planning such changes, that could be a chance you are willing to take. Service firms will object to this billing method only if the claim volumes are subject to major seasonal fluctuations, which could cause them cash flow and staffing problems. This is sometimes dealt with by combining a per-claim charge with a fixed monthly fee, which guarantees the service firm minimal payments in slow months and keeps the client's cost from skyrocketing too much in the heavy season. A catch to watch out for is different types of claims: Simple literature or merchandise orders should not be charged at the same rate as claims requiring more thorough auditing and processing.

- **Per ad.** Once growing in popularity, this is used less often now, because it causes too much conflict over how ads are counted, particularly in the ever-growing area of nonmedia claims. Also, it might be reasonable to pay $3 per ad, but do you really want to pay $3,000 to audit a Kmart claim with 1,000 ads?

- **Percentage of amount claimed (or paid).** It is statistically valid to argue that, if the other billing methods would work out to, say, 3 percent of amount claimed, why not just bill 3 percent of the amount claimed? It is clean and easy. The problem comes (again) when the client realizes that he or she is paying $3,000 to have that $100,000 Kmart claim audited. Soon the client stops sending the Kmart and Target claims to the service, then the reports are invalid because they do not include expenditures by the biggest customers. The service is upset because their income is much less than they expected, since they are only processing the little claims, which they lose money on. Nobody is happy.

Service firms will generally bid and bill in whatever manner you request. Many manufacturers seem now to prefer a monthly fixed fee, a billing per claim, or a combination. The problem, from the service providers' viewpoint, with such billing methods is that prospective customers often do not provide them with good estimates of the workload anticipated, and thus they are forced to commit themselves to a bid for a workload that might turn out to be very different from what they bid on.

If, however, you can give the service companies bidding on your business good numbers on the claim and phone volume they can expect, some sort of firm price is best for all concerned: It allows you to budget your costs and the administrators to plan their cash flow, and will minimize monthly billing disputes. Still, you have to make sure you are both agreed as to what is included in the fixed price and what sort of service or information request will be considered a "special project" that will be billed extra. Ask the references whether they feel they are treated fairly in such matters. Watch out for incredibly low bids, which might be followed up with equally incredible add-ons after the contract is signed ("Oh, you want us to *talk* to the dealers when they call? That'll be extra. We only bid on answering the phone.").

**STABILITY**

The stability of your service firm is of obvious importance; your marketing programs could be seriously disrupted if the company administering them goes out of business. This is a danger no one wants to talk about, but it is real, since all the major players in this field are, in fact, minor players; they are all relatively small companies. In addition, it is difficult to get good information on their financial status since all are privately held. You should, nonetheless, ask to see financials.

**TECHNOLOGY**

Have somebody from your MIS department check into the prospective services' technology. It is not always necessary to have the latest and greatest, but it is important that your service have the power to handle your database and the flexibility to grow and change with your program. Some of the older software is very inflexible and, if you make major changes in your program after hiring an administrator, you might find yourself hit with long delays and/or large programming bills to get modifications done. There are, of course, always trade-offs between power and flexibility, but these trade-offs have been ameliorated a bit in some of the more recent relational database programs.

Also, check into the qualifications of the services' programming staff. Further, find out whether they actually *have* a staff, or if they use contract programmers. Contractors are less likely to be familiar with marketing programs in general, and with your program in particular, to allow them to intelligently translate your instructions from marketing to computer lingo. They are more likely to just program what they have been told to program, even if it does not make technical or marketing sense.

Equipment is also important; failures can disrupt your promotions. Check into the age and quality of their equipment; find out how and how often they do back-ups and where they store them; ask what sort of equipment replacement plan they have with their supplier; and ask to see their disaster recovery plan.

**INDUSTRY AND MARKETING KNOWLEDGE AND INNOVATION**

Innovation and knowledge of trade promotion and marketing are difficult to assess, but vital if you are going to get any value-added service out of your administrator. There are really only two ways to check on this: Talk to the references and talk to the prospective services themselves. Ask the references for their assessment of the marketing ideas they have gotten from their service, how the service responds to changes, and if the service has come up with any innovative new service or reporting ideas.

Then make your own judgment by sitting down and talking with people at the administrators' offices. Find out how much they know about marketing, trade promotion, and your business, and then decide whether they sound like paper-shufflers or the sort of people who can be your marketing partners. It is important to talk with the management personnel; they will probably be the ones serving as your consultants. But *do not* limit these conversations to the salespeople and top management. Talk to some of the people who might actually be working on your account. Of course, they might not be as knowledgeable and/or as experienced as the managers, but they are the ones who are going to be at ground level on your program, and the insights they gain from that perspective can be invaluable to you. After you talk to some of them ask yourself whether they are capable of understanding the marketing implications of the things they will see and hear in the course of handling your program, and whether they have the ability and the initiative to bring their insights to their managers' attention and yours.

## PHONE SUPPORT

This leads into the last, but far from least, item: phone support. For many marketers, this is the most important single point in the decision process. Your dealers are going to be looking on your administrative service as an extension of your company. From their perspective, when they talk to your administrator, they are talking to you. The only way to judge how a prospective service will do is to talk with them and to observe them in action. After you ask the questions described in the previous section, you will have a good idea as to whether the administrator employs people who are sufficiently professional that you would want them on the phone representing your company. Another test might be to actually call a couple of times, pretending to be a dealer, and see how quickly the phone is answered and how well the call is handled. Besides dealers, of course, your field salespeople will be calling the administrator frequently, looking for information. The last thing in the world you want is to hear from field sales about getting inaccurate, garbled, or hard-to-understand information, or being on hold for a long time.

# Bids from Outside Administrators

As of this writing, the major administrative firms are in alphabetical order: Advertising Audit Service (AAS), Farmington Hills, Michigan; Advertising Checking Bureau (ACB), New York, with offices in Memphis and Phoenix; CoAMS, Chicago; Co-op Communications, Greenbrae, California; Medianet, Austin, Texas; Pinpoint Marketing (PMI), New York; and Shared Market Services, Chicago. There are a few other very small services with one or two clients. In addition, a few advertising agencies offer limited administrative services to their clients.

We have talked about some of the ways outside administrators can minimize their estimates to you. This can best be avoided by giving bidders a clear-cut and complete set of program specifications, preferably in writing. At least make sure all the bidders are bidding on the same specs.

To get the best possible estimates, give the prospective services as much of the following data as possible:

- How many claims and ads can they anticipate?

- What are the approximate accruals and payout?

- How many funds are there? Can payments cross over and use different funds?

- How will you provide sales or accrual information? How often? If it is a distributor program, will the distributors be providing sales-out information? In what format?

- What are the channels of distribution?

- How many dealers (or distributors) are there? How many are active in the program?

- If it is a distributor program, do they pass through money to the dealers?

- Are there a lot of chains, and if so, who earns and spends the money—the headquarters or the chain member? Does the composition of the chains change frequently?

- Are there a lot of exceptions in your program? Give some examples (such as dealers who get special handling). How will such exceptions be communicated?

- What department in your company runs the program (sales, marketing, or finance)? How are other departments involved?

- Who will the service be in contact with (dealers, distributors, or the sales force)?

- What is the anticipated amount of phone calls?

- Will there be an 800 number?

- What reports do you want? (Show samples if possible). How often do you want to receive each report (monthly, quarterly, year-end)?

- Do you want on-line access to your data? For what purpose (entry, update, read only, doing your own reports)? How will you be accessing? How often?

- Do you use prior approvals or commitments?

- Is the program fixed or rolling?

- What media and promotion types are used?

- Do you have pending? If so, how does it work?

- Do you want to pay by credit memo or check?

- Do you have deduction problems? How do you handle deductions?

- Is the program limited to the United States, or does it include Canada or other countries? Are there any special translation or currency conversion needs?

- Do you want services other than regular audit and payment (such as fulfillment or telemarketing)?

- Will your administrative service need to interface with other service providers (fulfillment service, telemarketers, and so on)?

- When will you be making your decision?

- When do you want the first claims audited? The first statements mailed?

Armed with this information, any service should be able to give you a pretty solid estimate within a week, two at the most. Make sure they are very detailed as to what they include and what they consider extra. We discussed the different ways a bid can be structured. Most manufacturers prefer to avoid time and materials, and with the data we have listed you can expect some form of fixed pricing. Ask for details on any charges that would not be included in the fixed fee (special projects, work on a volume higher than what is in the specs, materials, and so on).

Draw up a chart something like Exhibit 5.7. When you complete this form, you will have some idea of the comparative costs of the firms. Remember to include higher internal costs if you feel that one of the outside services might require more supervision or might cause additional internal expense through weaker dealer phone service, reporting inaccuracy, or some other weakness they may have.

Earlier, we looked at some estimates of what it might cost to bring a program currently handled by an outside administrator in-house. The costs of moving an in-house program to an outside administrator (or from one administrator to another) are generally covered by a set-up fee charged by the administrator, which may range from $2,000 or $3,000 to $100,000, depending on the size and complexity of your program and the length of the contract you are signing. Some services are willing to waive some or all of the set-up costs in return for a long-term contract. Additionally, of course, you need to factor in the very considerable costs on your side, mostly for your own time and that of your staff.

Something to remember about specifications and guarantees. While most people are properly reluctant to make choices about important things (like hiring outside services to handle their biggest marketing program) solely on the basis of cost, you should still consider that the more exact you make your specs and the stronger the guarantees you demand, the *closer* you come to being able to decide on price alone.

## Transition Trauma

As mentioned previously in regard to ongoing fees, you need to make sure that what the administrative service will do in return for the set-up fee is clearly defined. Most transitions include at least one dispute over a report needing special programming, which the administrative service says was not included in the specs they bid on, whereas you contend it was discussed in great detail.

Transitions, of any kind, are painful. Think back to the last time your company made a major change in its computer system. Expect the best-planned co-op transition, whether from in-house to a third-party, vice versa, or from one administrator to another, to cause at least three months of confusion and chaos. It is worth it if you made the right choice.

## In-House Responsibility

Even if you hire an outside service, you are going to have to do some of the administrative work inside. As a matter of fact, one of the important decisions in the course of deciding whether to go outside will be which functions to outsource and which to keep. In many cases, this decision will be driven in part by the capabilities of the outside service you select.

In any case, which department within your company should be in charge of your program's administration? This is one of those questions that has no right answer, because it will depend a lot on your internal politics, your structure, and your needs. These are some of the points to consider:

- Is the program to be administered inside or outside? If it is outside, how much is sent out?

- How tight do you want controls to be?

- How is the program budgeted?

- What are your program goals (for example, sell-in or sell-through)?

**EXHIBIT 5.7**  Worksheet for Comparison of External Bids

| | Service #1 ($) | Service #2 ($) | Service #3 ($) | Notes |
|---|---|---|---|---|
| BASE ANNUAL FEES | 120,000 | 5,000 | 200,000 | |
| PER-UNIT CHARGES | 75,000 | 175,000 | | |
| MATERIALS COST | 25,000 | 25,000 | 30,000 | MORE TRAVEL TO #3 |
| ANTICIPATED PROGRAMMING | 40,000 | | 20,000 | #1 WILL HAVE TROUBLE KEEPING UP WITH PROGRAM CHANGES |
| OTHER CHARGES | | 10,000 | | REFERENCES SAY #2 HAS LOTS OF EXTRAS |
| INTERNAL SALARIES/ BENEFITS | 70,000 | 70,000 | 70,000 | |
| OTHER INTERNAL COSTS | | | 20,000 | #3 WILL NEED HAND-HOLDING |
| OTHER | | | | |
| TOTAL ONGOING COSTS | 330,000 | 285,000 | 340,000 | |
| SET-UP CHARGES, SERVICE | 30,000 | 20,000 | 17,000 | #1 WILL NEED LOTS OF PROGRAMMING TO MEET SPECS |
| SET-UP COSTS, US | 20,000 | 20,000 | 30,000 | #3 WILL NEED HAND-HOLDING |

Marketers tend to think that, in most cases, control of the co-op program should be in the marketing department. It is, after all, a marketing program. Companies with a channel marketing structure should put co-op under the channel marketing manager.

Some companies look at it as a sales-support program, however, and put it in sales. The drawback is that sales personnel sometimes tend to be a bit cavalier about controls. Other companies, especially those with serious deduction problems, tend to look at co-op in accounting (and accounts receivable) terms and place it in the finance department. The problem is that finance people sometimes tend to look at co-op totally as a cost and to see benefits in reducing the cost by discouraging use of the program. Companies that manage the program internally could justify placing control of co-op in their administration department.

# CHAPTER 6

# *Budgeting*

In this chapter, we will cover how to integrate accrual rates, dealer usage rates, costs of incentives and bonus programs, and cost of administration into an overall budget for your promotional allowance program. (How to determine each of these costs is dealt with in other chapters of this book.) We will also explore other budgeting issues, such as ratios of national advertising to promotional allowances, and how to deal with promotional allowance expenses in the corporate budget.

## Where to Find Things

Setting accrual rates is dealt with in Chapter 3. Determining dealer usage rates, as well as how to increase those rates, and the sorts of incentives and bonuses you can use to do so, are all found in Chapter 4. Determining what your cost of administration is, and estimating what it would be if you were to move it from an outside service to in-house or vice versa, are covered in Chapter 5.

## Putting Them Together

Once you have figured out everything that needs to go into your budget and gathered all your data together, it is a relatively simple matter to put it into a spreadsheet and figure out what your program is costing.

Let us look at what a program budget might look like for 1995 for a large internally administered program. Do not look at these administrative figures as any sort of guide to what your administrative costs should be, they are just reasonable numbers for a program of this size and are serving as examples. Chapter 5, as mentioned, has some guides to determining your own administrative costs, which are so specific to each company's budgeting and allocation process that it is impossible for anyone to make a blanket statement as to what they should be.

**EXHIBIT 6.1**   Sample Budget for Internally-Administered Program

|  | Notes | Budgeted |
|---|---|---|
| Projected sales | 800,000 | |
| Co-op program (3%) | 24,000 | |
| Anticipated usage (57%) | 13,680 | 13,680 |
| MDF program (1%) | 8,000 | |
| Anticipated usage (94%) | 7,600 | 7,600 |
| Incentives and bonuses | 2,144 | 2,144 |
| Total funds paid out to dealers | | 23,424 |
| | | |
| Salaries | 520 | 520 |
| Space cost | 18 | 18 |
| Printing, postage, and materials | 50 | 50 |
| Phones | 15 | 15 |
| Travel | 25 | 25 |
| Programming support | 50 | 50 |
| Computer allocation | 60 | 60 |
| Equipment purchase and deprec | 25 | 25 |
| Allocated overhead | 100 | 100 |
| Other administrative costs | 86 | 86 |
| Total administrative costs | | 949 |
| Total budget | | 24,373 |

Note: Figures are in thousands of dollars.

**EXHIBIT 6.2** Sample Budget for Externally-Administered Program

|  | Notes | Budgeted |
|---|---|---|
| Projected sales | 1,000,000 |  |
| Co-op program (4%) | 40,000 |  |
| Anticipated usage (70%) | 28,000 | 28,000 |
| MDF program (1%) | 10,000 |  |
| Anticipated usage (95%) | 9,500 | 9,500 |
| Slotting program (2%) | 20,000 |  |
| Anticipated usage (100%) | 20,000 | 20,000 |
| Total funds paid out to dealers |  | 57,500 |
|  |  |  |
| Administrative fees | 1,150 | 1,150 |
| Salaries | 100 | 100 |
| Space cost | 5 | 5 |
| Phones | 5 | 5 |
| Travel | 25 | 25 |
| Equipment purchase and depreciation | 10 | 10 |
| Allocated overhead | 125 | 125 |
| Other administrative costs | 27 | 27 |
| Total administrative costs |  | 1,447 |
| Total budget |  | 58,947 |

Note: Figures are in thousands of dollars.

In our sample case (see Exhibit 6.1), the company has annual sales of $800 million, offers a 3 percent co-op program and has a 1 percent market development fund (MDF) budget. They anticipate 57 percent usage of the co-op program and 95 percent usage of MDF. Not pleased with the 57 percent, they have budgeted 20 percent of unused funds to pay for incentive and bonus programs aimed at increasing usage.

A budget for a program administered by an outside service might look like Exhibit 6.2 (again, the numbers are for demonstration purposes only).

111

# Accounting for Promotional Allowances

There are two principal ways promotional allowances are expensed in most companies: They are either costs or reversals of revenue. How they are viewed makes no difference to the bottom line, but it can make a great difference in somebody's bonus. If they are reversals on revenue, it will make the gross profit percentage look better; very important to, for example, a product manager who gets a bonus on that percentage. Let us look at it both ways, assuming for our example a product with $50 million in sales, $1 million in promotional allowance expenses, and $19 million in all other expenses (see Exhibit 6.3).

Most promotional allowances (at least the ones we have been discussing) should be considered expenses. Rebates, off-invoice programs, slotting allowances, and the like are probably more legitimately reversals of revenue. A good rule of thumb might be that if the Federal Trade Commission would consider it a Section 2(a) matter, it is a revenue reversal; if it is Section 2(d-e), it is an expense. Of course, the Internal Revenue Service and the Financial Accounting Standards Board may have different opinions on the subject.

**EXHIBIT 6.3**   Effect on Gross Profit if Co-op Is Considered

|  | Expense | Reversal of Revenue |
|---|---|---|
| Sales | 50,000 | 49,000 |
| Co-op | 1,000 | |
| Other expense | 19,000 | 19,000 |
| Total expense | 20,000 | 19,000 |
| Gross profit | 30,000 | 30,000 |
| Gross profit (%) | 60.00% | 61.22% |

Note: Figures are in thousands of dollars.

# Promotional Allowances to National Advertising Ratios

One of the most contentious issues in determining marketing budgets is allocating expenditures between national advertising and promotional allowance programs. Not only does this involve major turf wars and internal politics, it also becomes very emotional and personal because people's deeply-held beliefs about various forms of marketing are challenged. Go into this very carefully. Let us see if we can establish some reasonably dispassionate criteria for approaching this problem.

## THE BUYING PROCESS

National advertising influences different steps in the buying decision than do local advertising and promotion, and the decision on how to allocate resources between the two activities therefore comes down to understanding how the buying decisions concerning your product are being made at each level in the distribution chain and allocating funding at the steps where it can be most effective.

There is evidence (see "A Model for Predicting Advertising Effectiveness" in the *Journal of Marketing*, October 1991) that consumers

**EXHIBIT 6.4** Progression of Purchase Decision

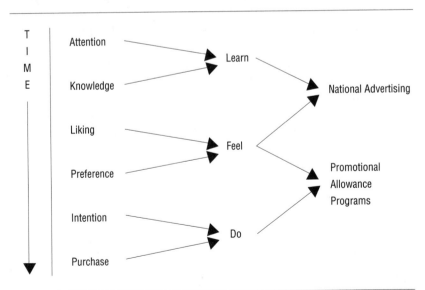

proceed through a series of steps on their way to a purchase. As they do so, their information needs and sources change (see Exhibit 6.4). Consumers use national advertising in the early stages of the purchase process, using local advertising and promotion in the later stages. The purpose of promotional allowance programs is to stimulate this local promotion.

General Electric's major appliances division describes its thinking about the use of local promotion in these terms. GE's model (from Dr. Robert Young's "The Uses and Effectiveness of Vertical Cooperative Advertising") is shown in Exhibit 6.5.

Due to the manner in which people reach purchase decisions (about, for example, a refrigerator), GE sees local promotion via promotional allowance programs as a vital tool to affect actual shopping behavior. They therefore budget substantially more money for promotional allowances than for national advertising.

Another approach is an advertising "planning grid" (see Exhibit 6.6) developed by Foote, Cone, Belding (see "How Advertising Works: A Planning Model Revisited" in the *Journal of Advertising Research*, Feb/Mar 1986). In this grid, the axes represent the mental processes used in consumer decision making and the varying degrees of personal involvement inherent in the purchase of different categories of goods.

For purchases that are high involvement and thinking, consumers need substantial marketing information at the local level. They perceive a significant risk in the purchase and they cannot put full faith in

**EXHIBIT 6.5**   GE Model: Purposes of National Advertising vs. Local Promotion

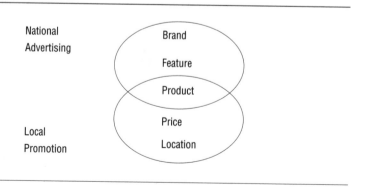

the product's brand name alone. They need local information and, possibly, face-to-face reassurance to reduce the perceived risk.

In this quadrant, most people make a fairly extensive search for information. Their decision process is prolonged and rational. They want brand-name reassurance but even more they want the brand linked to a credible local source. In other words, they need to tie together a trusted brand and a trusted local retailer. This is an obvious role for promotional allowance program expenditures.

In high perceived risk purchases, people look for credible sources of information. A magazine ad or television spot, no matter how well executed, cannot fill this need. Research in social psychology has shown that people are more persuaded when they consider the source of information trustworthy and to have a high level of expertise (see "The Persuasive Effect of Source Credibility" in *Public Opinion Quarterly*, Fall 1978). Consumers will respond to local ads if they perceive either or both the retailer and/or the brand as a credible source. They will respond *most* positively, obviously, if both are credible.

## THE PRODUCT LIFE-CYCLE

Besides the type of purchase decision being made about your product, you need also to consider where it stands in its life-cycle.

In the early part of the product life-cycle, the most important marketing goal is to establish product knowledge and brand awareness. This is primarily the role of national advertising. As the product

**EXHIBIT 6.6**   FCB planning grid

|  | Think | Feel |
|---|---|---|
| **High involvement** | Life insurance<br>Cameras<br>Refrigerators<br>PCs | Wine<br>Perfume |
| **Low involvement** | Detergents<br>Ballpoint pens | Popsicles<br>Beer |

matures, price competition, retail support, and smaller increments of differentiation become more important. Price and retail support can best be communicated with local advertising and promotion. Explaining small increments of differentiation, such as particular features and configurations, can best be done at the point of sale.

As products move toward maturity, therefore, local advertising and promotion become relatively more important than national advertising. In addition to increasing the tilt toward promotional allowance expenditures as the product matures, there should be a simultaneous tilt within the promotional allowance program away from purely traditional "co-op advertising" expenditures to a greater mix of infrastructure-building, in-store promotion, spiffs, and sales incentives.

## Summary

Few companies will reveal the finer details of their marketing budgets. Therefore, we cannot look at a lot of published data on how individual companies allocate their funding. There is, however, some such data. Michael Rothschild's 1987 book, *Marketing Communications,* (Chapter 4), for example, tells us that GE and Whirlpool spend six to eight times as much on cooperative versus national advertising for their appliances. These products are fully mature, high-involvement, thinking purchases where the buyer looks for the best deal and local support.

Most buyers know, for example, that GE makes good refrigerators. They want to know where to buy one and what it will cost, messages best carried by local promotion and support programs. Refrigerators are expensive, so buyers will do a lot of comparison shopping before getting one. Since it is impractical to do that sort of research through magazine or television ads, most buyers will use the Yellow Pages or the local newspaper, then visit the stores to gain enough confidence to make the purchase. As mentioned earlier, they want to see a credible brand name connected to a credible local retailer.

There are, of course, contrary examples. In most packaged goods categories, the brands have much more national advertising than local promotion. Tide, Coca-Cola, and Budweiser, for example, while having large trade promotion budgets, have even larger national advertising budgets. Consumer brand awareness is more important than retailer support. These products are relatively low involvement, and buyers are willing to trust the brand name as their only source of information. They do not need extensive information from the retailer in order to make a purchase. To cut through the jargon, people do not care who sells them a six-pack of Coke. They will buy it from whichever store is convenient or has the best price. They do care who sells them a refrigerator, because they may need service, because they do not know that much about the technical side of the product, and they need some reassurance that they are making the right choice.

Both national advertising and promotional allowance programs are difficult to evaluate for their exact numerical cost-to-benefit ratios (see Chapter 1). National advertising can be proven to have an effect on awareness, but it is very difficult to establish a credible and direct link between the level of national advertising expenditures and the movement of product. Promotional allowance programs are much more measurable in terms of their direct effect on sales, and can also leverage the timely entry of orders from remarketers when required, and be used to quickly respond to competitive efforts and local circumstances.

Another look at Young's list of product attributes lending themselves to co-op (see the Introduction) would help you in determining a ratio. Weigh into the equation the various studies examined in this chapter, especially the question of product maturity. The extremes are packaged goods, where the ratio is below 1:1; and high-involvement, thinking, fully-mature products like large appliances in the 8:1 range. For an example of a middle ground, consider personal computers, still in the growth stage of the product life-cycle, but perhaps nearing maturity. Their ratio probably should be around 3:1 or 4:1.

If you find, on analysis, that your ratio is out of balance, you can adjust by moving budgets for either activity up or down, although any marked change in the absolute amount of national advertising may have corporate image effects beyond the scope of this book. Although existing competitive situations and profitability goals may militate against major changes in budgets, in the long term the ratio will tend even higher for most products, and it would be best to plan incremental changes over several years in order to arrive eventually at the optimal level.

# Reporting

The computer age, which was supposed to do away with paper and put data at our fingertips, has too often buried us in paper (produced by the computers) and provided us with so much data that we are unable to deal with it.

Fifteen years ago, when practically all co-op programs were administered manually, the only data about the program provided to the marketing department was how much money had been paid out. Sometimes this data was broken down by product and by media (since newspapers, broadcast, and direct mail were the only permissible media, this breakdown was not too difficult to produce manually).

Today, the programs are much more complex, the goals are more ambitious, and the available data is far more extensive and detailed. So much data is available, in fact, that the challenge becomes determining how much data can be absorbed and understood, which data can be acted on, and in what format it should be presented.

Your administrative service or internal department can give you practically any information you want, as long as they capture it. And, of course, as long as you are willing to pay for it, because the more information you request, the longer it will take to process each claim, and the longer it will take to balance and quality-check the reports. (See Chapter 5 on comparing the costs of administrative services. The balancing of reports is an area where some administrative services will cut corners and costs.)

We will go over the most common data captured and reported. We will also discuss what you need for different purposes, and examine a few of the newest reports and some we see coming in the future.

## Standard Reports

### THE CUSTOMER STATEMENT

The most basic report, so basic you may not even think of it as a report, is the monthly statement you send out to your dealers. It is known by a variety of names, usually the dealer activity record or participant activity statement. The most important thing to remember about this report is that it is going to be read by people who are not co-op specialists and who have neither the time nor the inclination to try to absorb excess information. Keep the form as simple as possible, consistent with giving the customers the information they need. The most vital information is, "How much money do I have available?" If your program, as in a rolling fund program, has spending deadlines so that some of the money will expire if not used by certain dates, this needs to be clearly communicated; some statements have a "drop box," showing funds that are scheduled to "drop off" in 30, 60, and 90 days.

The second important element of the customer statement is the activity section. This tells the dealer which claims have been processed and what happened to them (if they were paid in full, in part, or rejected), with a code that *should* explain why. This is the portion that generally is most difficult to deal with, because it is where the balance between thoroughness and simplicity can most easily get out of synch.

The problem is, you have a limited amount of space and a lot of information to convey. Should you include only the claims processed since the last statement, or all the claims processed this year? If the former, you are relying on the dealer having kept the last statement (unlikely). If the latter, you end up with multi-page documents that will make even an accountant's eyes glaze over.

Should you list each claim as a single line item or, if it consisted of multiple elements, should you list each item separately? Again, you can have long lists of ads for some major dealers if you do a thorough breakdown, but if you do not, you may have a difficult time detailing which portions of a partially paid claim were paid and which were not.

And how do you handle claims that were resubmitted several times for additional payments—list each submission separately, or list only the most recent submission? Again, there are pros and cons: Multiple listings add to the clutter and confusion on the statement, but listing only the last submission does not create a good audit trail and may cause confusion.

There are no right or wrong answers, and the various factors that determine what might be right in your case are complex and often subjective. You need to go through these questions with your auditing service or your staff and determine what is right for you. In some cases, it is a coin-toss. Either way you will create some level of confusion among your dealers, so you just need to decide which set of problems and questions you want to deal with.

## THE BALANCE REPORT

This report summarizes the most important data from the customer statements. It details how much each dealer has earned to date, how much has been paid, how much has dropped off, what adjustments have been done, and how much is currently available. This might be subtotaled by region, sales rep, or other category.

This is the report that, if it does not balance, your controller will be coming after you, because finance uses this report to project liability. Your auditing service or internal department should be required to show you how they balanced your reports. This is the main report (everything else should be balanced against it). Insist they provide you with their reconciliation sheets, balanced to the penny, detailing the total available from last month's report, the total accruals they loaded this month, the total amount they paid out, any expired funds, any adjustments (with detail as to why the adjustments were made), and this month's new balance. It should look something like Exhibit 7.1.

The following horror story indicates the importance of checking this report. Several years ago, an administrative service took over management of a large program from another service. After they loaded the data from the new client and the historical data from the previous administrator, they found that they were unable to balance, a situation that persisted for almost two weeks. The client fumed at the delay, wondering, justifiably, if they had made a mistake and selected an incompetent service. At last, someone noticed that the amount out of balance was identical to the amount of accrual available to one particular dealer. On examination, it turned out that there was no such dealer, the previous administrator had created a dummy dealership to act as a "plug" to cover the amount they were out of balance, and each month they had added more to the dummy's account because each month they were further out of balance. By the time the situation was found the dummy account's fund was up to a couple of hundred thousand dollars.

While the administrator's action was clearly reprehensible, the lesson of the story is that the client could have caught the situation earlier if they had checked the balance report each month, and could have held the losses to a relatively small amount.

**EXHIBIT 7.1** Sample Balance Report Reconciliation

**February 1995 Balance Report Reconciliation for World Industries**
**Prepared 10 March 1995**

| | |
|---|---|
| Balance from January report | 12,643,654.96 |
| February accruals, loaded 3 March 1995 | 4,765,785.52 |
| Paid: check register #108, 2/3/95 | (1,101,032.68) |
| Paid: check register #109, 2/10/95 | (823,632.13) |
| Paid: check register # 110, 2/17/95 | (899,765.23) |
| Paid: check register #111, 2/22/95 | (954,231.48) |
| Paid: check register #112, 2/28/95 | (732,129.66) |
| Funds dropped 1 March 1995 | (1,954,378.62) |
| Adjustment: Kmart, special promo, per J. Smith memo 2/10/95 | 50,000.00 |
| Adjustment: Target, reduce funds for deduction, per L. Jones memo 2/15/95 | (43,321.72) |
| Adjustment: Little Store, reinstate 1994 funds, per J. Smith memo 2/21/95 | 116.85 |
| New balance | 10,951, 065.81 |
| Balance per report | 10,951,065.81 |
| Difference | 0.00 |

## THE DOCUMENT REGISTER

This is the "check register" mentioned in the balance report reconciliation. It could be for any type of document—check, credit memo, or other. You should get one each time your service or department is ready to send out a group of payments. It should list all payments being made and from which funds, if you have multiple programs. You use this to check for any obvious irregularities (payments going out to accounts on credit hold, for example). You then fund the bank account and authorize release of the payments.

## THE EXPENDITURE REPORTS

These are among the simplest reports to produce, but they will be very valuable for planning, and for determining whether dealers are using your program the way you want them to.

The standard expenditure reports break down the amounts paid out by media, by product, by class of trade, by ad date, and by combinations of these (for example, how much was paid out for January ads and promotions for your Widgets Lite line would be in the Expenditure by Ad Date by Product report; how much was paid out to department stores for radio ads would be in Expenditure by Media by Class of Trade, and so on).

These reports are vital for planning and fine-tuning your program. While anything can be overdone, it should not hurt to ask your service for every variation of these reports you think you might ever want because they are relatively easy to produce and quality-check. The reports that are time consuming, and thus expensive, to check are the ones involving accruals, adjustments, and balances. Reports involving only expenditures are easy, and your service should not charge you as much for them.

A variation on the expenditure reports you might ask for—it is not typically offered as a standard report by auditing services—is a report comparing the expenditures by month of advertising with your sales by month. This tells you if dealers are advertising in close correlation with sales.

## CLAIM ADJUSTMENT REPORT

Another simple report, this one lists what claims in what amounts are not being paid in full and why. It can alert you to problems with certain accounts, and can let you know which parts of your program are causing problems for the dealers.

The reports so far are pretty much the standard package. Any auditing service or internal department should be able to produce them. If your service or department cannot produce them accurately and on time, find another service.

Some reports not generally available now, but which more people ought to be asking for, are listed in the following sections.

## PROGRAM EFFECTIVENESS REPORTS

Have a report produced telling you what percentage of your dealers are using the program, what percentage of accruals those dealers represent, and what percentage of their accruals they are using. Get this broken down by sales territory and, if possible, by channel.

This report tells you whether your program is being used, whether it is being used by the big dealers, and whether those who are using it are using it fully. The territorial and channel breakdowns tell you where your strengths and weaknesses lie. It gives you the usage and participation rate information you need to get started on deciding whether you need to improve those rates, and where improvement might be needed (see Chapter 4).

## SALES AND USAGE REPORTS

On an annual basis, at the end of the program year, have a report produced like the ones described in Chapter 1, telling you whether the people who are using your program the most are growing the most. Have it done by channel, if possible, since that will tell you where your strengths and weaknesses are.

## RETURN-ON-INVESTMENT REPORTS

When you have started collecting ROI information on your major expenditures, get a report detailing and summarizing it (see Chapter 10). When you check your subtotals and cross-tabs showing overall ROI by dealer, sales territory, channel, and media, you will begin to know where your most effective investments are.

## PROFIT-ON-INVESTMENT REPORTS

The next step after ROI (see Chapter 10), this is the same type of report, with the same cross-tabs and subtotals, but this one tells you not only which types of promotion by which retailers produce the most incremental sales, but which ones produce the most incremental profits.

**PROFIT-BY-ACCOUNT REPORT**

This is the ultimate report that rolls together all the various payments and expenses you incur with each dealer, and analyzes your profitability by account. When you have this report, you are ready to move on to the next level of co-op, where you allocate accruals on profit instead of on sales. This report is shown in Chapter 10.

# Ad Hoc Reporting

One of the biggest fads of recent years in co-op advertising was the sudden demand for "ad hoc" reports. The problem was that many of the people who wanted them did not know what they were, they just wanted them because everybody in the business was talking about them. Some service firms began talking about their ability to provide ad hoc reporting, but again, since few people were clear on what they really wanted, the services weren't sure what to provide, and the clients were never sure whether what they were getting was what they thought they wanted or what they had been promised.

In actual fact, true ad hoc report writing does not exist in our industry today, although we are getting close to it (most of the supposed ad hoc systems are really just menus of canned, prewritten reports), and most manufacturers do not really want to get involved in writing their own reports, they just want quicker turnaround on their requests for data.

Recently, some report-writing packages have been developed for use with the leading fourth-generation databases that are more user-friendly than in the past, but these are still not at the Lotus 1-2-3 level most users are looking for.

# Co-op and the Economy

## Recession

Having just come through one recession, it seems unduly cruel to have to consider another, but the possibility is not remote that there will be another fairly soon. It is as near to certain as life gets that one will reappear eventually.

It is interesting to glance back through notes from the beginning of this last recession. An ACB executive was quoted in *Advertising Age* in 1990 as saying that he was not too concerned about the recession then looming because ACB had grown 7 percent during the 1979 recession. He was probably right about that number but wrong in terms of its meaning. Seven percent, if memory serves a considerable downturn from the company's growth rate of preceding years. It also was four points lower than the rate of inflation in 1979.

With the benefit of hindsight we know now that the recession and slow recovery was a bad time for every segment of the promotional allowance marketing business. All the administrative firms suffered, as manufacturers took their programs in-house or demanded huge price cuts, trimming margins to the breaking point. One administrator, CMA, hit by the death of its principal as well as the recession, closed its doors. All others made it through, but not without, in most cases, layoffs and restructurings.

Manufacturers were also hit by layoffs as programs were eliminated or scaled back, or simply downsized in line with shrinking sales. Some manufacturers brought administration of the programs in-house. Whether or not this generated a net savings (see Chapter 5), in most cases it represented a lower cash outlay, and also possibly averted some layoffs by absorbing internal personnel.

Retailers' woes are well known. The industry, already in bad shape when the recession began due to excessive leverage and the long-term decline of the department store channel, suffered numerous bankruptcies and store closures. The grocery and drug channels saw price-conscious customers flock to warehouse stores and clubs, and then were hit with everyday low pricing (EDLP).

Retail's problems exacerbated the problems of the newspaper industry, which, like department stores, was already in long-term decline when the recession hit. Several major dailies closed in the early 1990s. Broadcast also suffered, in large part from its own excessive leverage, although local broadcast outlets probably did better than their networks. We have gone through this painful recital to give you an idea of what to be ready for next time. Some of these problems may not recur, but most will. Most important is to think about what a manufacturer can do to keep a promotional allowance program moving ahead during a recession:

- **Pay by credit memo instead of check.** This helps your float tremendously; it forces reorders; and (most importantly) it saves you from having to explain to your credit department why you sent a check to a bankrupt dealer.

- **Educate your dealers.** This may be a long-term project (so do not wait until the next recession to get started on it), but try to convince your dealers of the importance of advertising and promotion. Numerous studies exist (the American Association of Advertising Agencies [AAAA] has one on the value of advertising); try circulating them to your dealers. Do articles on the value of advertising and promotion in your dealer newsletter. Provide seminars and workshops for your sales force on how to reinforce this message.

  The dealers, of course, will answer that they cannot spend money they do not have. You may have to consider bumping up market development funds (MDF) selectively and temporarily to allow dealers to maintain promotion levels on your products in the face of declining sales. Of course any such add-ons come out of *your* margins, but if you can afford it, do it.

- **Support your best dealers.** Here is a case study: There are two dealers in town. Dealer A is heavy on your product line and carries your rival as a secondary line; dealer B is heavy on your rival and carries you as a secondary line. Only one can survive the recession, the other is going to go bankrupt. The survivor, as a result, will come out of it bigger and stronger than ever. Which dealer do you want to see survive? You can help Dealer A survive by offering him or her extra help. Tie your MDF funds, at least in part, to something like shelf space. Dealers who give you more than X percent of their shelf space get a bigger piece of the pie. You may even allow your most committed dealers to use these funds for infrastructure expenses like interest, service technicians, sales training, and so on.

- **Promote value.** Value is one of the buzzwords that seems to crop up in every recession. In bad times, people look for value and for trusted brand names—good news if you are one of the top brands in your category; something you will have to battle if you are a "second-tier" vendor. Something you can do to capitalize on the drive for value is to determine which of your products is a "recession-beater"—a high-value product or one in a category that will do well in a recession (people entertain at home in a recession, they repair their cars, they repair and redecorate their homes, and so on). Offer increased accruals and/or increased payout on these items.

  The value idea is another to get across to your dealers in your educational efforts: The AAAA has published a study showing that advertising a product increases its perceived value. Therefore, the more a dealer advertises your product the better price he or she can get for it.

- **Maintain your perspective.** Just as recessions are almost inevitable, so is the end of the recession. This too shall pass.

## Economic Growth

After several years of recession and slow growth, it is good to be speculating on how much growth we are going to get and how long it will last. But how should promotional allowance marketers respond to growth?

The most important thing is to increase the amount of promotional allowances for your products. Higher sales will take care of some of this, but if possible, increase your accrual rate and/or MDF budget. If not, at least offer dealers incentives to spend more of the available funding. It seems likely that co-op moves product even better in good times than in bad.

At least that is what some recent research indicates. An example is Exhibit 8.1, a graph of two studies performed for a major housewares manufacturer. In the studies, the co-op usage rates and growth rates were determined for the manufacturer's top 50 customers in 1988 (compared to 1987), and 1991 (compared to 1990). Nineteen-eighty-eight was a good year with high growth rates, but 1991 was a poorer year. The results of this study, as performed for a number of manufacturers in various fields, all of which show that the heavier users of co-op have sales increases significantly higher than lighter users, were described in Chapter 1.

Exhibit 8.1 takes the study another step. It compares the degree by which the heavy co-op users' usage and growth rates exceeded those of the light users for the same manufacturer in a year of healthy growth and in a bad year. As you can see, in 1988 the heavy users' co-op usage rate was about 80 percent higher than the light users', while in 1991 it was about 50 percent higher. The significant numbers, however, have to do with sales growth—in 1991, the heavy users grew 20 percent faster than the light users. But in 1988, they grew more than 200 percent faster! The indication is that incremental co-op usage generates almost geometrically increasing amounts of incremental sales *in better selling climates.*

Another study, also described in Chapter 1, compared a weak selling environment with a stronger one. The sales growth and co-op usage rates for certain products for department stores and other channels of distribution were compared. Within each channel, as always, the heavier co-op users grew at faster rates. However, when channels were compared to each other, it was found that the troubled department store channel, while having (as expected) far higher co-op usage rates, had significantly *lower* sales gains. The conclusion again is that, while incremental co-op usage *always* produces incremental sales, its rate of payoff increases when the co-op is applied to situations where the sales potential is more elastic.

**EXHIBIT 8.1**   Comparison of Sales Growth and Co-op Usage Rates, Housewares Manufacturer

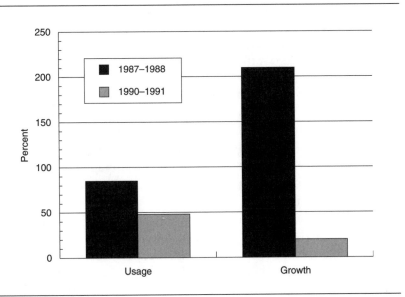

Source: MEDIANET, Inc.

In an improving economy, there are opportunities to get into more dealerships. If you have been locked out of some dealers by tight open-to-buy, a time of looser budgets might allow you to get in. Incentive co-op programs might help you take advantage of the opportunity. The flip side of this is that your competitors have the same opportunity to get into your top dealers. If you tie MDF funding to incremental orders you might be able to soak up enough of the additional open-to-buy to keep the competitors out.

A stronger economy might also be an opportunity to get some of your secondary product lines into stores carrying only your strongest lines, by pooling allowances or encouraging tie-in promotions. If you have a brand management structure, you might get resistance from the brand managers of the stronger lines, but maybe you can remind them that it is one company.

Another thing to remember, especially in the event of a boom, is to maintain your perspective. Many people start thinking they are marketing geniuses when sales are up, when really all they are doing

131

is riding a wave. Just as recessions do not last forever, neither do recoveries or booms. Do not commit yourself to things you cannot get out of if the economy sours again, and do not get caught in the market share trap again—your goal is profit. If you stay focused on essentials, you will not only take better advantage of the upturn, you will be in better shape to ride out the next economic storm.

## High Inflation

What happens to promotional allowance marketing when inflation reaches 12 percent to 15 percent annually, when the prime rate is 16 percent? Veterans of the late 1970s know, although they may have forced themselves to forget those days. But it could happen again. If so, what would it mean to co-op?

One thing it would mean is that you would be strongly tempted to slow down the payment of your claims. And if you are not tempted to do so, your finance department will be. Do not give in to the temptation. The finance people will come to you with figures like these: "We pay out $12 million a year in promotional allowance payments, and interest right now is 18 percent. That means each day we delay payments saves us about $6,000. If we can average two extra weeks in claim turnaround, we can save over $80,000 a year." Remind them that, as a $500 million company (which is probably roughly what you are if you have a $12 million co-op program), $80,000 represents 0.016 percent of sales, and you will lose far more than that in lost incremental sales if you do not treat your dealers fairly. Remember, if you are saving $80,000 by slowing payments, it means your dealers are losing $80,000. They will remember. At the very least, slowing payments will cut utilization of your co-op program, and less co-op usage means less sales.

Another point to mention to them is that slower payments mean more deductions. Get the credit department to tell them how much they spend each year chasing down deductions. That should be the end of the discussion.

You can compromise with finance and attain some savings, with fewer dealer-relations problems, by changing from check payments to credit memos. Since credit memos cannot generally be applied to their account by your dealers as quickly as they can deposit a check, you gain some of the delay factor the finance people want without actually delaying response to your dealers.

The best reason for paying by check is if you have indirect customers who cannot use credit memos. If you have both direct and indirect customers, however, you may want to consider splitting your payment system—paying the indirects by check and the directs by credit memo. There are administrative hassles involved with this, but a decent computer system should be able to keep it straight. Check on how much you pay out to each group; since the direct customers are usually the biggest, the savings may be enough to outweigh the administrative concerns.

If you must pay by check, and you use an outside service, make sure you use a zero-balance account to add a few extra days of float.

Returning to the subject of deductions, even if you do not slow down your payment cycle, if interest rates increase significantly you can expect more deductions as dealers try to fight their own cost-of-money battles. You may find that *speeding up* payments, though it is counterintuitive, is actually the way to save money, because cutting the number of deductions saves you more than the offsetting cost of money. This is just speculation, and depends on the deduction practices in your industry and your channels of distribution, but it may be worth considering.

Another way to battle deductions is with a commitment system in which you and the dealer plan out promotions in advance (see Chapter 11). With a commitment system, since claims are approved in advance and dealers know exactly what they will be paid for given activities, the claims move through your system more quickly. Also, if a deduction is taken, it is often easier to identify and clear. See more about deductions in Chapter 12.

There are just a couple of other minor points about inflationary co-op. One is to delete the clause in your co-op program saying "claims must be submitted within 60 days." If the dealer is not in a hurry to get the money, why should you try to speed things up? Those clauses came into being in the days when almost all the claims were for newspaper advertising, and the auditing services kept two or three months worth of papers on hand. That is not so important now, so just require them to submit the claims in time to close your books at year-end.

If media advertising is your major expense, you might consider tightening up your checking on rates; the media will be changing (increasing) their rates more frequently, and dealers will be tempted to use the most recent rate card on their claims, even if they are still on the old card.

# Supplier Control and Other Co-op Program Variations

Supplier control co-op programs have been around for a long time in various forms. Although often touted as "the programs of the future," they have never really caught on as much as their proponents have hoped. Nevertheless, in some forms and in some applications, they have been quite successful.

Perhaps one reason supplier control has not been as successful as hoped is because it is so misunderstood. And perhaps one reason it is misunderstood is because it is not one concept, but several, and discussions of it frequently end up at cross-purposes through mutual misinterpretation.

A definition of supplier control might be: Any program in which creative, production, media selection, media purchase, and/or media payment are done directly by the manufacturer (or supplier or co-op provider) instead of by the dealer (or co-op recipient).

In the broadest sense, all co-op programs contain some degree of supplier control. Every program has rules, and the rules are an attempt by the manufacturer to control in various ways the nature of the ad or promotion—most commonly through art and copy restrictions, and limitations on media choices. What is generally understood by the term "supplier control," however, occurs when the efforts by the manufacturer to control the final product become more direct and intrusive. The question that comes up is: How direct and how intrusive does the supplier need to be before it is a supplier control program?

We will leave that question to the co-op metaphysicians and deal with the substantive issues: What are the major forms of supplier control, what are their strengths and weaknesses, and how can you most effectively use them?

## Types of Programs

Before we go into the different types of programs, it might be good to examine the basic concept behind supplier control, and compare it to "regular" co-op. A useful metaphor might be to compare supplier control vs. regular co-op to a socialist (or centrally planned) economy vs. a capitalist (or free-market) economy. In both cases, each alternative has its strengths and weaknesses.

In a regular co-op program, similar to a free market, hundreds or thousands of dealers are spending their own co-op funds, often inefficiently or even stupidly. Often the amount available to a given dealer is so small it cannot be used or, if used, is too small to have any impact; these dealers are effectively shut out of the program. The biggest dealers are breaking the rules (and getting away with it), demanding more than their share of accruals (and getting it), and demanding payments for things they did not do (and getting them). On the positive side, the spending decisions are being made based on local knowledge and in response to a day-to-day feel for the current market situation. Once the decision has been made it can be acted upon and implemented quickly.

A supplier control program, like socialism, relies on a central planning mechanism. This central mechanism (in a word, *you*) is generally much more knowledgeable and sophisticated, at least about advertising and promotion, than local dealers. You can create better advertising and events than most dealers can. By pooling funds, you can make better media buys and allocate funds more efficiently. On the negative side, you do not understand local conditions in every market in the country. Nor is this type of program flexible; you cannot move as quickly as your dealers do to, for example, get an ad on the radio tomorrow to reflect a change in the weather that might represent a marketing opportunity for beach towels.

As the above paragraphs indicate, there are strengths and weaknesses to both approaches. The marketing question is how to maximize the strengths and minimize the weaknesses. Let us look at how the three basic forms of supplier control—full-control, direct deduct, and signback programs—match up.

## FULL-CONTROL PROGRAMS

These are programs in which all decisions about creative and media are made by the manufacturer. The dealer has no accrual. The manufacturer notifies the dealer about planned media and asks if the dealer wishes to participate. If so, the dealer's name is put on the ad (either singly or as part of a list). This is essentially a national advertising program, in which some of the ads are customized to include dealer names. It is co-op for people who do not like co-op.

Full-control programs are the rarest of the breed, for obvious reasons. Dealers have no cost generally (in rare cases the dealers are asked to pay the manufacturer for a portion of the cost), and no creative concerns. However, they also have no control and little choice about the advertising, and never perceive it as "their" ad. The manufacturer has total control of the creative and media, and minimizes administrative problems by just giving the dealer a yes or no decision on involvement. Dealers generally do not like it. Some manufacturers like it except for the fact that their dealers do not.

## DIRECT DEDUCT

A direct deduct program is one in which the dealer places an order for advertising, promotion, or materials with the manufacturer or an authorized third party. When the work is performed, the cost is deducted from the dealer's co-op accruals. Such programs are generally run in conjunction with a regular co-op program, and are most often found in 100 percent paid programs. Direct deduct is the most popular and successful form of supplier control.

The benefits to the dealers of this type of program are that they need to do little or no work, and there is no cash outlay. The drawbacks are the loss of control and the limited menu of choices. For manufacturers, the benefits/drawbacks are essentially reversed: They gain control of the creative and can direct expenditures to desired media/events, but there is a large administrative burden and cost. (Manufacturers offering direct deduct programs in commissionable media may be able to use the commissions to offset some of the administrative cost).

Many programs have direct deduct elements—most commonly for materials, such as premiums, literature, signage, and point-of-purchase. It is also common to have direct deduct programs for Yellow Pages, with listings, or sometimes display ads, being placed by a Yellow Pages specialist agency. In such cases, typically, the dealer calls the manufacturer or the co-op service firm and places an order for an ad. The dealer's co-op funds are frozen and the order is faxed to the Yellow Pages agency. When the agency confirms placement of the order, they notify the manufacturer or service, who deducts the funds from the dealer's allowance, sending confirmation of the placement and the fund deduction to the dealer. The dealer also sometimes places the order with the Yellow Pages agency, who then checks with the manufacturer or co-op service to confirm availability of funds, but this can cause extra steps if the order costs more than the dealer has available.

Similar programs allow dealers to order direct mail pieces imprinted with their name and address, and/or mailing lists in appropriate zip codes, again with the costs deducted from allowances. Direct deduct programs are also used for seminars and workshops for salespeople and technicians in programs allowing payment of those types of costs from co-op funds.

Where direct deduct has been used least is in traditional media (newspapers, radio, and television). Given direct deduct's popularity in other types of promotion, this may say something about the reasons for the decline of traditional media in the co-op mix.

For many years, direct deduct programs could not be applied to newspapers, the largest medium for retail advertising, because of the newspaper industry's archaic billing practices, specifically their refusal to allow placement by and billing to a third party at a dealer's local contract rate. As newspapers' share of the co-op market has plummeted in recent years, most newspapers have abandoned this silly attitude, and now there are only a few holdouts.

There are other problems with direct deduct in this medium, however, that may continue to limit its applicability. An example is a major computer manufacturer who inaugurated a direct deduct program for, among other choices, newspaper advertising. Their ad agency produced a series of attractive ads in various sizes, from which the dealers were allowed to choose. The dealers needed only to call the manufacturer's co-op service, which would customize the ad to the dealer's specifications with logo, store hours, and so on. The service would place the ad in the dealer's chosen paper, send the ad to the paper, and pay the bill. The cost to the dealer was the space cost at his or her usual rate, plus materials and postage, plus a 7 percent fee paid to the co-op service, all of which could be deducted from their co-op funds.

138

Not surprisingly, the 7 percent fee met with universal disapproval from the dealers, and was soon dropped. But even after its disappearance, the program, which logistically worked quite well right from the beginning and can be considered a success in that regard, was little used by the dealers. The reasons tell a lot about the limitations of this type of program.

The first reason was the type of dealers. A large portion of the manufacturer's dealer base was made up of value-added resellers. These resellers generally do not have storefront locations and are little interested in walk-in traffic; they typically sell complete systems rather than just computers. They live off solution sales done face-to-face to businesses by outbound salespeople. Right or wrong, they do not see much value in newspaper advertising.

Secondly, most of those computer dealers who *do* use newspaper advertising want to do multi-product ads, showing perhaps a brand A computer with a brand B printer and several pieces of software. Better yet, they want ads with a bunch of boxes with various competing brands of computers, printers and associated items. They are seldom interested in single-product ads.

The lesson learned from this experiment is that such programs *can* work in traditional media, but only if the media is appropriate to the dealer base and if the dealers see value in running single-product ads. (See the section of this chapter dealing with multi-vendor programs for a discussion of exceptions to this rule.) There is no reason you could not put together a successful direct deduct program in newspaper or other traditional media if you keep these rules in mind. The other lesson, of course, is that you will have to bear the full administrative and production costs of the program.

The typical direct deduct program allows dealers to call in if they wish to use it, as described. Some involve varying degrees of proactivity, most often telemarketing, but occasionally visits. Another variation makes direct deduct the only option. This is similar to full-control programs, but allows the dealer a certain amount of say in choosing among media and creative options. However, the dealer is *not* given the option of running his or her own ads.

### SIGNBACKS

In a signback program, a number of dealers authorize their manufacturer (or, sometimes, distributor or media) to spend a given portion of their co-op funds on a specific project. Signbacks are most typically utilized in putting together dealer-list ads or promotions.

Signbacks are most popular among smaller dealers, because they allow them to get advertising impact and buying efficiency they could not attain on their own. Manufacturers like them for the same reasons, and because they can control the message and the media (in manufacturer-organized signback programs). The major negatives are the usual advertising-by-committee drawbacks, getting everybody to agree to the content of the ad and overcoming competitive conflicts among the dealers.

Signbacks are frequently organized on a local basis by media. In a common scenario, a radio station will put together a spot for a widely-distributed product, get approval for it from the manufacturer, and then do the rounds of local dealers, getting them to sign over specified amounts of their co-op funds. The station then runs the spots, rotating tags among the dealers in proportion to the amount of money signed over. The station then submits the claim and gets reimbursed, the payment being deducted from each dealer's co-op funds.

Distributors will also sometimes be the originators of signback programs, frequently working together with a group of media reps on a regional basis. Many newspapers have banded together in regional organizations to promote this type of advertising.

Manufacturer-originated signback programs are often attempts to coordinate co-op advertising with national advertising, and in effect are efforts to funnel money from co-op into the national budget. The danger is that, if used too much, signbacks will drain the co-op budget to such an extent that local promotional support will dry up. Signbacks also need a lot of advance notice. Given advance notice, however, and used on a spot basis, signbacks can be effective promotional tools.

How do you run a signback program? It is November, and you have a major new product coming out next spring. You need more money to support your national advertising goals for the introduction. You check the co-op balance and utilization reports, and they show the funds are there. You can raid the co-op budget a bit without doing too much damage to local support (which is also essential, obviously, to the success of the introduction).

You will need to put together an attractive package for the dealers, something they cannot buy for themselves. We will say you decide to do full pages in the top 30 metro editions of *Time*, *Newsweek*, and *Sports Illustrated* on May 1, 15, and 29. Without checking any rate cards, we will say the media cost is $250,000. You also budget $25,000 for production, and $25,000 for administrative costs.

A question here is what your total package is going to be—is it just a listing or is there more to the promotion? The more attractive the overall package, obviously the more you can charge and the more interest you will get. But given that the potential signees are mostly small dealers, you cannot make the package too expensive. A way out of this is to provide a menu of choices, but that complicates the administration and pricing. We will assume the simplest case—magazine listings only—for this example.

Your goal is to sign up an average of ten dealers per metro, or a total of 300 dealers. You cannot expect (in most cases) the dealers to pick up the whole cost, but you have to make a judgment on what the traffic will bear, depending on your dealer base. We will say in this example that you hope to get half the cost ($150,000) out of the dealers. This means an average of $500 per dealer. If this sounds reasonable you can continue with your planning. Otherwise, you need to go back and start over.

The pricing has to vary by market, according to each market's cost and number of expected signees. If you have some markets where the space costs are inordinately high and/or your number of dealers is low, the price per dealer may go too high. At that point, you have to make a decision: Do you cut the market, or do you subsidize it?

Next, you do a mailing to the dealers in each of the markets. A decision to make here is how to define the markets. The magazines will tell you which zip codes their metro editions cover, and typically you would mail to dealers in those zip codes. The mailing includes a sample ad and a pitch that tells the dealers how much you are putting behind the promotion compared to the paltry sum they are being asked to contribute, and a signback form, something like Exhibit 9.1.

On the form, the underlined places for market name (Phoenix) and amount ($500), would be blanks to be filled in for each dealer. If there were a menu, instead of one package, then you would have some boxes listing the menu options and prices, and the dealer would select one option.

The deadline, shown as January 31, would depend on the magazines' requirements. Certainly you would want to give the dealers a deadline at least two weeks in advance of the real one. Probably you would do the mailing about 30 days in advance of the announced deadline, around New Year's Day. This might be affected in this example (a new product introduction) by disclosure concerns.

As the enrollments come in, you track them by market. As you get close to the deadline, you may need to start calling some markets, or have the local rep make some visits and twist some arms. Some markets may get overcrowded, more dealers sign up than you can fit in without making the ad look bad. You can close these markets off or decide to run extra ads.

Proofreading is critical. It is best to have the dealers approve their names, addresses, and phone numbers as typeset. If this is not possible, at least have them approved by your local rep. Otherwise, there will be errors, anger, and recriminations. Figure heavy proofing into your cost estimates and time schedules.

An important adjunct to a signback program is to offer a special allowance or payment option to encourage dealers to run their own ads during the same time frame. This encourages dealers (especially large ones) who choose not to participate in the signback to nonetheless support your new product introduction. Chapter 4 offers some ideas on how to encourage additional promotion during specific time periods.

These are the major forms of supplier control. Which is best for you is something for you to answer, but some form of supplier control should be in most manufacturers' arsenals, ready for at least occasional use.

Besides supplier control, there are some other variant types of program features you might want to consider.

## Demographic Limitations in Co-op Programs

Although almost all national and spot media purchased for manufacturers by their advertising agencies is endlessly analyzed to make sure it is reaching the proper demographics (and even psychographics), the same manufacturers pay no attention at all to demographics in their much larger co-op expenditures. What's wrong with this picture?

The manufacturers are trusting, of course, that the retailers, who know their own markets, are making the right demographic decisions.

And this is probably generally true. Certainly Kmart's and Target's media buying capabilities are at least equal to any manufacturers'. And even smaller retailers, while less sophisticated, can be presumed to have a good feel for their customer base.

Still, given that manufacturers will put all sorts of other restrictions on co-op programs—in terms of art, copy, and media choices—it is surprising that so little has been done in regard to demographics.

One example was a program run by the Olympia Brewing Company in the late 1970s. Olympia had three brands of beer: Olympia, Olympia Gold, and Hamm's. The program, which was aimed at distributors (because of legal restrictions against breweries or distilleries offering promotional allowances to retailers), was limited almost entirely to radio. The distributors were required to advertise each brand on stations whose formats attracted audiences that matched most closely the target customer of the brand. Olympia, for example, was to be advertised on middle-of-the road formats and news/talk stations; Olympia Gold, the yuppie brand, was on light rock formats; and blue-collar Hamm's on country and rock stations.

The program was almost impossible to administer, because stations changed their formats so often SRDS could not keep up with them. Olympia finally decided to keep the requirements in the program, but to take distributor compliance on faith.

Such a program would be even tougher today, because of the profusion of radio formats. But the basic idea is still an attractive one, if only in terms of guidelines to the dealers instead of requirements (which is what effectively happened to Olympia's program).

Today, it might be more effective, in specialized cases, for use in regard to cable television, which attracts even more finely segmented audiences, demographically and geographically, than radio, and which does not change format overnight. A manufacturer seeking local television exposure, but limited to upper demographics, could provide customized spots to dealers, to be run on cable systems in the dealers' immediate area on A&E or Discovery. Another product might be limited to sports channels. Such a program limits dealers, and therefore might be perceived negatively by them. The larger dealers who are most likely to make such a complaint, however, are not the ones who could most effectively use such a program. It is, however, a good possibility for smaller local independents, and should be considered as another alternative to supplier control programs in certain cases.

The problem is that many of the local cable operators are only beginning to deal with co-op and often do not understand co-op documentation requirements. In some markets advertisers are lucky to get a handwritten invoice; log information and scripts with affidavits are out of the question. These system operators apparently think only in terms of subscribers and do not understand the potential of advertising as a supplemental revenue stream.

Still, this situation is rapidly changing, and most cable operators, as they near full penetration of their markets, recognize that future growth will come from advertising. This means that soon marketers will be able to use the possibilities inherent in the combination of the geographic targeting of local systems, with the demographic targeting of specific cable channels.

## Multi-Vendor Programs

From time to time, programs involving more than one vendor are offered to dealers. These programs have obvious appeal (split the costs more ways), and obvious problems (advertising by committee almost never works).

Some examples of this type of approach are airlines and/or hotels and/or car rental firms and/or credit cards jointly advertising through travel agents. In the early 1980s, Digital Equipment Corporation, during their first disastrous foray into the personal computing business, ran a series of ads in local and regional editions of magazines, combining their computers with some of the more popular software packages and adding lists of dealers (for example, the ad might feature a DEC computer and Lotus 1-2-3, and list ten dealers in the metro area who carried both). Given DEC's subsequent withdrawal from the PC market, this campaign might not be a good example, but it is doubtful if it was the ads that caused DEC's problems.

The concept is good, and should probably be used more often, but the problems are those related to any sort of supplier control program, multiplied by two. But, if you can find a compatible product, and a compatible director of marketing with whom you can work without too often stepping on each other's toes, you might be able to make your co-op budget go twice as far.

# Ingredient Co-op

Similar to multi-vendor programs in some ways, this is a concept in which suppliers to manufacturers offer promotional funding either to the manufacturers or through the manufacturers to retailers, for ads featuring the ingredient name as well as the manufacturer and retailer name.

The best-known of these programs is the long-running cotton program, which gives money to makers of cotton apparel and funnels money through apparel manufacturers to department stores. There is a similar program for wool, and duPont has had programs for many of its fibers and fiber treatments (Stainmaster is their most prominent current program). A recent major addition to this field has been the Intel Inside program, in which Intel has reimbursed computer manufacturers for advertising the fact that their computers are built around Intel chips.

The ingredient manufacturers, in most cases, see these programs in the same terms as end-product manufacturers see their programs—they are efforts to help their customer market more effectively and thereby sell more product for both of them, to tie their product name to other products which might be more familiar to the public (just as regular co-op programs are designed to tie product names to retailer names), and to build customer loyalty.

Intel's program is interesting in that it was originated as an effort to build a brand name. Intel had invested most of its efforts throughout the eighties toward promoting its chips by name, the 286 and 386. At the height of the 386's popularity, however, and just as Intel had begun promoting the 486, a court ruling held that their competitors could also use the x86 names. Intel was faced with a situation in which the only name by which the public knew them had been declared a generic term.

Intel's response was to launch the Intel Inside program, primarily through co-op, but strongly supported by national advertising and later by point-of-purchase, to promote awareness of their chip as the key ingredient in computers, and to build a brand preference for the chip. Intel's market research indicates that they have been successful in building both awareness and preference.

Robinson-Patman rules apply to ingredient programs in the same ways as to other programs; the act applies to all products. (If the ingredient is a service, then Robinson-Patman does not apply, which we will discuss later). Since the end-product manufacturer is the ingredient manufacturer's customer, the ingredient manufacturer is required to give allowances to all such manufacturers on equal terms. When the allowance is passed through to retailers, the ingredient manufacturer's responsibilities are the same as any other manufacturer's responsibilities when selling through distributors. They are required to monitor the pass-through to ensure that all retailers are receiving proportionate allowances. In this instance, the retailer is viewed as the ingredient manufacturer's indirect customer.

The allocation of allowances among manufacturers is complicated, from a Robinson-Patman perspective, since purchases may be made in the United States for use in products being sold both domestically and in foreign markets. The FTC has never said whether the ingredient manufacturer in such a case is legally required to deduct from the end-product manufacturer's allowance a proportion equal to what is being exported, or to require that proportion of the funding to be spent overseas. Nor have they dealt with whether an ingredient manufacturer who exports its products to foreign manufacturers has to give allowances if the foreign manufacturers' end-products are subsequently imported into the United States. Since the Commission, in the commentary accompanying their 1990 revisions to the Guides, admitted that they were ducking the question of product diversion as it related to co-op on the grounds that trying to deal with it would be a legal and logistical nightmare (they referred to "the daunting difficulties the seller might encounter in tracing the diverted goods . . . . An administrative morass could ensue."), it might be best to assume they would take a similar stance in regard to exports.

# Nonrelated Co-op

Another variation on ingredient co-op is programs in which there is no direct relationship between two entities, but A gives support to B because something about B's product encourages greater use of A's product.

In a recent example, in mid-1994, Cotton Inc. approved of the use of their symbol on Procter & Gamble's Cheer and Tide ads and packaging. P&G's inclusion in these detergents of "carezyme technology" improved their color protection on cotton clothing. Since this would give manufacturers more reason to use cotton in their products and consumers more reason to buy cotton products, Cotton Inc. felt it was in their interest to help P&G promote the new feature.

# Nonproduct Co-op

Although we generally think of promotional allowances in terms of products, the concept can be applied to services. Some examples are credit cards, such as American Express and Visa, and travel, including hotels, airlines, and car rental companies, all of whom frequently offer allowances to travel agencies.

Some of the Baby Bells, most notably US West and Pacific Telesis, have offered co-op programs to agents who resell their business phone services, such as Centrex and digital communications.

The biggest and oldest nonproduct co-op programs have been run by insurance companies, who offer promotional support to their agents. Often these are variations of signback and direct deduct programs in which the insurance company places advertising for the agents, or provides him or her with customized mailing pieces.

The important point about promotional allowance programs for services is that, as mentioned above, Robinson-Patman does not apply. Otherwise, such programs generally operate similarly to product programs.

Another important point, relating to the future of the promotional allowance business, is that the manufacturing sector has been in long-term decline, in the United States and most other economically developed countries, as a percentage of gross domestic product (GDP). According to an article in the *The Economist* on February 20, 1993, between 1970 and 1991 manufacturing in the United States declined from 26 percent of GDP to 21 percent. During the same period, in Japan it fell from 36 percent to 29 percent, and in what used to be West Germany from 41 percent to 28 percent. Services, meanwhile, rose to 72 percent of U.S. GDP, and are in the 55 percent to 65 percent range in all other developed countries. The message, for those in the promotional allowance business, is clear: Spread promotional allowances to more of the service sector, or be consigned to a declining market segment.

**EXHIBIT 9.1**  Sample Signback Form

---

**The XYZ Company New Product Introduction Program**

I agree to participate in the XYZ New Product Introduction promotion scheduled for May 1995. Please include my store name and address, exactly as shown below, in the ads to appear May 1, 15, and 29 in the <u>Phoenix</u> editions of *Time, Newsweek,* and *Sports Illustrated.* My share of the cost for these ads will be <u>$500.</u>

I understand that this form must be returned to XYZ by January 31, 1995, and inclusion in the program cannot be guaranteed after that date. I also understand that the program may be canceled at any time, without liability to either party, but that XYZ agrees to notify me promptly if the program or any portion of it is canceled.

I also understand that the program is limited, and participation is available on a first-come, first-served basis.

I authorize XYZ to deduct the agreed amount from my current and/or future co-op allowances earned under the terms of the XYZ Co-op Program. If sufficient allowances are not earned to cover my cost by June 30, 1995, I authorize XYZ to invoice me for any remaining balance, and I agree to pay the invoice in accordance with my usual credit terms.

Signature of Authorized
Representative of Dealer:

_____

Name: _____

Title: _____ Date: _____

Store name and address (Please type or write legibly *exactly as you wish it to appear in the ads*):

Store Name: _____

Address: _____

City/State/Zip: _____

Phone (Include Area Code): _____

---

CHAPTER 10

# Vendor Support
# Programs and Return
# on Investment

This chapter deals with seemingly unrelated subjects—vendor support programs and return on investment (ROI)—but you should be able to see their relationship by the time we finish. We will also go beyond ROI to profit on investment (POI).

Let us first define terms: *Vendor support programs* are requests for additional funding beyond what is provided by your published co-op program. These programs change names every few years, as fashions change—they have been called, at various times, key city funds, key account funds, market development funds (MDF), over-and-above money, and many others. Some of these terms are still popular, but we will use vendor support programs (VSPs) since this is currently the most fashionable. The term is used almost exclusively to describe requests by co-op recipients, and is almost never used to describe offers by suppliers, as some of the other terms are. For example, many manufacturers, especially in the computer industry, have MDF programs in which, typically, they offer funds beyond normal accruals, often to support retailer efforts to achieve specific types of goals.

What has changed in recent years about VSPs is the degree of sophistication with which retailers pursue the funding, and the degree of support they get from the media in this pursuit. Retailers prepare elaborate presentations, sometimes including limousines, catered meals, agency (or media) produced audiovisuals, and personalized packets detailing the coming program and the degree of support expected from the manufacturer.

As an example, the following item appeared in the February 1, 1993 issue of *Computer Retail Week*: "The Good Guys! . . . hosted its traditional co-op ad dollar fund drive at the recent Consumer Electronics Show, and those who were limo'd, wined and dined at its five suites at the Alexis Park said it was the usual extravaganza. It works like this: The Good Guys! sends a limo for the prospective vendor, who finds inside the car his respective buyer in a tux. Calculations are done regarding how much business the chain can do with the [vendor], and a figure is released representing how much co-op ad money will be required to pull it off. Sources said the percentage is in the 10 percent range."

Retailers often have considerable assistance from media, especially newspapers, in this type of presentation. This is especially so with local and regional retailers.

Few manufacturers enter these meetings anywhere nearly as well prepared as the retailer is. Therefore, the odds are excellent that the decision to approve or (less often) disapprove the request will be based on whether or not the money is available rather than whether or not the program proposed meets the manufacturer's marketing needs.

In the Good Guys! example cited, the retailer was at least presenting anticipated sales figures as well as a funding request. Not all retailers do this, but it is the data we would expect a manufacturer to seek in determining whether to approve the request. The article does not say whether the purchase figures are guaranteed, or if the manufacturer is entitled to make funding contingent on achieving the goals.

Getting anticipated sales figures, based on the requested additional funding, though, is the first step a manufacturer must take in determining the value of a VSP request. The next step is to determine what the manufacturer would expect to sell without the VSP. The difference is the return on investment for the program.

# Return on investment

We talk about this a lot, but what do we do about it? Why approve a vendor support program (or do anything else related to marketing) unless it produces additional sales in a reasonable multiple of the expenditures? Obviously there is no reason to do so, but why then do so many otherwise reasonably intelligent companies spend billions of dollars on promotional allowance marketing without a clue as to what they are getting in return? Maybe it is because they do not know how to find out, or because they do not know it can be done. Maybe it is because they just never thought about it.

Let us assume you are the director of marketing for the Continental Widgets division of Intergalactic Enterprises Inc. You have a co-op program for your 3,000 dealers. Available funds this year will be about $10 million, of which you have budgeted $6 million to be used. You also have a discretionary fund of $1 million. This is to cover special requests for VSPs from the 20 big chains who do most of your business.

Tracking ROI should begin with this discretionary fund. When the buyer from Widgets R Us calls you in for the presentation requesting $50,000 extra funding for their fourth-quarter promotion, it is reasonable to ask what sort of product movement they expect the promotion to generate. Over-and-above funds should produce over-and-above results. If they say they expect to sell $3 million at wholesale in the fourth quarter, and you would normally expect them to move $2.5 million, you are getting a 10:1 return (a $500,000 increase generated by a $50,000 investment). If they say they do not know what the promotion will produce, then they are not professional marketing people. Surely they would not invest $50,000 of their own money without some idea of what it was going to buy them.

In cases where accounts are projecting exceptionally large sales increases, some sales reps ask for an extra order on the grounds that normal stock would be insufficient to cover the anticipated demand, and they would not want to run out of stock. Their response might be a good measure of the sincerity of their projections and you might actually get an extra order.

Follow up after the promotional period and see whether fourth-quarter shipments (minus first-quarter returns) really did show a $500,000 increase. Keep records on this sort of activity (see Exhibit 10.1). Then you can use this information when negotiating Widgets R Us' request for $60,000 next year.

After a while you will have enough data to cross-reference the different types of promotions and see which types by which chains are producing the best return, so you can put more of your future over-and-above funds where they will be most productive. That is your discretionary fund. What about your regular co-op program?

**EXHIBIT 10.1**

PROMOTIONAL COST ANALYSIS REPORT

AREA: CENTRAL

REG: CHICAGO

TERR: LYNCH

PROD: ALL

PROMOTIONAL COST ANALYSIS

BY SALES AREA

PERIOD ENDING: JUNE 1995

| ACCOUNT | PERIOD | UNITS COMM | RETAIL PRICE | RETAIL COMM | W'SALE COMM | COMM COST | % TO W'SALE | W'SALE ACTUAL |
|---------|--------|-----------|--------------|-------------|-------------|-----------|-------------|---------------|
| | | | | COMMITMENT DATA | | | | |
| DOMINICK'S | 5/15–6/15 | 135,000 | 0.50 | 67,500 | 60,000 | 5,000 | 8.33% | 70,315 |
| JEWEL | 5/25–6/8 | 166,000 | 0.48 | 78,680 | 72,000 | 7,000 | 9.72% | 75,411 |
| KROGER | 5/20–6/11 | 112,000 | 0.52 | 58,240 | 52,000 | 4,000 | 7.69% | 44,982 |
| WINN-DIXIE | 5/20–5/26 | 225,000 | 0.46 | 103,500 | 92,000 | 12,000 | 13.04% | 75,121 |
| TOTALS | | 638,000 | 0.48 | 308,920 | 276,000 | 28,000 | 10.14% | 265,829 |

In most cases it will not make sense to track ROI on all claims, you do not want to pay your co-op service to track return on every $200 claim, and you do not want to do it yourself.

However, on a program of Continental Widget's size, you might get about 200 to 300 claims a year of more than $5,000 each, and these claims probably represent close to half of your total co-op payout. When your ROI tracking system is in place, amend your program to require prior approval on expenditures of more than $5,000.

One of the items on your prior approval request form should ask for anticipated sales during the promotional period. Compare this to the dealer's average sales for the past few months or in the comparable period the previous year to get your anticipated ROI figure. When the claim is submitted, check your sales figures to see whether the dealer made his or her numbers.

The information you gain from this exercise will help you in a number of ways. As mentioned before when we were discussing the vendor support part of your program, you will gain information on what works and what does not—helping you in updating your program. For example, if the ROI on radio promotions is consistently low, perhaps your program should not allow radio, or you need to look at how radio is being used or misused. If direct mail works exceptionally well, you want to encourage more mail, perhaps by offering turnkey packages of some kind.

| | | | | | ANALYSIS DATA | | | | |
| PERFORMANCE DATA | | | | | | | | | |
| % VARI-ANCE | PROMO COST | % TO SALES | VARI-ANCE | % VARI-ANCE | PLUS SALES | ROI | PLUS COG | PROMO PROF | % PROFIT | POI |
|---|---|---|---|---|---|---|---|---|---|---|
| 17.19% | 6,092 | 8.66% | 1,092 | 21.84% | 30,111 | 4.94 | 15,056 | 8,964 | 12.75% | 1.47 |
| 4.74% | 7,000 | 9.28% | 0 | 0.00% | 41,206 | 5.89 | 20,603 | 13,603 | 18.04% | 1.94 |
| -13.50% | 4,511 | 10.03% | 511 | 12.78% | 10,311 | 2.29 | 5,156 | 645 | 1.43 | 0.14 |
| -18.35% | 10,825 | 14.41% | -1,175 | -9.79% | 21,018 | 1.94 | 10,509 | -316 | -0.42% | -0.03 |
| -3.69% | 28,428 | 10.69% | 428 | 1.53% | 102,646 | 3.61 | 51,323 | 22,895 | 8.61% | 0.81 |

One benefit, not to be denigrated, is internal politics; you can sell the importance of the co-op program (and your importance in running it) by demonstrating that it produces measurable results. Since there are a lot of people in your organization who do not currently believe this, it can be a boost for the program and your career.

Measuring ROI is a major step forward for most manufacturers, but it does not go far enough. The next step beyond return on investment is profit on investment.

## Profit on Investment

After you have developed your ROI reports, you need to work into them your cost of goods (COG). When you deduct the incremental COG from the incremental sales and divide by the cost of the promotion, you have POI.

Exhibit 10.1 is a sample POI report, integrating dealer commitment data (see Chapter 11) with actual results from a promotion. The report can be used as shown, with COG worked into the equation, to produce a POI number, or used partially, leaving out the COG, and generating only a sales return on investment. If POI sounds too ambitious to you for now, settle for ROI, until you are ready for more.

Profitability is a theme we have addressed many times already, but it is one that cannot be overemphasized, because it is why we are in business. Too often, those who are involved in promotional allowance marketing, and marketing in general, focus excessively on market share. The result is that they become slaves to the major retailers and distributors, believing they have to give them everything they ask for, because they represent such a big share of the business.

The argument most often cited for giving Target huge vendor support payments, for example, is that they will produce bigger incremental sales with the money, a bigger ROI. (Note: In this and succeeding paragraphs we will use Target as a generic example of big retailers). Most marketers would say that, if they had a spare $50,000 in their budget, they would rather give it to Target than give it out in $1,000 chunks to 50 local dealers. There are no studies to support the assumption that the big retailers are, in fact, more productive with co-op funds, but let us for the moment accept the idea, because whether or not the big stores produce bigger incremental sales is not the important point. The big question is: Do they produce more incremental profits? If, in the example cited, Target produced twice as much in incremental sales as the 50 locals, but the locals' sales were three times as profitable, where would you want to put your money?

Is this the case? No one knows. And that means most manufacturers' promotional allowance programs are flying blind; money is being given out without reference to whether it is producing profits, or just sales.

Support for the idea that the locals might produce more profit comes from "Managing Price, Gaining Profit" (*Harvard Business Review*, Sept/Oct 1992), which demonstrates that a 1 percent increase in price will, for an average company, yield more than three times the profit gain of a 1 percent increase in volume. So the local stores, which are probably paying you higher prices for your goods than Target is, are better positioned to offer you more profits, even if the incremental sales they generate for you are substantially less than Target's.

Retailers, especially the biggest ones, are coming to you constantly, requesting additional funding, and not just promotional allowances—slotting, failure fees, returns, markdown money, higher volume discounts, and on and on. At what point does giving them everything they want mean they are no longer profitable for you? At that point, increased market share becomes a negative—the more they sell, the more you lose.

If you do not know what that point is, you need to find out. You need to design, or have someone design for you, a system to bring together all the various advertising, slotting, and display allowances, the discounts and rebates, the redemption cost of coupons, the costs of clearing deductions, and everything else that goes into doing business with your customers. As much as possible, tie specific expenses to specific dealers. Where that is not possible, allocate expenses as fairly as you can. When you have all the data together, you will begin to know how much profit you are making on a given account. When you know that, you will know whether to give them their latest over-and-above request, or whether giving it to them will put you under and below.

When you have enough of this data on enough accounts, you will begin to see whether you are making more profit on your big accounts or your little ones. There is a growing suspicion among many marketers that small accounts are often more profitable, and that they should be given more of the over-and-above funding.

## FUNDING LOSERS

If in fact the smaller accounts are more profitable, and you are giving all your extra promotional money to the giants, you are losing two ways: You have lost an opportunity to grow the more profitable accounts; and, not only have you not helped the profitable accounts grow, you are probably taking sales away from them. Where, after all, did many of those "incremental" sales at Target come from? Some, at least, were incremental only to Target, not to you, because if your promotional dollars had not been used to lure the customers to Target, *some* of the customers would have bought your product anyway, from another (more profitable) dealer. Target has used your promotional funds to trade some of the more profitable sales you would have made through other dealers for less profitable sales through Target. Not a very good trade from your standpoint, is it?

Consider this possibility: You gave Target the extra $50,000 for a promotion producing $1 million in incremental sales, and $150,000 in incremental profit. You are a hero. However, if some of the sales are not really incremental to you, but are sales Target took from other dealers who would have given you better margins, and if those lost profits were subtracted from the $150,000 in incremental profit Target gave you, would the promotion look as successful? If you had given that $50,000 to smaller dealers, would they have perhaps returned you less in incremental sales, but more in net incremental profit?

Another reason for considering giving more of your extra funding to smaller dealers is more long term, but one you might want to consider carefully: It is in your best interest to keep them in business.

At the Newspaper Advertising Co-op Network meeting in January 1990, Joe Blocker of General Electric's major appliance division described some programs GE had devised to help local appliance dealers, and added a plea to the newspapers to help their local retailers find niches, pointing out that these dealers (in appliances as in other categories) were being squeezed between the mass merchandisers and the national chains.

If you think it is tough making a profit now, think about what the future might be like if current trends in retailing continue. *Computer Retail Week* (March 1, 1993) reported that Zeos, a second-tier computer manufacturer, had decided to "deemphasize" the mass merchandising channel. A spokesman was quoted as saying "It's tough to make money dealing with Sam's—unless you're Sam's."

Steps are being taken, halting steps at this point, toward providing the answers to the questions in this chapter. In the article mentioned earlier, "Managing Price, Gaining Profit," Michael V. Marn and Robert L. Rosiello of McKinsey Company wrote about the importance of determining how much each account is actually paying for the product they purchase. Marn and Rosiello call this the "pocket price," defining it as the invoice price minus all the subsequent allowances and rebates. Marn and Rosiello, in the cases they presented, found that there was no relationship between pocket price and the size of the accounts. They found there was a wide range in this price, meaning that taking steps to identify the accounts with higher pocket prices (whether large or small) and driving more sales through them is well worth the effort. (Caution would, of course, have to be taken not to give these accounts so much help that they became substantially less profitable. Some ideas on tilting a program toward profitability are explored in Chapter 12).

Marn and Rosiello also touch on the reason that few manufacturers are currently determining profitability by account: It is an incredibly complex task, involving inputs from many different departments, some of which are maintained on separate systems in noncompatible formats. It is difficult to understand how manufacturers can justify *not* making the effort to assemble this data, particularly in those industries that are now beginning to talk about "account-specific marketing." Without knowing how profitable each account is, how can you know how (or whether) to market to the account? As Marn and Rosiello say: "Pocket price should be the sole yardstick for determining the pricing attractiveness of products, customers and individual deals."

The information can be obtained. You can develop a system internally or have an outside service provide you with one. A sample report is shown in Exhibit 10.2.

The point is to try to capture *every* cost related to the manufacture, marketing, advertising, and sale of your products, and then report those costs on a per-product, per-dealer, per-region, per-sales rep, and so forth, basis. (McKinsey's study dealt only with the comparative sale price of the goods by account, which is an excellent starting point and certainly far beyond what most manufacturers are currently doing. Ultimately, however, you want to go beyond that to include all costs, thus producing a net profit figure, and to judge sales reps and regions on their ability to produce profits.)

When these figures are drawn together, the manufacturer knows exactly what their margin is with every dealer, making possible intelligent decisions on, for example, whether to give an additional allowance or to cut prices. Some of the items are truly account specific, others are arrived at via allocations of various kinds. National advertising costs, for example, could be allocated among markets based on their size and then among dealers within each market. In Exhibit 10.2, the notes at the bottom of each column refer to the lower section, where it is indicated how each number would be derived, and/or which department of a typical manufacturer would probably provide the data.

Developing such a reporting system may be a legal necessity. If you are not making approximately the same percentage of net profit from every account, it could mean your pricing structure involves discounts you cannot cost justify, which would indicate violations of Section 2(a) of Robinson-Patman.

If you make a 10 percent profit on sales to Joe's Corner Market and only 5 percent on sales to Target, you might feel the lower return is offset by Target's volume. But the Federal Trade Commission might

## EXHIBIT 10.2 Profit by Accounts Reports

PROFITABILITY ANALYSIS REPORTS

REPORT 1—PRODUCT BY DEALER
DEALER:    XYZ STORE          REGION:   TEXAS           PERIOD:   Y-T-D
DEALER#:  12345              REP:      J. SMITH        THRU:     30-JUN-95

| | | MARKETING PROGRAMS | | | | | | | | | | SALES EXPENSES | | | | |
| PRODUCT | TOTAL SALES | NAT ADV | BUS CO-OP | SLOT DEV | COUP FUND | REDEM | MDF | DISP/ DEMOS | OTHER | TOTAL | % OF SALES | SAL/ COMM | TRAV/ ENT | MEALS/ GIFTS | MEET COMP | OFF INVC | OTHER |
|---|---|---|---|---|---|---|---|---|---|---|---|---|---|---|---|---|---|
| RFH99 | 1254.8 | 50.2 | 62.5 | 30.6 | 35.7 | 12.5 | 50.0 | 21.0 | 5.0 | 267.5 | 21.32% | 8.0 | 1.1 | 0.3 | 31.6 | 25.1 | 4.5 |
| UTL42 | 654.2 | 25.6 | 33.1 | 15.8 | 20.6 | 5.9 | 30.0 | 12.0 | 0.0 | 143.0 | 21.86% | 4.2 | 0.6 | 0.1 | 0.0 | 13.1 | 3.8 |
| RLH621 | 963.5 | 41.8 | 49.2 | 23.3 | 25.8 | 8.9 | 42.0 | 14.1 | 0.0 | 205.1 | 21.29% | 6.1 | 0.8 | 0.0 | 0.0 | 28.9 | 3.0 |
| X-LINE | 421.8 | 20.0 | 19.6 | 10.5 | 10.6 | 4.5 | 15.0 | 9.5 | 0.0 | 89.7 | 21.27% | 2.7 | 0.3 | 0.1 | 12.3 | 8.4 | 2.8 |
| OTHER | 359.9 | 19.5 | 12.5 | 9.9 | 10.3 | 5.0 | 25.0 | 8.2 | 0.0 | 90.4 | 25.12% | 2.3 | 0.2 | 0.0 | 3.0 | 7.2 | 1.9 |
| TOTAL | 3654.2 | 157.1 | 176.9 | 90.1 | 103.0 | 36.8 | 162.0 | 64.8 | 5.0 | 795.7 | 21.77% | 23.3 | 3.0 | 0.5 | 46.9 | 82.7 | 16.0 |

REPORT 2—DEALER BY REGION
REGION:   TEXAS                              PERIOD:   Y-T-D
DISTRICT: SOUTHCENTRAL                       THRU:     30-JUNE-95

| | | MARKETING PROGRAMS | | | | | | | | | | SALES EXPENSES | | | | |
| DEALER | TOTAL SALES | NAT ADV | BUS CO-OP | SLOT DEV | COUP FUND | REDEM | MDF | DISP/ DEMOS | OTHER | TOTAL | % OF SALES | SAL/ COMM | TRAV/ ENT | MEALS/ GIFTS | MEET COMP | OFF INVC | OTHER |
|---|---|---|---|---|---|---|---|---|---|---|---|---|---|---|---|---|---|
| 12345 | 3654.2 | 157.1 | 176.9 | 90.1 | 103.0 | 36.8 | 162.0 | 64.8 | 5.0 | 795.7 | 21.77% | 23.3 | 3.0 | 0.5 | 46.9 | 82.7 | 16.0 |
| 67890 | 3012.5 | 121.2 | 102.6 | 89.9 | 71.0 | 30.3 | 95.2 | 55.0 | 3.0 | 568.2 | 18.86% | 21.0 | 3.2 | 0.4 | 30.6 | 65.0 | 13.5 |
| 45678 | 1254.8 | 59.4 | 25.3 | 25.2 | 11.2 | 13.6 | 15.8 | 25.4 | 1.1 | 177.0 | 14.11% | 8.6 | 1.8 | 0.3 | 20.3 | 28.1 | 6.8 |
| 54321 | 789.5 | 30.2 | 15.0 | 9.0 | 8.3 | 9.9 | 7.5 | 20.6 | 3.0 | 103.5 | 13.11% | 5.5 | 1.5 | 0.2 | 6.9 | 16.8 | 5.8 |
| 98765 | 2585.3 | 100.6 | 75.5 | 65.8 | 29.7 | 28.5 | 60.6 | 51.5 | 2.1 | 414.3 | 16.03% | 18.1 | 2.9 | 0.5 | 30.3 | 55.1 | 13.0 |
| TOTAL | 11296.3 | 468.5 | 395.3 | 280.0 | 223.2 | 119.1 | 341.1 | 217.3 | 14.2 | 2058.7 | 18.22% | 76.5 | 12.4 | 1.9 | 135.0 | 247.7 | 55.1 |

| NOTES: | 1 | 2 | 3 | 4 | 5 | 6 | 7 | 8 | 9 | 10 | 11 | 12 | 13 | 14 | 15 | 16 | 17 |
|---|---|---|---|---|---|---|---|---|---|---|---|---|---|---|---|---|---|

1: Provided by Accounting Department.

2: Provided by Advertising Department, allocated on formula devised by Marketing Department (probably combination of ADI size and total commodity volume).

3: Captured by administrative service (internal or external) through payment of claims.

4: Captured by administrative service through payment of claims.

5: Captured by administrative service through payment of claims.

6: Reported by coupon redemption service.

7: Captured by administrative service through payment of claims.

8: Captured by administrative service through payment of claims.

9: Captured by administrative service through payment of claims.

10: Sum of 2 through 9.

11: Product of 10 divided by 1.

12: Reported by Sales management, together with allocation formula.

13: Captured by administrative service through payment of claims.

| | | OTHER EXPENSES | | | | | | | | | PROFIT ANALYSIS | | | | | |
|---|---|---|---|---|---|---|---|---|---|---|---|---|---|---|---|---|
| | % OF | FRE- | RET- | MARK | DDCT | | | % OF | GRAND | % OF | | % OF | ALLOC | % OF | NET | % OF |
| TOTAL | SALES | IGHT | URNS | DOWN | COST | OTHER | TOTAL | SALES | TOTAL | SALES | COG | SALES | EXPS | SALES | PROFIT | SALES |
| 70.6 | 5.62% | 25.1 | 23.7 | 106.5 | 3.3 | 5.1 | 163.7 | 13.05% | 501.8 | 39.99% | 511.0 | 40.72% | 94.5 | 7.53% | 147.5 | 11.76% |
| 21.7 | 3.32% | 13.9 | 14.6 | 58.9 | 3.0 | 3.2 | 93.6 | 14.31% | 258.3 | 39.49% | 280.8 | 42.92% | 48.6 | 7.43% | 66.5 | 10.16% |
| 38.8 | 4.03% | 18.5 | 20.2 | 88.7 | 3.1 | 1.6 | 132.1 | 13.71% | 376.0 | 39.03% | 400.5 | 41.57% | 71.2 | 7.39% | 115.8 | 12.01% |
| 26.7 | 6.32% | 11.0 | 8.8 | 31.2 | 2.5 | 5.6 | 59.1 | 14.01% | 175.5 | 41.60% | 180.6 | 42.82% | 33.8 | 8.01% | 31.9 | 7.57% |
| 14.6 | 4.06% | 10.2 | 7.1 | 35.5 | 1.9 | 3.9 | 58.6 | 16.28% | 163.6 | 45.46% | 145.9 | 40.54% | 28.2 | 7.84% | 22.2 | 6.17% |
| 172.4 | 4.72% | 78.7 | 74.4 | 320.8 | 13.8 | 19.4 | 507.1 | 13.88% | 1475.2 | 40.37% | 1518.8 | 41.56% | 276.3 | 7.56% | 383.9 | 10.51% |

| | | OTHER EXPENSES | | | | | | | | | PROFIT ANALYSIS | | | | | |
|---|---|---|---|---|---|---|---|---|---|---|---|---|---|---|---|---|
| | % OF | FRE- | RET- | MARK | DDCT | | | % OF | GRAND | % OF | | % OF | ALLOC | % OF | NET | % OF |
| TOTAL | SALES | IGHT | URNS | DOWN | COST | OTHER | TOTAL | SALES | TOTAL | SALES | COG | SALES | EXPS | SALES | PROFIT | SALES |
| 172.4 | 4.72% | 78.7 | 74.4 | 320.8 | 13.8 | 19.4 | 507.1 | 13.88% | 1475.2 | 40.37% | 1518.8 | 41.56% | 276.3 | 7.56% | 383.9 | 10.51% |
| 133.7 | 4.44% | 65.2 | 64.1 | 288.0 | 10.7 | 14.9 | 442.9 | 14.70% | 1144.8 | 38.00% | 1261.3 | 41.87% | 228.1 | 7.57% | 378.3 | 12.56% |
| 65.9 | 5.25% | 31.1 | 30.6 | 114.1 | 5.0 | 8.1 | 188.9 | 15.05% | 431.8 | 34.41% | 526.4 | 41.95% | 95.5 | 7.61% | 201.1 | 16.03% |
| 36.7 | 4.65% | 19.5 | 19.8 | 80.5 | 1.3 | 4.1 | 125.2 | 15.86% | 265.4 | 33.62% | 331.7 | 42.01% | 60.3 | 7.64% | 132.1 | 16.73% |
| 119.9 | 4.64% | 54.5 | 50.6 | 255.8 | 9.5 | 12.5 | 382.9 | 14.81% | 917.1 | 35.47% | 1080.9 | 41.81% | 196.2 | 7.59% | 391.1 | 15.13% |
| 528.6 | 4.68% | 249.0 | 239.5 | 1059.2 | 40.3 | 59.0 | 1647.0 | 14.58% | 4234.3 | 37.48% | 4719.1 | 41.78% | 856.4 | 7.58% | 1486.5 | 13.16% |

| 18 | 19 | 20 | 21 | 22 | 23 | 24 | 25 | 26 | 27 | 28 | 29 | 30 | 31 | 32 | 33 | 34 |

14: Captured by administrative service through payment of claims.

15: Provided by Accounting Department.

16: Provided by Accounting Department.

17: Provided by Accounting Department.

18: Sum of 12 through 17.

19: Product of 18 divided by 1.

20: Provided by Shipping/Receiving Department.

21: Provided by Shipping/Receiving Department.

22: Provided by Accounting Department.

23: Provided by Accounting Department (unless administrative service handles deductions).

24: Provided by Accounting Department.

25: Sum of 20 through 24.

26: Product of 25 divided by 1.

27: Sum of totals (10, 18, 25).

28: Product of 27 divided by 1.

29: Provided by Manufacturing Department, on per-unit basis.

30: Product of 29 divided by 1.

31: Provided by Accounting Department, allocated by formula devised by Marketing and Sales Departments (probably based on sales).

32: Product of 31 divided by 1.

33: Remainder of 1 minus 27 minus 29 minus 31.

34: Product of 33 divided by 1.

feel you are giving Target five too many points. The difference could be accounted for by programs made available to both Joe and Target, which Joe does not take advantage of (in which case you have no problem) or by offers to Target you were forced into in order to meet competition. If, however, the difference is caused by special deals you are giving Target that are not available to Joe and that are not covered by meetcomp, you had better talk to your attorneys. Since you currently do not know whether you make more profit from Joe or Target, let alone why, you *might* be able to plead ignorance for any past violations. But since the ability to capture such data now exists, you might not be able to make such a defense in the future.

Obviously, putting together such a system would require a great amount of interdepartmental cooperation. More such cooperation than normally exists in most companies, which means it would require a commitment from top management to force compliance. Also, it should be noted that the system as shown would be a final product. The project could be undertaken with only pieces of the data (as in the McKinsey study). However, even a step toward producing profit-by-account data is a step in the right direction.

CHAPTER 11

# Commitment
# Systems

Vendor support programs, as we discussed in the preceding chapter, are programs initiated by the dealer to elicit funding from the supplier. They place the supplier in the position of having reactive promotional programs. Many manufacturers, wishing to be more proactive and maintain some measure of control over their programs, have turned to commitment systems or, in the latest terminology, plan-based programs.

Commitment systems, under a variety of names, are nothing new. Broadly defined, a commitment system is any program under which the manufacturer and reseller make advance agreements as to the advertising or promotion to be performed and the payment to be made. In its simplest form, it has been around for decades in every program requiring prior approval. The most advanced forms of "old" commitment systems have been in the record industry, where recording companies and music stores have long agreed in advance on exactly which records would be promoted on what days and how large the ads would be.

The record labels (who called these "authorizations" instead of commitments) had particular problems with co-op. They had products that needed ads as soon as they were out, and that needed to be advertised very intensely for the short period of time they were popular. Therefore, the advertising needed to be planned in advance. In addition, the labels had contractual arrangements with their recording artists to provide specified levels of promotional support to each of the artists' releases. Finally, each release was a separate profit center, and the labels had to account to each artist for the costs connected with promoting his or her release. So, they developed the authorization system. Deals were made in advance with record stores for each ad the stores would run. The authorization form that was filled out specified exactly which releases were to be featured, exactly how much space each would get, and exactly what the retailer would be paid.

The record industry version of the commitment system was, of necessity, extremely inflexible. No divergence from the approved plan was allowed. The WEA (distribution arm of Warner Brothers, Electra, and Atlantic records) co-op program in the late 1970s was willing to pay out thousands on the basis of practically no documentation, as long as the authorization had been complied with exactly as written. But any changes (for example, a change in which releases were to be advertised) required high-level approvals, and the amount authorized to be paid could *never* be exceeded. A claim for $10,000 for handbills might be approved on the basis of a photocopy of the alleged handbill as long as $10,000 was the authorized amount, but a fully-documented claim for $301 on an authorization for $300 would result in a form letter being sent to the retailer that the claim had been reduced by $1.

The record industry's particular needs and eccentricities aside, the idea was picked up in the 1980s by other industries to which timeliness of promotions was of overriding importance. The pharmaceuticals and health and beauty aids trade, with their "deal periods," were already halfway there and have since developed the most comprehensive commitment systems.

Others now are developing various types of commitment systems, aiming to improve their marketing planning and the handling of vendor support requests, and to fulfill the buzzword of "partnership" with their retailers. Commitment systems can also help in the development of return on investment tracking systems. These systems, unlike the record industry programs, generally deal only with the big-money claims or with market development funds (MDF), rather than trying to do commitments on every promotional allowance expenditure.

## How it works

In a commitment system, a portion of the promotional allowance budget is allocated down through the system to the regions, the reps, and finally the accounts. The rep works with the customer's buyer to plan a season's major events. Together they determine what level of promotion will be needed to hit desired sales levels. The document created moves back up through the levels and, with necessary approvals, is logged into the computer as a commitment.

The commitment typically details a number of promotional events that will take place at specified times. It often includes committed sales levels. As the events take place, the retailer, or in some cases the rep, submits claims, which are generally signed off on and paid with minimal checking.

For the manufacturer's finance department, commitments can be a windfall of information. Whereas the most common method of projecting liability has always been historical promotional expenditures, there is now a more exact set of figures representing the expenditures that have been agreed to. This information can been used to forecast liability more exactly.

The principal benefit to the retailer is preapproval on a season's worth of promotion. For the sales rep, it is the opportunity to be part of the retailer's promotional planning process and the creation of customized programs. If every retailer is different, according to the thinking of manufacturers now implementing commitment programs, a real partnership arrangement cannot depend on a one-size-fits-all co-op program. For them this means the promotional allowance program (or at least the commitment piece of it) moves beyond being a set of rules—it becomes guidelines expressing their promotional goals. This is part of what many marketers, particularly in the grocery and drug channels, are calling "account-specific marketing" (see Chapter 12).

### PLAN-BASED PROGRAMS

Mostly just a commitment system under another name, the idea of plan-based systems is that, rather than giving dealers accruals, a supplier asks them to submit a plan (or, more proactively, sits down with the dealer to draw up a plan) which is approved and, when executed, paid.

### LEGALITY

No one could read this chapter without asking, "But isn't it all illegal?" The answer is a resounding "maybe" (with perhaps a shading toward "yes"). The commitment or plan-based system itself is neither legal nor illegal—it is simply a mechanism for tracking deals. It is the deals that might be (and in many cases, are) illegal. A commitment system that gives all dealers an equal opportunity for MDF support, or a plan-based system that considers all submitted plans by objective criteria, could be perfectly legal. The danger, of course, is that sales reps will be tempted to favor their biggest customers.

These types of plans are the value standard that was proposed and rejected by the FTC (see Chapter 2) in 1990. The Commission did not fully reject the idea however. They admitted that it could be used, but warned suppliers using it to be careful.

The commentary released by the Commission when the new Guides were published said: "The law may also permit use of the value standard. . . . However, the vast majority of the comments addressing this issue are concerned that the value standard creates indeterminacy and thus the potential for abuse by sellers. These comments have merit. Unless carefully monitored, sellers may use elastic, expansive measurements of value which could help disguise persistent, systematic discrimination."

## Case Study: Upjohn

The following case illustrates the reasoning behind the use of commitment systems in the health and beauty aids industry, as well as some of the system's strengths and weaknesses.

Judy Huth, Manager of Information Services and Administration for the Consumer Products Division of Upjohn, says that the difference between their co-op program and their MDF program is that co-op is accrual based and offers fewer spend options (mostly media), whereas MDF is commitment based, negotiable, and is open to more innovative proposals that the reseller and Upjohn both think will work. "We'll work with the reseller in developing their business. We're willing to try new things—new types of promotions."

This flexibility is both the strength and weakness of commitment systems, says Huth. The benefits of flexibility are plain: It allows the resellers, who know their market, their business, and what will increase sales, to work with their sales reps to design successful promotions. Huth says that Upjohn's program "helps develop the concept of partnership. There's more dialogue than with a regular co-op program."

The downside is that the resellers and reps can get too creative. "Control is important," Huth says. "We have to keep track of commitments by salespeople, we have to know our liability. And it's very important that we make sure it's equitable. There's a danger in a program that isn't accrual based that everything could go to a few big dealers—we've instituted controls to prevent that."

To assist in controlling the program, Upjohn had to make changes in administration. The intent was to get more reliable, more informative reports. "We run a lot of tracking reports," Huth says, "and we use them to take action to keep the program on track."

Some commitment systems require specific orders from the resellers as a *quid pro quo* for the manufacturer's funding. Huth says that Upjohn's program has no such feature, but they do watch the reorders resulting from a promotion and, if the results are poor, "next time maybe we won't participate."

Most internal departments at Upjohn like the commitment system. "Sales loves it," according to Huth. "It gives them a tool to work with their customers; they have more flexibility." She adds that Finance "appreciates being able to determine future liabilities, allowing better budgetary controls."

Marketing has reservations. "They have less control over what the dealers put in their ads. Under this system, we no longer audit for content according to preestablished guidelines. Marketing has had to relax their control over the message of the ads and promotions."

Overall, Huth feels that Upjohn's commitment system is a success. For the future, she would like to see even more control moved down to the regional level. "I'd like to see them each have their own budgets," she says, adding that such a move would increase the need for tight reporting and tracking to ensure that overall program goals are met.

CHAPTER 12

# Trends, Problems, and Opportunities

No guide to promotional allowance marketing would be complete without an examination of some of the current trends in our industry and related areas, and attempt to project what they will mean in the future. These are, of course, educated guesses.

## New Media

New media, the subject of a great amount of talk in advertising and marketing circles (namely, Ed Artzt's speech to the American Association of Advertising Agencies in May 1994, which was all the buzz in *Advertising Age* for weeks after), has only tangential importance to the promotional allowances business. It matters little to the process of co-op what media or promotional format carries the co-op message. Whether an ad is in the daily paper or on the Internet does not change its nature as a co-op ad, nor does it change the relationship between the co-op supplier and recipient.

Where new media will have an effect on co-op is where the media *does* change that relationship, as for example on cable shopping networks, where the medium becomes the dealer, or similarly on the new interactive computer shopping networks. In both these instances, however, as the medium becomes a dealer, it will be treated by the manufacturer as a dealer and be given promotional support funding in one form or another. In the form of their relationship to their suppliers, shopping networks are no different from catalog dealers.

The real importance of interactive computer and/or television shopping is that they might herald the end of the reign of the retail giants. Some analysts predict that such channels might account for as much as 15 percent of the retail market in ten years. While all such predictions are open to question, even a much smaller loss of market share could prove disastrous to many traditional retailers, given their low margins. Since these new channels would make their biggest inroads in the sale of undifferentiated products to consumers who demand little service, they would take most of their share from mass merchandisers who currently dominate such markets.

Having mentioned the Internet, we should point out that it will have (and is already having) an effect of co-op, not as an advertising medium, but as a communications medium. The Internet and other such networks are already being used to carry purchasing data from manufacturers to their third-party administrators and to carry reports back. These networks will be used to tie together administrative services, retailers, distributors, manufacturers, and media in the rapid exchange of data to make co-op more effective and efficient. Some of those uses are described later in this chapter.

## Pay for Performance

One of the hottest topics in grocery marketing circles currently is pay for performance (PFP) programs. These programs, first proposed by Information Resources, Nielsen, and other scanner data companies in 1993, are based on the idea of using scanner data to offer retailers X cents per unit for each unit of specified product sold during a specified period. The benefits to the manufacturer are elimination of diversion and amelioration of forward-buying and deduction problems (since the retailer will be paid, according to the promises being made, within a few days after the completion of the period). The benefits to the retailer are more nebulous, but certainly quick payment and elimination of deductions are important to retailers, and retailers who do not engage in diverting will cheer its elimination.

What PFP does not do is reward promotion (meaning actual promotion of brand names, such as advertising and displays, as opposed to price promotion). This type of performance continues to be ignored and that *must not be*, for the good of the industry.

When stripped of its high-tech veneer, PFP is simply a rebate for selling merchandise as opposed to buying it.

The problem with PFP is that the grocery channel does not need more rebates in any form. The entire grocery channel, not just manufacturers, needs to return to brand-building. Manufacturers, led by Proctor & Gamble, are moving in that direction, but P&G at least appears to be planning to do its brand-building through the relatively inefficient method of national advertising. Perhaps the company despairs of getting real promotion from their retailers, however much it pays. Certainly such an attitude would be justified: Grocery retailers have long made a living out of gouging their suppliers' promotional allowance programs. Some grocery chains make more off their promotional allowances than their total net profits, which leads to the conclusion that they are really in the business of collecting promotional allowances, with selling groceries as a mere sideline.

There is nothing wrong with rebates *per se*, and PFP rebates are better than rebates for purchases, which have led to trade-loading excesses. But the grocery channel already has more than enough of them, and sustainable growth—real improvements in sales, brand performance, and profit—will come from a recognition that retailers and manufacturers are partners in the joint promotion of their brands and stores. Retailers should be willing to perform (that is, to truly promote the manufacturers' brands together with their stores' brand names) and manufacturers should be willing to pay for it.

As of mid-1994, the PFP idea had not caught on to the degree expected by its proponents, though it did have some degree of acceptance. It should be mildly successful over the coming years, but will ultimately be seen as a great idea that came along a bit late. It is basically a more efficient form of paying rebates at a time when rebates are beginning to go out of style. If, however, manufacturers tie PFP as a payment and measurement mechanism to requirements of joint brand-building activities by the retailer, the practice could have a greater degree of success.

## Proportionality

The Robinson-Patman Act requires that allowances be proportionate. But there is nothing except habit requiring the proportionality to be based on the dealer's purchases. It is one of those cases of "that's how we've always done it."

The purpose of giving promotional allowances is to help your dealers sell more of your product so you can make more profit.

Therefore, it makes sense to give the biggest co-op allowances to the dealers who give you the biggest profits. When you have put together the profitability-by-account information described in Chapter 10, you can begin giving your dealers their allowances based on X percent of the profit you made from them, instead of X percent of their purchases. For example, you currently give an allowance of 3 percent of sales. You make a 10 percent net profit. If you know how much profit you make on each account, you could give your dealers an allowance equal to 30 percent of the net profit you make from them. The amount of the allowance is the same, but it would be directed to the most profitable accounts.

An alternative is to give dealers a percentage of their purchases, but base the percentage on a sliding scale according to profitability, that is, the dealers showing the highest profit percentage get the highest allowance percentage. The two approaches would work out to be about equal. For example, you give an allowance of 5 percent of sales to accounts on which you make 20 percent or more profit, 4 percent to accounts in the 15 percent to 20 percent range, 3 percent to the 10 percent to 15 percent accounts, and so on, down to no allowance for those who are not profitable.

This sort of approach could be a way of at least partially redressing profit differentials the Federal Trade Commission might see as violations of Robinson-Patman (see Chapter 10), and thus be a way of showing that you are making an effort to bring your overall pricing and allowance structure into compliance. Consult your company's attorneys about this.

Allowances, especially bonus allowances, can be used to drive desired behavior. Take for example, display space. If your product sells in the type of retail environment where there is a direct correlation between the number of units displayed and the number of units sold, you obviously want to get more units displayed. If your line consists of four products, and you have an extra 2 percent of sales you can use for bonusing, offer to give dealers 0.5 percent for each product they display.

Another good way to calculate bonus allowances is on return on investment (ROI). When you are setting up your over-and-above budget, go back to your ROI figures on last year's over-and-above. If you have a 2 percent budget and you find that your dealers averaged a 10:1 ROI last year, try giving 3 percent to the ones who did 15:1 or better, 1 percent to those who were 5:1 or below, and 2 percent to those in the middle.

In both of these examples, you can multiply the effect by combining it with a profit basis. For example, if you give an extra percentage to dealers who give you extra shelf space, and you apply the percentage to a profit figure instead of a sales figure, you are giving most of your extra allowances to profitable dealers who are cooperating in building sales. For example, if, again, you make a 10 percent net profit on sales, your 2 percent of sales bonus fund equals 20 percent of profit. Thus, you give dealers a 5 percent-of-profit bonus for each unit they display. The biggest bonuses go to the most profitable dealers who display the most merchandise. The smallest bonuses go to the least profitable dealers who display the least merchandise.

In the ROI example, if the allowance percentage is applied to a profit figure, and the amount of the percentage is determined by how much the account has succeeded in using previous funds to generate additional sales, you are rewarding two elements (profits and increased sales) that interrelate to give you not only more sales, but more profitable sales.

Commitment systems, plan-based programs, and other value standards (see Chapter 11) are other forms of allocating allowances on bases other than sales.

## Co-op by Channel

One of today's biggest marketing buzzwords is "customer-focused." It is amazing to consider, however, how noncustomer-focused most promotional allowance programs are.

The great majority of programs are totally undifferentiated; they are one-size-fits-all co-op. If there is any differentiation, it is by product. This is self-focused, reflecting the product or brand management structure of so many companies.

In this regard, there is good news in the 1993 *Nielsen Survey of Manufacturer Trade Promotion Practices*. It says that brand management controls the trade promotion budget in only 24 percent of the respondent companies, down from 42 percent in only two years. Meanwhile, trade marketing departments, which did not even show up in the 1991 survey, now have control of the budget in 29 percent of the companies. Although this refers only to packaged goods, that industry is the birthplace of brand management and is still its stronghold. If control of trade marketing is slipping away from the brand managers, even in packaged goods, it is a good sign for the future of trade marketing everywhere. This is because any marketing program, regardless of fads and buzzwords, should reflect the needs of the target market. In the case of promotional allowance programs, this target is the channel. Programs therefore should be differentiated by channel. Note that this does not mean programs should not also have product differentiations, as *co-operative* programs, they should reflect the marketing needs of both partners.

Many companies have shied away from channel differentiation because of a misunderstanding of the Robinson-Patman Act. There is a widespread belief that the act requires all customers (and therefore all channels) to be treated the same, although in fact it requires only that they be treated equally. Even many people who know this, however, fear that the only way to make sure the FTC does not fault them for treating different channels unequally is to be safe and treat them all the same.

This fear is valid if your idea of channel differentiation is to come up with different programs and tell each dealer which program they get based on *your* definitions of channels.

It would be better to design the different programs and then offer all programs to all dealers, allowing each dealer to choose the program that is most appropriate. This approach avoids any charges of discrimination because the dealer discriminates among programs, you do not discriminate among dealers. If you have designed the programs properly for each channel, you should find few dealers choosing the "wrong" program.

As an example, say you have two channels: value-added resellers who sell your product as part of a total solution package to businesses, and mass merchandisers who sell it in a shrink-wrapped box off the shelf. Offer two programs. The resellers need seed units to place in customer locations for trial; the mass merchandisers need floor display and demo units. The resellers need telemarketing programs and turnkey direct mail segmented for vertical markets; the mass merchandisers need newspaper ads, point-of-purchase materials, and spiffs.

Give each what they need, and offer an accrual percentage appropriate for the channel—meaning a higher percentage for the mass merchandisers. The resellers will not be happy about getting a lower co-op percentage, but they still will not sign up for the mass merchandiser program because it offers them nothing on which they could reasonably spend the money.

You can overcome charges of unfairness from a channel to which you offer a lower co-op percentage by having different dealer agreements, of which the promotional allowance program is only a part. In these dealer agreements, the different channels are offered entirely different packages of services and terms. A channel offered a lower promotional allowance percentage might be offered better technical support or lead-referral as an offset.

This approach would appear to be perfectly within Robinson-Patman (as always, check with your lawyers) as long as the overall effect is equal. In fact, similar approaches have been used on a few occasions. You would want to include in the dealer agreement a clause indicating that the dealer has been shown all the various offerings, otherwise disgruntled dealers could later say they chose one offering without being aware of all the possibilities.

Channel-differentiated programs are a way of structuring trade promotion programs to meet both your needs and the widely varying needs of your dealers, which is what co-op is supposed to do.

## Account-Specific Marketing

Some manufacturers, particularly in packaged goods, are talking about a step beyond co-op by channel to account-specific marketing.

Such an approach might make other industries rather nervous. Grocery and health and beauty aids have always been rather cavalier about Robinson-Patman, however, and the FTC has generally allowed them a wide berth, probably figuring that almost anything in the grocery trade could be justified as "meeting competition," since anybody who was caught could probably point to somebody doing something worse. (It is interesting that almost 60 years after passage of Robinson-Patman, the act has had the least effect on the industry at which it was specifically directed. This is a measure of how poorly it was written.)

If dealt with in a structured way, with a centralized mechanism in place to watch for abuses, such an approach could be followed in almost any industry. The necessary corollary to any sort of decentralized authority is centralized data collection and reporting.

Most companies are looking for ways to push authority and responsibility down to the level nearest the customer, and account-specific marketing is the logical outcome. Although such programs are wide open to abuse, appropriate reporting procedures can minimize the dangers. It is not an accident that the packaged goods companies most widely adopting account-specific marketing are also adopting commitment systems, since the latter are designed to offer the best hope of controlling the potential abuses inherent in account-specific marketing.

## Warehouses, Clubs, Category Killers, and Everyday Low Pricing

The grocery chains are running scared. It is tough to compete with someone whose costs run 13 points lower than yours. Grocers are looking over their shoulders, wondering if the explosive growth of the warehouses and clubs will continue, or if things will level off with the newcomers merely occupying a niche in the channel. As of mid-1994 it appears that warehouses and clubs have reached a plateau. Even at this plateau, they have taken a sizeable bite out of traditional grocery chains' profits. But they are not the worst news.

Deciding that the everyday low pricing (EDLP) format is here to stay, Proctor & Gamble decided to match their pricing with that of the channel. The idea, dubbed "value pricing" by P&G but generally called EDLP, has spread among packaged goods manufacturers. The latest Nielsen survey says that 73 percent of packaged goods companies now practice some form of EDLP.

The effect on the typical high-low retailer will be huge, possibly more severe than that of the warehouses. The reason is the comparative impact on profits of prices and volume. As mentioned earlier (from "Managing Price, Gaining Profit" in the *Harvard Business Review*), a 1 percent increase in price will yield more than three times the profit gain of a 1 percent increase in volume. Unfortunately for grocery chains, the effect is the same in reverse, and EDLP is attacking their pricing at the same time the warehouses are chipping away at their volume.

In the early days after P&G announced its EDLP strategy, there was speculation that there would be massive cuts in trade promotion spending. This has not been borne out. What P&G and other packaged goods companies appear to be moving toward is a situation in which they are cutting back on price-cutting, both at the trade and consumer levels, but not cutting back on support for actual promotion and advertising of their products by the trade.

The Nielsen study shows that total trade promotion spending by the respondent companies was 13 percent of sales in 1993, exactly the same as in 1991 and 1992. Moreover, when asked about their expectations for the future, the respondents said that they expected to see increases in MDF and accrual programs and decreases in off-invoice allowances.

This would be consistent with P&G's stated goals when introducing the new policy, which were to redirect money toward brand-building endeavors and to reduce the constant price-cutting that was eroding the images of its flagship brands. Ross Love, P&G's Worldwide Vice President of Advertising, wrote in *The Advertiser* that "As businesses move away from price promotions and trade enticements, there will be the opportunity to channel more resources to the best tool for building brand equity—advertising."

Although the impact of warehouses and clubs has been felt most severely by the grocery chains, all retailers are feeling the pinch, and all may eventually be afflicted with competitors practicing some form of EDLP. Most of the category killers (such as Builders Square and Toys R Us) practice EDLP to some degree.

One response by the grocery channel has been a new willingness by both manufacturers and retailers to discuss ending some of the practices that result in the 13 percent cost bulge—including trade loading, diverting, and deductions through their Efficient Consumer Response (ECR) initiatives.

As noted previously, the spread of EDLP and value pricing, while having a tremendous effect on who wins and who loses in the distribution channel, will not have a major direct effect on the practice of promotional allowance marketing as long as the cuts are in pricing as opposed to promotional support.

# Deductions

Deductions may turn out to be the Black Death of the promotional allowance business, totally destroying the concept in entire industries. Is this an exaggeration? Probably, but there's a measure of truth behind it. The following are some facts about deductions in just the grocery industry from the report of the grocery manufacturers' and retailers' Joint Industry Committee on Invoice Deductions, published in 1990:

- Invoice deductions represent 3 percent to 7 percent of a manufacturer's sales, adding up to about $10 billion per year.

- Deductions grew in the 1980s at about 15 percent to 20 percent annually.

- Direct costs to the industry were estimated at 0.10 percent to 0.15 percent of sales. Remember, this is the grocery trade, where profit margins generally run in the low single digits. Remember also that this is an industry measuring sales in hundreds of billions, so a tenth of a percent means hundreds of millions of dollars.

- One major wholesaler reported having eight full-time people per division processing deductions.

- The administrative costs to a large supplier could run as high as $3 million to $4 million per year.

- Buyers and sales reps reportedly spend 10 percent to 50 percent of each appointment working through deduction problems.

This is only one industry, but others have similar problems.

The deduction problem is not solely related to promotional allowances, of course. Retailers deduct for a variety of causes (freight allowances, markdown money, and so on). But the Committee found that the largest number of deductions were for promotion. Timothy M. Hammonds, Senior Vice President of Research and Education for the Food Marketing Institute, speaking at a seminar on the subject in February 1991, said: "Approximately 80 percent of invoice deductions are caused by not understanding the terms and conditions of promotional programs."

The deduction plague, if not brought under control, could cause serious cutbacks in promotional programs. Some people believe the move toward everyday low pricing by so many packaged goods manufacturers has been partially motivated by a desire to limit their horrendous deduction expenses. A major food broker was quoted in the December 2, 1991, issue of the grocery trade journal *Supermarket News*: "[D]eductions are the reason more and more major manufacturers are planning to go to an EDLP program." The most recent Nielsen survey says that 73 percent of the responding companies were practicing some form of EDLP in 1993, up from 54 percent in the preceding year.

There are two powerful forces driving the growth of deduction problems. The first is that deduction problems are more serious where retailers are more dominant. A good rule of thumb is the bigger the retailer, the more they deduct. Current trends are toward larger and larger retailers and more and more retail dominance. The second impetus toward more deductions is the likelihood of higher rates of inflation and interest over the next few years. The higher these rates are, the greater the retailer's incentive to deduct.

Consider these numbers: A grocery retailer buying $1 billion in goods earns about $130 million in promotional allowances. If interest rates are 1 percent monthly and the retailer can get its money 30 days earlier by deducting, the annual savings is $1,300,000.

Why do retailers deduct? The biggest reason is that manufacturers are too slow in paying. Retailers justifiably ask why manufacturers who demand payment on their invoices within 30 days think it is acceptable to hold a claim for a promotional allowance 60 or even 90 days. The grocery industry's committee found the other chief reason for deductions was simple misunderstanding or miscommunication of the terms of trade promotion programs between the buyer and the sales rep, particularly as the industry's programs have grown more and more complex.

For both these reasons, the grocery industry is putting a great deal of faith in electronic data interchange (EDI) as a major part of the solution to their deduction problems. The Joint Industry Committee recommended that the industry expand usage of the industry-standard communication system, known as UCS (department stores and their suppliers have a similar system known as VICS), to transmit promotional data in advance of buyer-rep meetings, so the terms are clearly expressed in writing. A few chains, such as Super Valu (Minneapolis), are adapting UCS to download promotional data directly into their pricing system.

Similarly, PFP programs and the various types of paperless and claimless systems we discuss in this chapter are intended to cut claim payment time from months or weeks down to days or even minutes (if the payment is made by electronic fund transfer). If implemented successfully, these approaches could have a positive effect on the deduction problem.

Meanwhile, until the problem is solved, a number of companies offer software packages intended to help manufacturers in tracking and clearing deductions as efficiently as possible.

One thing is certain: If the deduction problem is ever to be solved, the industries with the problem are going to have to do it themselves. Any hope that the FTC would take a strong stand against deductions was crushed when the 1990 revisions of the Guidelines were released. The Commission's position is that deductions are a violation only if the deduction was taken in an effort to induce unfair treatment. Since it is unlikely this will ever be shown, there is little likelihood the FTC will soon proceed against a retailer for taking deductions, despite the language, written into many manufacturer's programs, saying retailers must not take deductions and that such deductions might be a violation of FTC Guidelines. The FTC states that it is not convinced deductions upset the competitive balance of the marketplace.

Some lawyers have argued that a co-op program, when used by a retailer, constitutes a contract between the manufacturer and the retailer, and that if the retailer takes a deduction forbidden by the program, it constitutes a breach of contract. This may be true from a legal standpoint, but in marketing terms it is totally irrelevant, because manufacturers do not make a practice of prosecuting their customers.

A few manufacturers occasionally have taken strong stands on deductions. In the mid-1970s, Levi Strauss stopped shipping to Goldwaters department stores in Phoenix, because Goldwaters had ignored repeated warnings to stop deducting. Goldwaters promptly settled the open issues and stopped deducting—from Levi's. In the same era, London Fog is said to have lost patience with the Strawbridge & Clothier chain in Philadelphia. London Fog waited until the first day of Strawbridge's fall coat sale, backed their trucks up to the stores' doors, and repossessed all of their merchandise. In some cases, according to legend, removing the coats from customers' backs. Again, the store backed down.

One lesson we can learn from these examples is that manufacturers *can* enforce their antideduction policies, though it takes determination. But there are two other lessons as well. Levi Strauss and London Fog were the leaders in their categories, brands the stores could not do without. Lesser brands probably could not get the same results. Also, both of these examples come from the 1970s, illustrating how the balance of power between manufacturer and retailer has changed.

## Trade Loading

In an article published in the October 5, 1992 issue of *Fortune* magazine, titled "The Dumbest Marketing Ploy," the magazine attacks "trade loading" (also known as "channel stuffing"), the practice of offering periodic deals and discounts to pump up sales into the channel.

The principal reason for loading is a drive for market share and/or a need to hit quarterly sales targets. The problem, of course, is that such practices are addictive and, like other addictions, require ever larger fixes to achieve the same effect. In the standard scenario, a promotion has succeeded, meaning it has stuffed more product into the channel than can normally be absorbed, thereby depressing sales for the next period. However, the same desire for share growth will exist in the next period, so another, even more generous, promotion must be scheduled.

The practice is most prevalent in the packaged goods business and, according to the article, results in the average grocery product taking 84 days to travel from the factory to store shelves. Which means $75 billion to $100 billion in product is in the distribution pipeline at any given time, the inventory cost of which is said to add $20 billion to consumer costs. Additional costs result from the peaks and valleys the promotions create in production.

The *Fortune* article, of course, featured Proctor & Gamble, but the Nielsen report that 73 percent of respondents are practicing some form of EDLP indicates that trade loading may be a dying practice, since the two are incompatible. Among other packaged goods companies who were reported to be changing their marketing practices away from trade loading were Duracell and Quaker Oats. However, these companies were not reported to be cutting trade promotion spending, merely spreading their spending more evenly over the year to try to even out the expensive peaks and valleys. Quaker, in addition, is reported to be changing its employee bonus plans so that managers are rewarded less for sales increases and more for efficiency of manufacturing and distribution. They have implemented a program called Supply Chain Management, aimed at allowing them to replace inventory as needed rather than having huge amounts of inventory in the pipeline (see "Just-in-Time" in this chapter). Since implementing this system in 1991, Quaker's operating margins have risen from 9.4 percent to 12.1 percent.

The difficulty in eliminating trade loading, as *Fortune* points out, is that most major packaged goods manufacturers are publicly traded companies whose officers keep a sharp eye on their stock price (for many, that is where they get their bonuses). Wall Street, in turn, keeps a sharp eye on quarterly results. To unstuff the channel requires accepting a quarter, or maybe two, of sharply reduced sales and even more sharply reduced profits. One example cited is Bristol-Myers Squibb, who unstuffed in early 1992, and had a 9 percent drop in its stock price when it announced its quarterly results. Duracell and Quaker also suffered sales and earnings losses as a result of their strategies. In addition, eliminating the deals and discounts leaves marketers vulnerable to hardball tactics from competitors.

Those who defend trade loading argue that the practice works because wholesalers, having stocked up heavily, will push the product on to retailers. *Fortune* disputes this, quoting wholesalers as saying that loading generally does not lead to additional push at the retail level, although the article does not address promotional practices that might accomplish this goal.

Pay-for-performance programs, as mentioned earlier, offer some possibilities in regard to both trade loading and another industry problem, diverting. Because retailers would get their payments based on sales rather than purchases, they would buy only what they could reasonably expect to sell in the promotional period. In addition, if the promotion pays on sales, it would do no good to buy goods in a regional promotion and divert them outside the region.

Given the widespread acceptance of EDLP, it appears that the worst excesses of trade loading are behind us. The dangers exists, of course, that as a new generation of marketers comes along, the lessons will be forgotten, and when pressures build to meet quarterly sales goals, the new marketers will gradually bring back some of the practices of the past. Senior management needs to be vigilant to avoid backsliding.

# Just-in-Time and Automatic Inventory Replenishment

One of the more important developments in manufacturing in recent years, pioneered by the Japanese but now almost universally embraced, is the concept of just-in-time manufacturing (JIT). Simply put, this is the idea of having suppliers ship as the parts are needed instead of maintaining stockpiles of parts. The effect, of course, is to tremendously reduce inventory costs.

It is the sort of idea that is so simple, one wonders why it took so long to think of it. The benefits are so obvious that the concept has spread past manufacturing and caught on in retailing.

While JIT would probably have moved into retail anyway, its acceptance was quickened by the widespread credit problems of the retail industry in the early 1990s. We constantly heard during the recession of resellers placing smaller orders not only because of recession-induced lower demand, but because they could not get enough credit for the orders they would have liked to place. We might have expected such a situation to change as the recession ended and credit problems were overcome, but JIT has meant resellers are continuing to hold inventory down.

Just-in-time is interrelated with automatic inventory replenishment (AIR), and sometimes the two terms are used almost interchangeably. Automatic inventory replenishment, however, refers more specifically to a particular aspect of JIT—an arrangement between a manufacturer and its customer for the manufacturer to monitor the customer's inventory levels and automatically ship product, without specific purchase orders, to maintain specified inventory levels. This benefits the customer by keeping inventory levels low and benefits the manufacturer by evening out production and delivery schedules. The negative effect on manufacturers is that *their* inventories increase, as do costs related to making more, smaller shipments.

So what are and will be the effects on promotional allowance marketing of just-in-time retailing and automatic inventory replenishment? The changes we might see include the following:

- Inventory costs will be shifted from the reseller to the manufacturer. Will the manufacturer be tempted to offset these costs from co-op? This might be done by offering higher promotional allowances to resellers who order in advance of busy seasons,

who do not demand quick shipment, or who maintain specified inventory levels. While this would be presented as bonuses
to these resellers, it would actually be a penalty against resellers
who practiced JIT.

- The biggest effect of JIT may be on the planning and spending
  cycle. If ordering and shipping is followed immediately by
  promotion and sale of the merchandise, manufacturers are
  going to have a less defined picture of their liability, and
  resellers of their promotional allowance balances. This will
  mean manufacturers will put pressure on their co-op administrative services (or internal departments) to drastically upgrade
  their reporting capabilities and shorten the reporting cycle.

  One way of addressing this might be to extend the EDI
  ordering systems already in place at most major resellers and
  manufacturers so accruals are networked into the ordering and
  shipping system. For example, the reseller places (or cancels)
  an order through EDI; the EDI system (as now) notifies the
  shipping department; simultaneously, the co-op system is noti-
  fied and accruals are updated immediately. The up-to-the-minute
  co-op balance is available to the reseller at all times through
  EDI and/or voice response systems. This might take place over
  the Internet or another such network.

  Implicit in this scenario is that promotional allowance accruals are generated from orders or shipments. Many (maybe
  most) promotional allowance programs currently base accruals
  on invoices or even payments. This will probably have to
  change in response to JIT.

- Manufacturers may want to base accruals on orders above AIR
  levels. The logic here would be that AIR is intended to maintain
  the levels of merchandise required to meet normal demand.
  Promotional periods would usually require orders beyond
  these levels. Therefore, the promotional allowances ought to
  be tied to these promotional orders. It might be too radical a
  step to discontinue allowances entirely on AIR shipments (and,
  in any case, some amount of promotion is needed to maintain
  the "normal demand" AIR is intended to fulfill), but a good
  compromise would be to offer one level of accrual on those
  shipments, with a higher level on orders for promotions.

This would have the effect of tying retailer requests for over-and-above funding for promotions more closely to the orders placed for those promotions, thus generating some very direct tie-ins to the commitment systems discussed in Chapter 11, and the discussion of vendor support programs and return on investment and profit on investment in Chapter 10.

## Growing Channel Concentration

Much of what has been covered in this chapter, because it is dealing with on-going trends, is speculative. We do not know what all the effects of EDLP, EDI, JIT, AIR, warehouses and clubs, value pricing, and trade loading will be or how they will interact. One thing that *is* clear, though, is that more and more power is being concentrated in the hands of a very few retail giants. The growing power of these giants, and their ability and willingness to use that power to demand and get promotional and other allowances far beyond what is available to their competitors, is reminiscent of the situation existing immediately prior to the enactment of Robinson-Patman. Is history ready to repeat itself?

There are, of course, differences between then and now. One of the most important is the budding ability of manufacturers to determine profit by account. The end of this cycle *might* not have to be government intervention which, besides leveling the playing field, would probably also kill all the innovation that has made promotional allowance marketing so exciting and successful in recent years. If manufacturers move quickly enough to determine and act on profit-by-account information, they might end the retail giants' reign of terror simply by deciding it makes sense to say no to unprofitable customers, and to nurture smaller customers (because they might be more profitable and because they provide a defense against the giants).

As mentioned earlier, if shopping by computer and/or interactive television catches on to the extent some analysts believe it will, and the market share the new channels capture comes from the retail giants, the effect on co-op could be tremendous, as the balance between manufacturers and retailers swings back more in the manufacturers' favor.

# Electronic Data Interchange and Paperless Co-op

We have already mentioned ways in which EDI and the Internet could be used to speed processing and dissemination of promotional allowance accrual information. They also could be used also for the submission and payment of claims.

"Paperless co-op" has recently become a major buzzword. The problem is, as so often happens when everybody starts saying "I want _____" only because everybody else is saying the same thing, it quite often turns out that they mean very different things. So when somebody else offers to provide it, it is quite possible that what the provider is offering may not be what the requester wanted (or thought they wanted).

Some people talking about paperless co-op are looking for the ability to have sales reps gather data and input commitments on their laptops. Others want to eliminate the need for retailers to submit claim documentation. Still others want payment by electronic fund transfer, or the ability to file claims and invoice data on imaging systems to cut filing costs. All these and other goals are considered paperless co-op by somebody.

There are programs being tested or in limited use for implementing each of these ideas. But none is doing all of them. And even these ideas leave a lot of paper in the system. What would a true, fully paperless co-op system look like?

First, as mentioned in the just-in-time section, the accruals would be calculated automatically as orders were placed, and communicated to the dealer over the network. Where accruals are not used, commitments would be entered as the deals were made by sales reps using laptops.

The print media would need to put data on their ads including product name, reseller, size, rates, and copy content (features, prices, and so on) onto the network. This data would be in a standard format and data layout and could be accessed by any manufacturer. Broadcast media would electronically verify performance of each script including dealer, product, date, time, and rate.

Manufacturers and third-party administrators would need a retrieval system that would search the network for ads for their products. Verification for print would be an online image of the ad, verification of broadcast would be electronic station logs showing time, date, copy, and image (in the case of television) along with actual audio for documentation. All media performance would be electronically accessed and stored with the performance cost data.

Ads retrieved off the network would be audited through a system that allowed a human auditor to quickly check performance, compliance with program terms, and cost. Once completed, the system would issue payment via electronic fund transfer to the dealer's bank or credit to the dealer's account with the manufacturer. (A variation would have the payment go directly to the media.)

The cost of administration, either internal or through a third party, would be calculated on a transaction basis and immediately billed and paid via electronic fund transfer.

Preformatted reports would be generated in real time and constantly updated, available to both the field sales organization and corporate executives for planning and marketing program development. Management and sales force would be equipped with data extraction tools to access the data and generate ad hoc reports. Scanner data would be tied in with promotional activity to generate a complete picture of promotion, results, and cost on a real-time basis.

All of this is possible today, but nonetheless it will not be happening for a while yet. The media currently have no incentive to participate, and their role is clearly essential. They can presumably be persuaded if it is pointed out to them that such a system would give dealers an incentive to choose media over nonmedia spend options in using their promotional allowances (nonmedia promotions could be tied into such a system, but verification would be trickier, though not impossible).

There are other problems that will delay full implementation of such a system, primarily its cost. In addition, all the various hookups are not in place.

So what can be done now? Reports are already being sent to many manufacturers via the Internet by their administrative services, and many are accessing their data and producing their own reports. Sales reps are accessing this data either via laptop or touchtone phone systems and using it in their planning sessions with clients; in some cases, they are entering commitment data on their laptops. Payment is being done via electronic fund transfer, but maintaining a complete database of bank accounts for each reseller is currently unrealistic. Most people who are using this method are doing it for only a few resellers.

The next step we can expect to see will be the gradual implementation of real-time accruals. The whole system will be in place only when the media sees its benefits.

CHAPTER 13

# International
# Co-op

Promotional allowance marketing is still primarily an American phenomenon, though it has spread to other countries over the last couple decades, and the spread seems to be gaining speed. Only in Canada, however, does co-op play a role in marketing similar to that it plays in the United States.

Promotional allowance marketing, to whatever extent it exists, is practiced very differently outside North America, primarily because of custom and law. Custom is the major reason for the differences. Co-op is not important in India, for example, simply because it has never been important. We tend to underestimate how much of what we do is ruled by the credo "that's the way we've always done it."

Law also plays an obvious role. Although most developed countries have something similar to a Federal Trade Commission, few have the equivalent of sections 2(d) and 2(e) of the Robinson-Patman Act or a *Fred Meyer* decision, which played such a big role in the growth of co-op in the United States. In much of the world, governments take a much more interventionist role in the economy. Although this can make things much more fair in terms of marketing practices (witness some of the abuses the United States sees these days), it can also deaden competition and the resulting innovation in marketing programs.

None of this is to say that co-op will never catch on outside North America, only that it will not soon reach U.S. levels, and that it will probably always be practiced differently.

The growth of international trade and multinational corporations, in fact, seems to guarantee that something like co-op will take root and grow in most parts of the world. As U.S. firms enter foreign markets, many of them introduce promotional allowances in some form. Some foreign companies operating in the U.S. have seen the effectiveness of co-op and taken it home.

## The United Kingdom

As with so many things, the United Kingdom is the European country with practices most like the United States. Even there, however, co-op is still fairly primitive. Giving dealers an allowance based on purchases is the exception; almost all "co-partnership" (the British term) is based on specific requests from dealers to manufacturers, similar to market development fund and vendor-support programs.

PressAd, the newspaper association most active in British co-op, puts out a book describing available co-op programs. The overwhelming majority use the word "discretionary" to describe their funding. PressAd's 1991 convention demonstrated both the rudimentary conditions of British co-op and its growth and potential. The representative of Hitachi, for example, revealed that his company would soon begin sending out statements of co-op balances to its dealers, an idea presented (and received) as something of an innovation. Another speaker revealed that her advertising agency had been hired by IBM to increase use of their program, which was running at 30 percent. Although these examples show how far the United Kingdom has to go to catch up with North America, they also show an intention to do exactly that.

It should also be noted that the conference was attended by over 200 people and addressed by representatives from a number of major manufacturers, most of them multinationals, like Hitachi, IBM, Hoover, and Phillips. In addition, the conference was addressed by Gerrit ter Heege, Advertisement Manager of *De Gelderlander* in Nijmegen, The Netherlands, who described the status of co-op there in terms reminiscent of reports from the British when they first started attending Newspaper Advertising Co-op Network meetings in the early 1980s.

We could make a plausible argument that the absence of the Robinson-Patman Act and the lack of a "that's the way we've always done it" attitude relative to co-op may allow the United Kingdom to move beyond its current co-op conditions, bypass the intermediary steps, and advance directly to the next level—commitment systems based on return on investment and profit. The United States, because of Robinson-Patman and entrenched practices, may have a harder time making such changes. In five or ten years, we may arguably see the United Kingdom as the leader in promotional allowance marketing.

Putting aside speculation on the future, let us try to guess the current size of the British co-op market. In 1993, PressAd estimated that co-op in regional newspapers accounted for £250 million, with national papers adding approximately another 20 percent, for a total of £300 million. In the United States, we estimate newspapers to be 38 percent of all promotional allowances and all media 65 percent. Because there is practically no broadcast co-op in the United Kingom, we will say that newspapers are 65 percent of British promotional allowances. That makes the total of co-op about £460 million or close to $700 million, using an exchange rate of about $1.50 per pound. Therefore, although the British economy is about 16 percent the size of the United States', the United Kingdom's promotional allowance spending is only a bit over 2 percent of American spending.

# Mexico

As the North American Free Trade Agreement (NAFTA) takes effect, we should see more American-style co-op programs in Mexico and, perhaps, Central and South America, as other countries join NAFTA and/or begin to change their marketing practices in preparation for it.

Mexico has a few large national retail chains, including Liverpool stores, Cifra, Palacio de Hierro, and Sears, which has been operating in the country since the 1930s. Wal-Mart has opened a Mexico City outlet (larger than any of its American stores), and has followed with stores in Monterrey and Guadalajara. They currently plan 60 stores in Mexico, all to be operated as a joint venture with Cifra. Dillard's has announced they will open 50 stores in Mexico, in a joint venture with Wal-Mart and Cifra. J.C. Penney has opened a Monterrey store and plans others, Price Club has opened in Mexico City, and Saks Fifth Avenue says they too will open a Mexico City store. These retailers will demand promotional support from their American suppliers, and their Mexican suppliers will be forced to follow suit to remain competitive.

The major hindrance to development of co-op in Mexico will come from the media situation. Dr. Alex Zaragoza, Associate Professor of History at the University of California at Berkeley, and director of the school's Berkeley Programs for Studies Abroad, a specialist in Mexican economic history, notes that "advertising venues are very limited." In most countries, co-op development is being driven by the newspapers, who see in it a major new revenue source. Zaragoza describes Mexican newspapers as "a total bust." He estimates the total circulation of all Mexico City's papers as about one million, in a city of 20 million or more. Circulation outside Mexico City is even smaller. Magazines are small and tend to be short-lived. Television consists of one major network, Televisa, and a weak competitor drawing less than 20 percent of the audience. Televisa discourages its local outlets from running local programming and advertising, which has the effect of shutting most retailers out of the television market. Cable is limited to a few areas of a few cities, and is too expensive for most Mexicans. Direct mail is a tool used by some retailers, although the Mexican postal system is not as reliable as it could be. Zaragoza says that many retailers in Mexico City, faced with these choices, resort to handing out flyers on street corners, "like the pizza parlors in Berkeley."

Radio may be the best hope, at least for smaller retailers. The radio market, as in the United States, is fragmented by the large number of stations, a factor that larger retailers may find discouraging, but that works to the benefit of smaller retailers by holding down rates and segmenting the audience.

In summary, the Mexican co-op situation offers considerable promise. The difficulty will be in overcoming the media problems; media and co-op professionals in the United States could have an opportunity to assist Mexican media outlets, especially the newspapers, in developing the co-op expertise they need.

## Other Countries

Given the previous comment that British promotional allowance practices are most like ours, we have some idea of how far behind most other countries are. The Netherlands, as we already mentioned, is beginning to develop a co-op infrastructure through its newspapers, and New Zealand and Australia have developed along the same lines. In most countries that have any sort of co-op, the newspaper industry is at the center of it.

Several U.S. companies marketing in Japan offer co-op programs there, as do many Japanese companies, many of whom learned the practice in the United States. The development of co-op in Japan, however, has been hampered by the dominance of Japanese retailing by thousands of small mom-and-pop stores. Japanese law has hindered the development of big retailers, and American and other foreign retail firms seeking to enter the market have run into numerous roadblocks. Much of the negotiation to close the trade gap between the United States and Japan has centered on these points, since many American (and Japanese) trade experts believe that larger retailers would be more likely to sell more imported products. The development of co-op in Japan will depend on the success of efforts to open Japanese markets to foreign goods.

Trying to describe how to offer co-op on an international basis is virtually impossible and beyond the scope of this book—each country is different, to say nothing of the varying market positions of each marketer. However, Appendix 2 includes a list of organizations in several countries (mostly provided by Marilyn Beadle of PressAd) that you may contact for specific information.

## Currency Questions

If you are involved with international co-op, it is wise to guard against currency fluctuations. The best way to protect yourself completely is to handle each country's program within that country. This may not be practical, however, since it means duplicating functions in each country and giving up all economies of scale in administration. Also, it is possible that, despite your best prevention efforts, each country or region may develop and use its own system of record keeping and reporting, making it difficult or impossible to report on world-wide promotions, or to compare program effectiveness by regions and countries.

If you are handling various countries from the United States, the next best way to protect against currency fluctuations is to accrue in the local currency at the time of sale. This is complicated, but it can be done. It is, of course, much simpler administratively to keep accruals in dollars. If you believe that the administrative advantage of keeping accruals in dollars and making the conversion at the time of payment outweighs the currency risks, you will need to consult with your finance department and let them decide if the risks are large enough to include these amounts in their hedge funds.

If you accrue in dollars and pay in other currencies, make it plain to the dealers what date and what rate source will be used to make conversions. Typically, the rate source is something generally accepted and readily available, like the foreign exchange tables from *The Wall Street Journal*. The date used for conversion can be the date of the ad, the date of the claim, or the date of the payment. The date of the ad is probably the fairest, since it is the day the dealer incurred the expense. The date of the payment is also good, although some dealers may accuse you of sitting on a claim to take advantage of rate changes. If your database keeps the accruals in dollars, your auditing will have to convert the claim documentation from the local currency to dollars and then back again.

Another possibility is to pay in dollars and let the dealer convert it. This can, however, cause hardships on dealers in some countries, and could even raise legal questions in others.

It is also necessary to be conscious of the difficulties and delays inherent in dealing with banks in various countries. A program with its bank account in the United States, may make payments by wire transfer to dealers' accounts in various European countries. Depending on the American bank's correspondent status with the dealers' banks, some of the transfers may have to move through three or four banks. In theory, this should not be a problem, since wire transfers should move as fast as data can cross a wire. However, each bank in the chain may hold the money for a couple days, meaning that transfers can take one week to two weeks to reach the dealers' accounts.

However frustrating it may be, international co-op offers many exciting challenges and opportunities and its inevitable growth will make it more necessary to address these challenges creatively.

# Glossary

$M$uch of this addendum has been adapted or reproduced (with permission) from Ed Crimmins' *Cooperative Advertising,* although items have been added, deleted, or changed to reflect changes in the field.

**Account-specific marketing.** The practice of tailoring marketing programs to specific customers. (Chapter 12)

**Accrual.** The amount of funds earned through purchases over a stated period. Usually earned on the basis of so much per dollar (or per unit) purchased.

**Accrual period.** The period during which purchases accrue allowances. *See also* Spend period.

**Ad scrip.** A certificate entitling a retailer to a specified amount of co-op funding. Often used as a means to provide allowances to indirect customers. Sometimes called "co-op in a box." (Chapter 3)

**Administrative services.** *See* Auditing and payment services.

**Advertising deadline.** The last date by which advertising may take place if it is to qualify for reimbursement.

**Affidavit of performance.** A sworn statement that provides information (time, place, cost, content, and so on) about certain advertising. Typically refers to a statement from a medium, such as a radio, cable, or television station or an outdoor supplier.

**ANA/CAB, ANA/RAB, ANA/TvB.** *See* Electronic tear sheet.

**ANA/IOA affidavit.** Documentation of performance provided by outdoor advertising companies in a format developed jointly by the Association of National Advertisers and the Institute of Outdoor Advertising.

**Audit.** A process by which a claim is analyzed and a determination made as to whether a claim falls within program guidelines and, if so, how much should be paid.

**Auditing and payment services.** Companies with specialized facilities for handling auditing and payment of claims for promotional allowances. Also called "administrative services" or "third-party administrators." (Chapter 5.)

**Authorizations.** *See* Commitments.

**Automatic inventory replenishment.** An arrangement by which a retailer authorizes a manufacturer to monitor the retailer's inventory of the manufacturer's products and automatically ship additional products when inventory reaches certain levels. *See* Just-in-time. (Chapter 12.)

**Barter.** The trading of merchandise instead of paying cash for advertising. Suppliers sometimes trade goods for national broadcast advertising time. Retailers and distributors often trade goods for local broadcast time (*see* Trade agreement). Barter houses are companies that trade goods and services, chiefly to radio and television stations for air time which the barter houses then either sell or trade to advertisers.

**Carryover period.** A period after the end of a co-op program during which a retailer can spend funds left over from the program. A program running from January through December might allow dealers to use funds through March of the following year. Also called an "overlap." (Chapter 3.)

**Category killers.** A relatively new class of exceptionally large retail store that is devoted to one category of merchandise; examples are Builders Square and Circuit City. Also called "superstores".

**Channel.** A group of retailers or distributors through whom a product moves. In some cases called "class of trade." A manufacturer often has several channels, each of which is used to reach different types of end-users or to sell separate categories of merchandise.

**Channel stuffing.** *See* Trade Loading.

**Claim.** The invoice from a retailer or other intermediary for reimbursement of the cost of advertising or promotion of a supplier's product or service.

**Class of trade.** Type of retailer or distributor. *See* Channel.

**Column inch.** Unit of measure in newspaper advertising. The width of an advertising column by one inch in depth.

**Commitments/Commitment system.** Advance agreement between a manufacturer and a retailer on what promotion will be done and what payment will be offered. The agreement might cover specific promotions or a series of promotions over a period of time. (Chapter 11)

**Co-op in a box.** *See* Ad scrip.

**Cooperative advertising.** Any arrangement by which a product or service is brought to public notice over the names of both the supplier and any intermediary who comes between that supplier and the ultimate purchaser. The intermediary may be a retailer who buys a product for resale a distributor who sells to retailers or other form of intermediaries. This arrangement results in consumer advertising as well as (frequently) other forms of promotion. The cost of the promotion may be shared by the supplier and the intermediary, or the supplier may pays all costs. The process commonly it involves reimbursing retailers for advertising they create and place, but it also includes the supplier creating and placing advertising over the retailer's name.

**Co-op period.** The period during which a specific co-op offer is in effect.

**Credit advice.** A form of payment by which the manufacturer advises the retailer that a given amount has been credited to the retailer's account and that the retailer may deduct it from invoices. Similar to a credit memo. (Chapter 3)

**Credit memo.** An alternative to cash as reimbursment to customers for cooperative advertising. The supplier issues a credit memo that authorizes the retailer to deduct that amount from the next payment to the supplier. (Chapter 3)

**Customer-controlled co-op.** An arrangement by which a retailer or other intermediary creates and places advertising featuring a product or service and is reimbursed for that advertising, in whole or in part, by the supplier. The most common form of co-op; also called "retailer-controlled co-op". The opposite form "supplier-controlled co-op".

**Customized magazine ads.** Ads designed so they can be changed to fit the needs of major retailers in markets across the country. Beyond changing the store name, customization can include the individual retailer's price, store logo, store slogan, information on store hours, locations and parking facilities, and changes in models featured. Customized ads commonly appear in city and regional magazines, in independently edited Sunday newspaper magazines, and in regional and metropolitan issues of national magazines.

**Customized radio and television spots.** Spots created by a supplier and designed to be customized to fit the needs of major retailers in markets across the country. Distinctly different from tagged commercials that leave a few seconds at the end to identify one or more retailers in the market who carry the product advertised. Can be customized to include several mentions of the store (in both audio and video for television), the individual retailer's price, store logo, slogan, location, and hours, and the store's own choice of models to be featured. In the packaged goods industry, spots commonly co-feature other noncompetitive private labels or nonbranded items such as meats, produce, or dairy products that are being offered at special prices. Sometimes called "doughnut" or "sandwich" spots.

**Deal/Deal period.** A time frame during which a manufacturer offers products to its customers at unusually low prices and/or with other inducements, such as increased co-op accruals or volume rebates. Most common in the packaged goods industry. Some deals may induce a customer to buy more product than can be sold during the deal period, leading to diverting. *See* Diverting and Trade loading.

**Dealer-listing ad.** A newspaper or magazine ad featuring a supplier's product or service and more than one retailer. Commonly created and placed by the supplier through an agency specializing in this technique. Tagged radio and television rotation spots are the broadcast equivalents of this technique. (Chapter 9)

**Deduction.** A retailer's subtraction of co-op charges from the supplier's invoice. The FTC Guides indicate that deductions may be unlawful. (Chapter 12)

**Demographics.** In general use, the study of population patterns and characteristics of population groups. In marketing and advertising, demographic information is used to target programs toward specific groups. *See* Psychographics. (Chapter 9)

**Direct customers.** Customers who buy directly from the manufacturer without going through a wholesaler.

**Direct deduct.** A program in which the manufacturer pays directly for a promotion or ad, deducting the cost from the retailer's allowances. A form of supplier-control program. Also called "direct-to-media." (Chapter 9)

**Display allowances.** Payment by a manufacturer to a retailer for in-store displays or for preferential shelf space or positioning. *See* Slotting allowances.

**Disti.** Distributor. A term used in some industries.

**Distributors.** Intermediaries between manufacturers and retailers. Also called, in some industries, "wholesalers," "jobbers," and "W/Ds" (wholesaler/distributors). In many industries, the distributor is a conduit for promotional allowances from the manufacturer to the retailer, and the major questions about them relate to the most efficient way to track purchases and accruals. In other industries, however, the distributor is the co-op recipient or, in a few cases, the co-op provider.

**Diverting.** The practice of buying a product on deal in one area and reselling it in another area where it is not on deal. Often done by retailers who resell to other retailers or to other divisions of their own company. Also done by distributors. *See* Deal, Gray market, and Trade loading.

**Documentation.** Evidence that permits the supplier to know the advertising appeared and that the amount claimed is proper. *See* Proof of performance.

**Double billing.** An illegal practice in which an advertising medium provides a retailer with two bills, one at actual cost and one at a higher rate. The retailer can use the latter bill to collect co-op reimbursement in excess of the supplier's offer. This practice is specifically forbidden under the *FTC Guides* and is subject to criminal penalties under a variety of state and federal laws. (Chapter 3)

**Efficient consumer response (ECR).** A catch-all term covering a variety of actions undertaken by many food and packaged goods manufacturers, distributors, and retailers to improve distribution practices and clean up abuses in the industry. Trade allowance practices, including deductions, are a major component of the process.

**Electronic data interchange (EDI).** A variety of techniques by which firms communicate with each other, generally through computers tied into dedicated networks using standardized formats. Planned co-op applications include paperless claiming and more efficient payment procedures. (Chapter 12)

**Electronic fund transfer (EFT).** Payment by one of a variety of means, through which money is transferred directly from one party's bank account to anothers, without using paper, such as checks. The co-op application is to speed claim turnaround by making EFT payments directly into retailers' accounts.

**Electronic tear sheet.** The ANA/CAB, ANA/RAB, or ANA/TvB documentation provided by broadcasters on a script itself to certify the number of times that particular script was broadcast and at what cost. The initials stand for Association of National Advertisers (ANA), Cable Television Advertising Bureau (CAB), Radio Advertising Bureau (RAB), and Television Bureau of Advertising (TVB), the organizations which created this form of documentation.

**Everyday low pricing (EDLP).** Originally a retailing concept, most often practiced by warehouses and clubs, in which there are no or few off-price promotions; any "deals" are averaged into the everyday price and products are offered at the same price consistently. Has now spread into manufacturing, where Proctor & Gamble calls it "value pricing." (Chapter 12)

**Failure fees.** Payments made to retailers (primarily in the grocery and drug channels) when a product is discontinued due to lack of movement. (Chapter 2)

**Fixed program.** A co-op program that runs for a fixed period of time, usually six months or a year. The opposite of a "rolling fund." (Chapter 12)

**Forced combination.** Two or more newspapers that will accept only advertising that runs in all the papers.

**Fred Meyer.** A retail chain in the Northwest that held that it could properly induce and receive promotional help from manufacturers from whom it bought directly although such help was not offered to retailers who bought from the same manufacturers through wholesalers. This position rested on the belief that Fred Meyer was the manufacturer's customer, while the retailers who bought through wholesalers were the wholesalers' customers. The U.S. Supreme Court found against that position and ruled that manufacturers who sell both directly and indirectly must make the same offer to retailers who buy their products through wholesalers as they make to those who buy directly from the manufacturer. This decision led to revisions in the

*FTC Guides* which state the FTC's view of the responsibilities of suppliers, retailers and media in dealing with cooperative advertising. *See* FTC Guides. (Chapter 2)

**Free standing insert (FSI).** An advertisement that is delivered as part of a newspaper, but is not printed at the same time as the regular pages of the newspaper. May be printed by the newspaper or supplied to the newspaper by the retailer or supplier of the products featured. Sometimes billed on a cost-per-thousand basis, sometimes at the publication's run-of-paper rate. Also called "circular" or "preprint."

**FTC Guides.** Full name is the *Federal Trade Commission Guides for Advertising Allowances and Other Merchandising Payments and Services.* The Guides present the FTC's view of how suppliers, retailers, media, and others can comply with the terms of the Robinson-Patman Act as it relates to promotional allowances. Issued in 1960 and reissued with major modifications in 1969 after a Supreme Court decision in the case of *FTC v. Fred Meyer, Inc.* Sometimes referred to as the "Fred Meyer Guides." Reissued with minor revisions in 1972 and 1990. (Chapter 2)

**Full-control programs.** Supplier-controlled programs in which the manufacturer makes all decisions concerning media selection and production and content of advertising. The retailer is given the choice of having its name included in the advertising. (Chapter 9)

**Gray market.** In industries, such as computers, where it is common to have authorized dealers or other forms of limited distribution, some retailers buy more units than they can sell, reselling the extra units to unauthorized dealers. In addition to making a profit on the resale, the authorized dealer achieves higher volume levels, better discounts, and more promotional and other allowances than would otherwise be possible. *See* Diverting.

**Guides.** *See* FTC Guides.

**Hedging/hedge fund.** A practice in international currency transactions involving the purchase of foreign currency to offset liabilities in U.S. currency. A consideration in operating foreign co-op programs. (Chapter 13)

**Holding.** *See* Pending.

**Indirect customers.** Customers who buy from a wholesaler or other intermediary instead of buying directly from the manufacturer.

**Ingredient co-op.** Programs in which an "ingredient" manufacturer offers to pay part of the cost of advertising a finished product containing their product. Examples are cotton and Intel Inside. (Chapter 9)

**Jobbers.** *See* Distributors.

**Just-in-time.** The concept of cutting inventory costs by ordering supplies only as needed. Pioneered in manufacturing by the Japanese, now increasingly popular among retailers. *See* Automatic inventory replenishment. (Chapter 12)

**Key market funds.** Funds, over and above the normal co-op allowance, made available by suppliers for use only in certain markets in which they have a strong interest. Often used incorrectly as a synonym for market development funds (MDFs go to specific retailers, whereas true key market programs go to all retailers within a given market on a proportional basis).

**Market development funds (MDF).** Extra funding given to specific retailers for specific purposes, such as a major seasonal promotion, by the manufacturer's sales and/or marketing management. These funds generally are not given out on a proportional basis; when this is the case, they are of questionable legality.

**Marriage mail.** The mailing of several pieces of promotional literature in one package to reduce the costs of mailing for each of the participating retailers. Packages sometimes include advertising by retailers featuring branded products for which they claim payment under co-op programs. Term is used sometimes even when the package is not mailed, for example, when the items are combined in a plastic bag hung on door handles.

**Multi-vendor programs.** Programs in which two or more manufacturers jointly offer a promotion to their retailers. Common in travel, where hotels and/or airlines and/or credit cards offer joint programs to travel agents. (Chapter 9)

**No-charge spots.** Radio or television spots that are offered at "no cost," complicating co-op because they have value and many suppliers feel their value must be determined in order to reimburse the claim properly. Sometimes called "bonus spots."

**Nonproduct co-op.** Co-op for services (such as credit cards, insurance, and so on.) Not subject to the Robinson-Patman Act. (Chapter 9)

**Nontraditional media.** Spend options (which are frequently nonmedia) not available in co-op programs prior to the 1980s, for example, inventory financing, sales and service training, and seminars and workshops.

**Off-invoice.** The practice of taking an allowance directly off the price of the product, rather than submitting a claim for payment of the allowance. For example, a retailer offered a 3 percent advertising allowance and purchasing $10,000 of product might simply pay the supplier $9,700, rather than pay the full $10,000 and then submitting a claim for the $300.

**Omnibus ad.** A retail ad featuring the products of more than one supplier.

**Open-end programs.** *See* Unlimited programs.

**Over and above.** Funding beyond what is earned through normal co-op accruals. *See* Market development funds and Key city funds.

**Overbill.** A practice among some retail buyers who ask suppliers to bill in excess of the regular price and hold the excess funds at the buyer's disposal to be used for promotional or other purposes. Sometimes stimulated by management pressure on the buyer to seek money over and above the supplier's regular allowance. In other cases, buyers use this approach when they want to promote an item for which no store funds are available. In some industries, called "price loading."

**Overlap.** *See* Carryover period.

**Participation.** The percentage of the customer's advertising cost the supplier agrees to pay.

**Participation rate.** The percentage of eligible dealers who use a program. *See* Usage Rate. (Chapter 4)

**Pay for performance.** Programs offering to pay retailers a specified amount for each unit of the manufacturer's product sold during a specified period, usually based on scanner data.

**Pending.** The practice of making additional payments on a claim if the dealer does not have sufficient accruals to pay in full at the time it is submitted. (Chapter 3)

**Plan-based program.** Program in which there are no accruals; instead, the dealer submits a plan for promoting the product. The manufacturer then approves, rejects or negotiates the plan. Similar to commitment programs. (Chapter 11)

**Preapproval.** Advance approval for an ad or promotion given to a retailer by a manufacturer. May be approval of a media selection, an ad's concept, or both. Also called "prior approval." (Chapter 3)

**Price loading.** *See* Overbill.

**Profit on investment (POI).** The amount of incremental profit generated by a promotion divided by the cost of the promotion. Generally expressed as a ratio; for example, a promotion costing $5 and yielding $25 in incremental profit would have a POI of 5:1. *See* Return on investment. (Chapter 10)

**Proof of performance.** Evidence of the content and cost of advertising placed by a retailer or other intermediary for which reimbursement is claimed from a supplier.

**Psychographics.** Attitudinal and behavioral characteristics of population groups. Some marketers attempt to use psychographic data to further segment geographic and demographic groups.

**Push money.** The practice by which a manufacturer offers cash or other inducements to a retailer's salespeople to encourage them to recommend its products to potential buyers. Most common format is to offer the salesperson a certain amount per unit sold during a specified time period. A common variant is to offer points, which the salesperson can use to buy various merchandise from a manufacturer-supplied catalog. Also known as "spiffs". *See* Sales contest and Push money rule.

**Push money rule.** Guidelines issued by the Federal Trade Commission in 1962, detailing the terms under which push money (spiffs) and sales contests are allowable under the Robinson-Patman Act.

**Rate.** What the retailer is charged or what the supplier is billed. Most broadcast stations have only one set of rates (and most rates are negotiated). Some may have different rates for national and local advertisers. There are many kinds of newspaper rates, among them:

*Combination rate.* A rate for buying space in more than one edition, zone, newspaper, and so on.

*Commissionable rate.* A rate that provides a commission to an advertising agency.

*Local rate.* Rate paid by a retail advertiser. Also called "retail rate."

*National rate.* Rate paid by a national advertiser.

*Net rate.* Rate after discounts are taken.

*Open rate.* Rate for only one newspaper insertion within a calendar year. Commonly, but not always, lower than the national rate and higher than net local rates. Sometimes called "open local."

*Vendor rate.* The rate at which some large retailers bill for cooperative advertising. Ostensibly based on the rate paid by the retailer plus a charge for advertising overhead. In practice, reflects the retailer's desire to charge more than the advertising actually costs.

**Redistribution.** The practice of using unused funds to give bonuses to other dealers; for example, redistributing unused funds among dealers who have met sales goals.

**Regional marketing.** The practice of offering special deals (or special products) in one section of the country, to reflect particular marketing needs in that area. Sometimes abused by diverters.

**Return on investment (ROI).** The amount of incremental sales generated by a promotion divided by the cost of the promotion. Generally expressed as a ratio; for example, a promotion costing $5 and yielding $25 in incremental sales would have an ROI of 5:1. *See* Profit on investment. (Chapter 10)

**Robinson-Patman Act.** Federal legislation requiring that all competing customers of a supplier who offers promotional help to those customers must be treated on an equal basis. See FTC Guides. (Chapter 2)

**Rollbacks.** In some programs in which accruals are passed through a distributor to indirect customers, the manufacturer allows unused dealer funds to "roll back" to the distributor.

**Rolling fund.** A type of program in which accrued funds are available to a dealer for a specified period (such as six months) after they are earned. Opposite of a "fixed program." (Chapter 3)

**Run of paper (ROP).** Any part of a regular newspaper printed on the paper's own press. The publisher has the option of placing the ad anywhere within the newspaper. Also called "run of press."

**Run of schedule (ROS).** The broadcast station has the option of running the spot in any time slot it chooses.

**Sales contest.** A form of push money in which, instead of offering cash incentives, the manufacturer offers participating retail salespeople the opportunity to win some kind of prize, either through a drawing (for example, each unit sold earns one entry into the drawing) or by achieving defined levels of sales (such as, ten units sold earns a television, 100 units earns a trip to Las Vegas). *See* Push money and Push Money Rule. Some common forms of sales contests may be illegal under the Push Money Rule.

**Sales out.** Most often used to refer to a distributor's sales to dealers. Manufacturers frequently want data on these sales in order to determine allowances for the indirect customers. This term is now sometimes used to refer to the dealers' sales, as some manufacturers want to base allowances and/or payments on sales to end-users. This usage is still rare, but becoming more common.

**Signback program.** A type of supplier-controlled program in which dealers return a portion of their accruals to the manufacturer, with the manufacturer using the accruals (often combined from several dealers) for the dealers' benefit. May also be a program in which the signback goes to a distributor or a media outlet instead of the manufacturer. (Chapter 9)

**Slicks.** Printed material furnished to retailers or other intermediaries from which they can create their own layout for advertising a supplier's product or service.

**Slotting/Slotting allowances.** Payments by a manufacturer to a retailer for the retailer's shelf space. Sometimes also used incorrectly to refer to payments for displays or preferential shelf space. *See* Display allowances. (Chapter 4)

**Soft dollars.** Promotional allowances. Sometimes used in computers and some other industries to encompass co-op, MDF, and other payments made to dealers.

**Spend options.** The various ways in which a manufacturer allows the retailer to spend allowances, including both media and nonmedia options.

**Spend period.** The time during which a dealer is allowed to spend a co-op accrual. Often different from the accrual period.

**Spiffs.** *See* Push money.

**Stock-keeping unit (SKU).** Each item inventoried by a retailer. For example, Tide might represent several SKUs for a typical grocery store, one SKU for each size, liquid and powder, with or without bleach, and so on. The more SKUs, the more shelf space required, the more inventory cost, and so on.

**Submission deadline.** The date by which a claim for co-op reimbursement must be submitted. Usually 60 or 90 days after an ad or promotion, or at the end of the spend period.

**Superstore.** *See* "Category killer".

**Supplier.** Any company that sells a product or service to its ultimate consumer through one or more intermediaries.

**Supplier-controlled program.** Programs in which suppliers create and/or place advertising featuring their product or service over the name of a retailer or other intermediary. Can take a variety of forms, including dealer-listing ads in newspapers and magazines, tagged radio and TV commercials, customized magazine ads, and customized radio and television commercials that give relatively equal treatment to the product and the retailer. *See* Dealer listing ad, Signback program, Direct deduct, and Full control program. (Chapter 9)

**Suspense.** *See* Pending.

**Tear sheet.** In print media, the entire page on which an advertisement appears.

**Third-party administrators (TPAs).** *See* Auditing and payment services.

**Trade.** Term used by manufacturers to refer to their customers collectively.

**Trade agreement.** An agreement by which an advertiser (often a retailer) trades merchandise rather than paying for the advertising in cash. *See* Barter.

**Trade loading.** The practice of inducing retailers or distributors to take on unusually large amounts of merchandise, generally by offering exceptional prices or terms. Often done at the end of a quarter or other financial reporting period in order to reach quotas. Sometimes called "channel stuffing". *See* Deal and Diverting. (Chapter 14)

**Traditional media.** Spend options that have always been available in co-op programs,such as newspapers and broadcast.

**Unlimited programs.** Programs in which retailers or other intermediaries are allowed to run as much advertising as they choose provided they pay their specified share of the cost (generally 50 percent). Also called "open-end programs."

**Usage rate.** The percentage of available co-op allowances used. *See* Participation Rate. (Chapter 4)

**Value-added reseller (VAR).** A dealer (in high tech) who specializes in "solution sales" (full service selling, including consulting, needs analysis, and bundling of turnkey packages). Opposite of a "retailer" who, in this business, is a dealer selling "shrink-wrapped boxes."

**Value pricing.** *See* Everyday low pricing.

**Value standard.** The idea, proposed in 1988 by the Federal Trade Commission, that manufacturers pay retailers for promotions based on the value of the promotion to the manufacturer, rather than on the cost of the promotion to the retailer or on a formula based on product purchases. This proposal was not adopted by the FTC. (Chapter 2)

**Vendor support programs.** Requests by retailers for extra funding for specified promotional efforts. Such programs are often illegal. *See* Market development funds , Key city funds. (Chapter 10)

**Vendors.** Name typically used by retailers to refer to manufacturers.

**W/Ds.** *See* Distributors.

**Wholesalers.** *See* Distributors.

# Resource Lists

The first section of this appendix lists major associations in the United States that may be able to offer co-op and/or marketing-related assistance or advice, the second section gives names and addresses for associations in other countries (mostly newspaper groups) that may be able to offer advice on co-op conditions in their respective area.

## U.S. Associations

Association of National Advertisers
155 East 44 Street
New York, NY 10017-5950

Cable Television Advertising Bureau
757 Third Avenue, 5th Floor
New York, NY 10017

National Association of Customer Accounting Administrators
   (NACAA)
520 Eighth Avenue
New York, NY 10018-6507

National Association for Promotional and Advertising Allowances
  (NAPAA)
245 Fifth Avenue
New York, NY 10016

National Retail Federation
100 West 31st Street
New York, NY 10001

Newspaper Association of America
400 N. Michigan Avenue
Chicago, IL 60611

Radio Advertising Bureau
1320 Greenway Drive, #500
Irving, TX 75038

Television Bureau of Advertising
477 Madison Avenue, 10th Floor
New York, NY 10022

Yellow Pages Publishers Association
820 Kirts, Suite 100
Troy MI 48084

# International Co-op Groups

### ARGENTINA

Asociacion de Editores de Diarios de la Ciudad de Buenos Aires
  (AEDBA)
Carlos Pellegrini 445, 3er Piso
1009 Buenos Aires

### AUSTRIA

Verband Osterreichischer Zeitungherausgeber und Zeitungsverleger
  (VOZ)
Schreyvogelgasse 3
1010 Wien 1

**BELGIUM**

Association Belge des Editeurs de Journaux (ABEJ)
20 rue Belliard, Boîte 5
1040 Bruxelles

**BRAZIL**

Associacao Nacional de Jornais
SCS Edificio Oscar Niemeyer, Salas 603/604
Brasilia

**CANADA**

Canadian Daily Newspaper Association (CDNA)
890 Yonge Street, Suite 1100
Toronto, Ontario M4W 3P4

**COLOMBIA**

Asociacion de Diarios Colombianos-Andiarios
Apartado Aereo 13663
Bogota

**DENMARK**

Danske Dagblades Forening
Pressens Hus, Skindergade 7
1159 Copenhagen K

**DOMINICAN REPUBLIC:**

Sociedad Dominicana de Diarios
Apartado de Correos 1455
Santo Domingo

**ECUADOR**

AEDEP
Mariscal Foch 510 y Diego de Almagro,
3 Piso, Oficina 3s
Quito

## FINLAND

Sanomalehrien Liitto
Kalevankatu 4
00100 Helsinki 10

## FRANCE

Syndicat de la Presse Quotidienne Régionale
17 Place de États-Units
75116 Paris

## GERMANY

Bundesverband Deutscher Zeitungsverleger e.V (BDZV)
Riemenschneiderstrasse 10
Postfach 205002
5300 Bonn 2

## GREECE

Athens Daily Newspaper Publishers Association
14 Mourouzi Street
10674 Athens

## HUNGARY

Magyar Lapkiadok Edysesulete
Ond vezer setay 9-11
1144 Budapest

## INDIA

Indian Newspaper Society
P.O. Box 69, INS Building
Rafi Marg, New Delhi 110 001

## INDONESIA

Serikat Penerbit Suratkabar
Gedung Dewan Pers
Jalan Kebonsirih 34, Floor VA
Jakarta Pusat

## IRELAND

National Newspapers of Ireland
89 Upper Leeson Street
Dublin 4

## ISRAEL

Daily Newspaper Publishers Association of Israel
Maua Building
74 Petah Tikva Road
P.O. Box 51202
Tel Aviv 61200

## ITALY

Federazione Italiana Editori Giornali (FIEG)
Via Piemonte 64
00187 Roma

## JAPAN

Nihon Shinbun Kyokai
Nippon Press Center Building
2-2-1, Uchisalwai-Cho
Chiyoda-ku, Tokyo

## KOREA

Korean Newspapers Association
The Korean Press Center Building
25 Taepyong-ro 1-ga
Chung-ku, Seoul

## LUXEMBOURG

Association Luxembourgeoise des Editeurs de Journaux
Tageblatt, 44 Rue de Canal
BP 147, 4050 Esch-Alzette

## THE NETHERLANDS

Vereniging de Nederlandse Dagbladpers
J Vermeerstraat 14 1071DR
Amsterdam

## NORWAY

Norske Aviisers Landsforbund (NAL)
Storgt 32
0184 Oslo 1

## PERU

Asociacion de Diarios del Peru (ADIPE)
Av Camino Real 159, Oficina 592
Lima 27, San Isidro

## PORTUGAL

Associacao da Impresa Diaria
Rua de Artilharia Um-69-2
1297 Lisboa Codex

## SPAIN

Asociacion de Editores de Diarios Espanoles (AEDE)
Espronceda 32-6a
28003 Madrid

## SRI LANKA

Independent Newspapers Ltd (INP)
P.O. Box 1257 No. 5
Colombo 12

## SWEDEN

Svenska Tidningsutgivareforeningen
P.O. Box 22500
104 22 Stockholm

## SWITZERLAND

Association Suisse des Editeurs de Journaux et Périodiques
(Schweizerischer Verband der Zeitung und Zeitschriftenverleger)
Baumackerstrasse 42
Case Postale
8050 Zurich

## TUNISIA

Association des Editeurs des Journaux en Tunisie
BP 46
Tunis 1000

## TURKEY

Turkiye Gazette Sahipleri Sendikasi
Cagaloglu Tükocagi Can no. 3 Kat 1,
Istanbul

## UNITED KINGDOM:

PressAd Co-op (The Newspaper Society)
Bloomsbury House
Bloomsbury Square
74/77 Great Russell Street
London WC1B 3DA

# Filing a Complaint with the Federal Trade Commission

What do you do if one of your competitors is violating the Robinson-Patman Act? Most people ignore it, possibly because they do not have time to deal with making a complaint or because they are afraid of attracting the attention of the Federal Trade Commission (because they are violating the act themselves). If you want to file a Robinson-Patman complaint but you do not know how, Kevin J. Arquit, former director of the FTC's Bureau of Competition, gave a speech to the National Grocers Association in 1991, titled *Antitrust Analysis of Slotting Allowances*. In the summation to this speech, he offered some advice to anyone who wished to file a complaint. Although it was directed to the grocery channel and referred to slotting allowances, much of the advice is generally applicable:

> It may come as a surprise to many of you, but in the Robinson-Patman area we receive only a dozen or so complaints per year of practices said to violate the Act. Unfortunately, a substantial percentage of these complaints are not accompanied by the kinds of specific information necessary for us to go forward, even with a preliminary investigation; in some instances the complaint does not even identify particular companies that are the subject of the complaint. In the case of slotting allowances, for example, a general complaint that a competing manufacturer is paying, or a competing retailer is receiving, a slotting payment does not help us distinguish a lawful arrangement from an unlawful one. When the complaint conveys sufficient information to give us reason to suspect that the law may have been violated, however, we investigate it.

After discussion of issues pertaining to 2(a) violations, Arquit went on:

Plaintiffs may be somewhat more likely to prevail in cases involving the second type of slotting allowance, because of the potential application of section 2(d) of the Robinson-Patman Act dealing with discriminatory promotional allowances.[1] This allowance is paid, not just in order to get into the store, but to get a favored position within the store. This position might involve a special display stand, or an advantageous location such as an eye-level shelf at the middle of a grocery aisle. These things have a fairly clear role in bringing the product (rather than competing products) to the attention of the public. Payments to achieve this exposure might therefore be shown to be closely related to the ultimate retail sale of the product,[2] since they have many characteristics of promotional allowances. The Commission has suggested that such payments may be judged by the standards of section 2(d).

These standards are somewhat different from those governing straightforward price discounts. Defenses are fewer and it is easier to find liability. Most notably, there is no need under section 2(d) to show harm to competition before liability will attach, and there is no cost-justification defense.

You should direct complaints of possible illegal activity in this area to our energy and food office or to one of the Commission's regional offices.[3] Here are some suggested ways that you can make your complaints more useful to us.

First, provide as much information as you can about the grocery retailing business in your area, which helps us establish the proper product and geographic markets in which to analyze the conduct that is the subject of the complaint. In cases involving single-firm conduct, it is important to know whether the payments in question are likely to have anticompetitive effects in a properly defined market. This is particularly true in the case of a manufacturer claiming that slotting payments are preventing it from being able to compete. We need to be able to determine what products compete with those at issue, what geographic area defines the boundaries of competition for sale of that product group, and what barriers or impediments exist to entry into the market. We have found in analyzing grocery mergers that some complex issues of market definition arise in grocery retailing, particularly in determining the relevant geographic market.

---

[1] In the recently amended *Guides*, the FTC indicated that "[t]he discriminatory purchase of display or shelf space, whether directly or by means of so-called allowances, may violate the [Robinson-Patman] Act, and may be considered an unfair method of competition in violation of section 5 of the Federal Trade Commission Act."

[2] Section 2(d) and 2(e) apply only to payments made in connection with the resale of a product.

[3] Marc G. Schildkraut, Assistant Director, Bureau of Competition, Federal Trade Commission, Room 3301, 601 Pennsylvania Avenue, N.W., Washington, DC 20580. The FTC has regional offices in Atlanta, Boston, Chicago, Cleveland, Dallas, Denver, Los Angeles, New York, San Francisco, and Seattle.

Second, if you are complaining as a competitor of one of the parties to a slotting arrangement, tell us as much as you can about the harmful effects on competition, not merely the harm that you believe you are suffering. If the harm you are experiencing falls within the category of exclusion from the market or suffering from higher entry barriers, that may be something we can act on. If, however, you are a retailer complaining that you are unable to command the slotting allowances received by your larger competitors, then we may have difficulty, without more, in making out a case that the slotting payments are unlawful.

# Further Reading

The following list of sources cited in this book may be of interest to readers who wish to find further information on promotional allowance programs and related subjects.

## Books

Crimmins, Edward C. *Cooperative Advertising*. New York: Gene Wolf & Co. in association with the Association of National Advertisers, 1984.

Rothschild, Michael L. *Marketing Communications*. Chap. 4. Lexington, MA: D.C. Heath, 1987.

Ward, Peter C. *Federal Trade Commission: Law, Practice, and Procedure*. New York: Law Journal Seminars Press, 1988.

Young, Robert F. "The Uses and Effectiveness of Vertical Cooperative Advertising," Ph.D. diss., Harvard Business School, 1980.

## Articles

"Dealing with Deductions." *Supermarket News*, 2 December 1991.

"Displays Pay Off for Grocery Marketers." *The Wall Street Journal*, 15 October 1992.

Jones, John Philip. "The Double Jeopardy of Sales Promotions." *Harvard Business Review* (September/October 1991).

Lavidge, Robert J., and Gary A. Steiner. "A Model for Predicting Advertising Effectiveness." *Journal of Marketing* (October 1991).

Love, L. Ross. "Brand Building/Advertising/Profit." *The Advertiser* (Summer, 1992).

Marn, Michael V., and Robert L. Rosiello. "Managing Price, Gaining Profit." *Harvard Business Review* (September/October 1992).

Sellers, Patricia. "The Dumbest Marketing Ploy." *Fortune*, 5 October 1992.

Sternthal, Brian, Lynn W. Phillips, and Rudy Dholakla. "The Persuasive Effects of Source Credibility." *Public Opinion Quarterly* (Fall 1978).

Vaughn, Richard. "How Advertising Works: A Planning Model Revisited." *Journal of Advertising Research* (February/March 1986).

Wilcox, Robert D. "Does It Pay to Advertise?" Armstrong World Industries newsletter (January, 1979).

Williams, Monci Jo. "Trade Promotion Junkies." *The Marketer* (October 1990).

## Reports and Speeches

Arquit, Kevin J. "Antitrust Analysis of Slotting Allowances." Speech given before the National Grocers Association, 12 November, 1991.

Food Marketing Association."Invoice Deduction Guidelines." Executive Report of the Joint Industry Committee.Washington, DC, 1990.

London Business School."The After Effects of Consumer Promotions." London, August 1991.

## Government Publications

Federal Trade Commission.*Guides for Advertising Allowances and Other Merchandising Payments and Services* Effective 3 August 1990; published with accompanying commentary in 55 Federal Register 33651. Proposed changes published in 53 Federal Register 43233 (26 October 1988).

# *Index*

# TITLES OF INTEREST IN
## ADVERTISING, SALES PROMOTION, AND PUBLIC RELATIONS

For further information or a current catalog, write:
NTC Business Books
a division of *NTC Publishing Group*
4255 West Touhy Avenue
Lincolnwood, Illinois 60646–1975